THE FORGERS

THE
FORGERS

E. Patrick McGuire

147814

Library of Congress Catalogue Card Number 73-77145

Padric Publishing Company
BERNARDSVILLE, N.J. 07924 U.S.A.

Acknowledgments

A book of this type cannot be written without the wholehearted cooperation and advice of the law enforcement community. To say that the following persons helped with the book would be a gross understatement. These people made this book possible.

A special debt of thanks is owed to Mr. J. Edgar Hoover, Director, Federal Bureau of Investigation and to those Special Agents who assisted the author in this project, with special thanks to the men of the FBI Laboratory.

The writer is also particularly grateful to the U.S. Postal Inspectors who courteously and without reservation cooperated in the education of the author in the ways and means of the forger. I would like to express my special thanks to Mr. Henry B. Montague, Chief Postal Inspector and also to Mr. Van Seagraves, Special Assistant to the Postmaster General, to Mr. Albert W. Somerford, Director of the Documents Laboratory, to Mr. Charles A. Miller, Director, Fraud and Mailability Division, to Mr. Marlin Brown, Bureau of Chief Postal Inspector and to Mr. Martin J. McGee, Inspector in Charge, Office of the Postal Inspector in Chicago.

In the United States Secret Service we appreciate the cooperation of Mr. James J. Rowley, Director, United States Secret Service and of Mr. John W. Warner, Jr., Assistant to the Director and of Mr. Paul E. Henne, Special Agent in Charge, Forgery Division.

In the Police Department of New York our thanks to Deputy Commissioner Jacques Nevard and to Lt. John C. Colleton, Commander, Forgery Squad.

The District Attorneys of New York provided extensive and valuable data on many forgery operations in the Boroughs of New

York. The author's thanks to Mr. Elliott Golden, District Attorney for Kings County and to Mr. Edward Panzarella, Chief Assistant District Attorney. To Mr. Thomas J. Mackell, District Attorney for Queens County and Mr. Joseph Monty, Chief Rackets Investigator and Lt. John Mahoney of the District Attorney's Office. To Mr. Frank S. Hogan, District Attorney of the County of New York and to Mr. Leonard Newman, Chief of the Frauds Bureau, Office of the District Attorney. And to Mr. Burton B. Roberts, District Attorney of Bronx County and Mr. Seymour Rotker, Chief of Frauds Division of the Office of the District Attorney.

Many executives and investigators in the banking community also deserve recognition for their contributions. The writer is indebted to Mr. William F. Owens, Director, Insurance and Protective Committee, American Banking Association. Also to Mr. Philip N. Cooper, Chief Investigator, The Chase Manhattan Bank. And to Mr. S.E. Bray, Director of Security, Continental Illinois National Bank and to Mr. Edward P. Meinhardt, Chief Special Agent, Bank of America. And to Mr. Gilbert D. Lawrence, Vice President, Manufacturers Hanover Trust Co.

Many police officers from urban police departments throughout the country also aided in this project. The author is particularly indebted to Detective Joseph Gibbons, Bank Squad, Boston Police Department and to Captain David J. Purtell, Director, Chicago Police Laboratory and to Sergeant Daniel Cook of the Los Angeles Police Department.

Security personnel from private industry have been equally helpful in this undertaking and the writer appreciates the help of Mr. John J. O'Toole, Vice President and Director of Security of Diners Club. And of Mr. James Miles, Director of Security and Mr. Harry F. Rote Jr., Special Investigator in Charge, United Air Lines. Also of Mr. Howard W. Brunn, Superintendent of Security, Eastern Air Lines and of Mr. W. C. Martinson, Director of Field Audits and Security, American Air Lines.

Also Mr. Edward B. Schneyer, Assistant General Auditor, Security, Sperry & Hutchinson Co. and of Mr. John Janssen, Manager-Criminal Div., William J. Burns International Detective Agency.

Special thanks also to Mr. Charles H. Rogovin, formerly Assistant Director (Organized Crime) of the President's Commission on Law Enforcement and Administration of Justice and now Assistant Attorney General, Commonwealth of Massachusetts.

With thanks to the U.S. Attorney's Office for the Southern District of New York and for the aid provided by Mr. Andrew J. Maloney and Mr. Robert L. Latchford, Assistant U.S. Attorneys.

Also to Col. James T. DeVoss, Executive Secretary, American Philatelic Society. And to Mr. Maurice Annenberg, President Maran Plastics Company and to Mr. R.P. Scott, Advertising Manager, Burroughs Corp.

And to Mr. C.P. Foote, Jr., Vice President and General Manager of American Bank Note Company. And to Mr. G.D. Gregory of New Scotland Yard. And to Mr. Luther M. Dey, Consultant, Law Enforcement Photography, Eastman Kodak Company and to Mr. Dey's assistant Mr. E.B. Reddoch, III.

And to one of the nations foremost private document examiners, Mr. Ordway Hilton.

Finally, I would like to thank all those detectives, FBI Agents, etc. whose names cannot be mentioned here but who made a real contribution to this book.

Preface

Anyone seriously studying the crime of forgery is immediately faced with several philosophical as well as practical problems. One of the first problems concerns the description of the crime itself. There is a feeling in some circles, and fortunately these people are in a distinct minority, that it would be best to ignore or at best gloss over the depradations of forgers. The advocates of this point of view would suppress information about the crime, the economic loss it creates, or the methods by which it is perpetrated. Their reasoning is that publicity about the crime will attract more criminals to this crime. Such persons are hopelessly naive about the nature of the criminal mind and about the communication facilities that exist within the criminal subculture.

On the surface there might appear to be some justification for such fears. We do know that a few master forgers, such as Courtney Townsend Taylor, have made an extensive academic study of their profession. However, this type of criminal is a rare breed indeed. Such a propensity for literary research certainly does not apply to the general criminal population.

In addition, my own research has completely convinced me that it is the business and sometimes the law enforcement communities, not the forgers, who are in need of education about the crime of forgery. The forgers themselves are only too well schooled in their profession. This book will add little to their education.

Beyond the latter points, there is an even more important reason for publishing this study. This reason goes to very nature of the forger himself. There is one thing and only one thing that discourages the professional forger. That is his inability to cash a check. He is not discouraged by fear of imprisonment. Imprisonment itself does little if anything to reform him. In fact the forger has one of the poorest records of rehabilitation of any class of criminal. The forger only turns from his crime when he finds it too difficult to practice. Failure to educate the business community to the methods and schemes employed by forgers simply proliferates the crime.

In the same vein, local police forces, who are sometimes less skilled in forgery detection than the forgers themselves, should benefit from a review of the basic M.O.'s and detection methods currently in use. Finally, the business and financial community should take a good hard look at its forgery losses. Most of these losses are preventable. All that is needed is knowledge and will.

Contents

THE BACKGROUND

"Forgery is the false making or materially altering with intent to defraud, of any writing, which if genuine, might apparently be of legal efficacy or the foundation of legal liability". (Bullock vs Commonwealth 13 SSE 2d 261).

The wall clock says exactly 2:30 P.M. It is a Friday afternoon and the supermarket is already crowded with week-end shoppers. A petite, brunette coed, wearing a University of Alabama sweatshirt and blue jeans, is checking out four items at the express check-out counter. The clerk registers a $5.67 sale. The coed rummages through her pocketbook and fishes out a Bell Telephone envelope. From the envelope she produces a check for $65.00. The check is made out from AT&T to Miss Madeline Brooks. Miss Brooks signs the check, exhibits a driver's license for the clerk's inspection and the transaction is completed. The check-out clerk returns $59.00 and some change to the coed and she walks smartly from the store.

An eight year old boy walks to a mail box and lifts out an envelope containing a postal money order. He removes the money order, endorses it with a ballpoint pen and mounts his bike for a short ride to the local Post Office. At the Post Office, he reaches up to the counter, passes the money order to the postal clerk, and receives his cash.

In Chicago, a group of fourteen housewives are engaged in a mid-morning coffee klatch. But they are not discussing fashions this morning, they are completing the details for opening a checking account at one of the local branch banks. Within a few days many of this group will begin drawing checks on this account.

Each of the above episodes involves a deliberate premeditated forgery. All of the individuals noted above were forgers and each of these cases is real. They have all occurred within the past few years. Because of their diversity, and the scope of criminal intent involved, they are perhaps typical of the crime of forgery and the extent to which it now permeates the American scene. Incidents like this, or variations of them, are taking place as you read this sentence. In fact, by the time you have read this far, the American economy has been defrauded out of $1500 through the cashing of fraudulent checks.

The total loss to the American economy through check forgery operations, may well exceed $600 million in this year. Some experts even predict a loss approaching the one billion dollar mark.

All segments of the economy are effected by the crime of forgery. Consider just the ordinary American food market.   It is   estimated that the supermarket portion of our economy lost $246 million dollars in 1966 alone due to fraudulent checks. A recent report on Detroit supermarkets, which are not as unusual in their business risk loss ratio, indicates that each week the supermarkets cash approximately $10 million in checks and sustain a weekly fraudulent check loss exceeding $100,000. In fact, any recent analysis of check frauds would have to conclude that we are rapidly being engulfed in a sea of "paper" (the term used by law enforcement officials to indicate worthless checks or securities).

In part we are perhaps paying the price demanded by an economy that rests almost wholly on faith. Faith is the essential element of our ordinary business transactions. The check, either personal or business, has no intrinsic value of its own. It is merely an instrument which confirms the faith of the payee in the payor's willingness and ability to settle a debt.

The period since World War II has produced a virtual nuclear explosion in check usage. For example, in the New York Federal Reserve Bank Clearing House four million checks were cleared in the calendar year 1943. By 1955, this figure had increased to 546 million checks. In 1949 there were an estimated 27 million checking accounts. By 1968 this number had increased to more than 60 million checking accounts. Not only had the number of checking accounts increased, but the number of checks issued on each account had multipled many times over.

This vast flood of paper produces a peculiar type of dilemma for both banking and law enforcement officials. It is technically possible to create conditions which would drastically reduce the number of forgeries presently encountered. However, these same restrictions would have such an adverse effect on the flow of credit that the cure might well be worse than the illness. Thus, it seems as if a certain amount of forgery is inevitable. The real question is whether or not the present rate of forgery can be reduced without seriously impairing normal business operations. As you read this report the answer to that question will become self evident.

Quite naturally, much of the statistical evidence on the national impact of forgery derives from the records maintained by the Federal Bureau of Investigation. During the past ten years, the FBI notes a 106% increase in fraudulent check operations. In the fiscal year ending June 30, 1967, the FBI received for examination 31,994 worthless company and personal checks. It also received some 32,013 money orders, travellers checks and similar items most of which were stolen in burglaries, forged and negotiated sometimes by two or more persons.

FBI files presently contain over 100,000 fraudulent check samples. The New York Police Department has 35,000 forged checks in its own file. The FBI has been particularly aware of the growth of the forgery menace and its Director, J. Edgar Hoover, noting the avalanche of check forgeries, has said that "fraudulent check passers are a national pestilence".

For the past few years the writer has travelled throughout the United States and England interviewing bank officials, economists, law enforcement officials, detectives, and many other persons directly or indirectly connected with the crime of forgery. From all of these interviews, a single overriding picture emerged. This picture is one of a business and financial community that is now being seriously threatened by the crime of forgery. As you will see in the following pages, there are all sorts of statistics to validate this impression. Consider for example the 100% increases in losses paid by insurance companies to banks for fraudulent checks in the period 1956 through 1963. A substantial increase, yet banks sustain, by their own estimates, only 5 to 7½% of the total loss due to fraudulent checks. The big losers are the supermarkets, the corner tavern, the restaurant, etc. Their exact loss, particularly in view of the fact that much of it is unreported, can never be exactly determined.

Recently, the Burroughs Corporation conducted a national survey of 4500 police and sheriff officials. This survey showed that check frauds had increased 20% within 1967 alone. Arrests increased 18% and thus failed to keep up with the crime rate. More significantly, the money amount in check crimes rose even faster than the total rate. They increased 22% during the past twelve months.

This same survey shows that check fraud activity is dominated by amateurs who account for 72% of the crime as compared to 28% for professionals. However, other studies put this ratio at anywhere from 60-40 to 50-50. This discrepancy is probably accounted for by the individual definition of what constitutes an amateur or professional check forger. However, from the author's own observation, it would appear that numerically the "amateurs" dominate the field.

These amateurs are particularly evident in large urban areas. A flood of social security, city welfare, pension, etc., checks provides a steady source of material for the small time urban forger. This type of forger works the postal boxes to particular advantage. In New York City, during 1964, the New York City Welfare Department reported over 1600 check forgery cases to the Police Department. The total loss in these cases exceeded $104,000. By 1968, the situation in ghetto areas such as New York had deteriorated to such a state that the postmen literally could not put down their delivery bags. In fact, postmen were being held up for the checks before they had even reached their destination. The local postal union complained to Washington requesting additional protection. Losses were then put at $1,000,000 per month.

As will be shown later, forgery is primarily an adult crime. However, recently the spate of urban ghetto check forgeries indicates that a younger group of criminals is moving toward this area of crime. This is a particularly significant development when we consider the following statistics as they apply to overall crime in the United States. Individuals under 18 years of age account for one-fifth of all non-traffic arrests during 1965. Those under 24 years of age account for 50% of all those arrested for major crimes of violence such as homocide, rape, robbery and assault. In addition, 75% of all those arrested for larceny, burglary and auto theft were under 24 years of age. Clearly the major emphasis on crime lies within the younger age group. Any discernible age shift in the crime of forgery, which accounts for large volume financial losses, is particularly hazardous to the financial and general business community.

The whole financial community and banks in particular, have been the subject of increased criminal attention during the past ten years. We do not have precise figures on the number of forgeries and their resultant increase within the banking community alone. It is fairly safe to say that they have doubled in the period from 1955 to 1965. This estimation can be derived from the Uniform Crime Report Statistics compiled by the Federal Bureau of Investigation. Forgeries against banks have generally paralleled the more violent crimes of bank robberies, but have not kept up a step-by-step pace. Bank robberies alone have produced a significant increase from 526 incidents of robbery in 1955 to 1,971 incidents of robbery in 1966.

Professional forgers, the courts, and over-burdened law enforcement authorities have combined in an unwilling alliance to contribute to the drastic forgery increase. Forgers have the highest rate of recidivism of any criminal group. The author has investigated cases where forgers have shown a 50 year history of continuous criminal activity in forgery. The professional forgers will be with us for a very long time. The courts do not always aid this situation. The difficulty in the courts lies in court calendar congestion, a shortage of prosecuting attorneys, and a recognized leniency by some jurists in dealing with forgery offenses. Federal prosecutors, who are frequently involved in professional forgery cases, are well aware of this problem. Since 1960 the pending criminal case loads in the Federal Judicial System has increased by more than 90%. Grand jury procedures have increased 31% and the Appeals Court has been swamped under a 153% increase in the last ten years. Yet, the men who bear the brunt of this load, that is the Assistant U.S. Attorneys, have only been increased 16% during the last 8 year period.

Each succeeding year seems to show an unchecked increase in forgery offenses. The ratio of increase is out of all proportion to normal population growths or even the growth of the criminal age section of the population. As far back as 1960, this trend was in clear evidence. A survey during that year showed a 20.5% increase in check forgeries over 1959. Check forgery, unfortunately, is the type of crime which is often reported by the press on the 15th page of a weekday newspaper. But even here, a brief search of the past several years newspapers, reveals again and again the existence of major check fraud operations. These operations have certainly taken more out of banks than all the robberies during the past decade. There are many examples of this movement, but let us consider just a few culled from metropolitan daily newspapers.

A Long Island, New York ring, consisting mainly of women, cashed over $100,000 in counterfeit checks in liquor, jewelry and furniture stores within a few months time. These checks ranged in size from $50 to $300.00. The checks were allegedly issued by the Humble Oil and Refining Company, the New York Life Insurance Company, or the International Ladies Garment Workers Union. A detective examining the checks described them as "near perfect". They carried seemingly identical signatures to the real paymaster of the companies involved. They were further described as "almost impossible to distinguish from the real thing".

During the same year another New York ring stole legitimate checks and used these to print useless models. They duplicated paper stocks, ink color, etc. This gang passed a total of $13,000 in counterfeit checks before being apprehended by U. S. Postal Inspectors. In the latter case, convicted members of the gang related that they were asked for identification in less than half of the cases where they passed fraudulent checks.

In 1964 the J. W. Mays, Inc. store, a Brooklyn, New York Department Store chain, was hit for nearly one million dollars within a single two-week period. Counterfeit checks on the First National Bank of New York and the Underwriters Trust Company were well utilized. At the time of this writing nearly $600,000 of this money is still unrecovered and the principals in the case, previously convicted, are about to be released. This particular case will be discussed further in the case history section of this report.

Nineteen sixty-three was a good year for check forgers basking in the sun in California. It is estimated that in that year alone California merchants were bilked out of more than $25 million through fraudulent checks. A single industrious group of forgers hit San Francisco merchants for $135,000 within an 18 month period.

In one recent case in New York a company employee defrauded his own company out of over $130,000 within a single year by creating fictitious payees and forging their signatures. This case is not unusual. A Monterey, California insurance broker recently sued the Bank of America for accepting $171,834 worth of checks that were forged with his signature and charged to his account.

Meanwhile in the center of America, the St. Louis Metropolitan area was also experiencing their own wave of forgery. St. Louis Circuit Attorney, James Corcoran, said that the number of bad checks cases had increased to 347 cases in 1966 from 219 in 1965. In the sprawling St. Louis County, Prosecutor Gene McNary, said that his office sent out as many as 1600 letters a month warning of prosecution for both check delinquencies and frauds. An average of 240 warrants per month are issued for check forgeries. The St. Louis County Forgery Squad notes that the previous image of the check forger as a highly sophisticated intelligent operator is now undergoing a slight change with even the uneducated finding it relatively easy to make a living with check forgeries. Within the City of St. Louis the police report about 300 bad check cases each month. Of this total 10% are for insufficient funds, bogus checks account for 65% and straight forgeries make up the remaining 25%.

Nearly all urban areas experience check forgery losses that must certainly exceed hundreds of thousands of dollars per month. Recently the author sat in the Squad Room of the Boston Police Department and quickly thumbed through a batch of forged checks which had arrived that day. There were over $20,000 worth of bad checks in a single envelope and envelopes like this, mailed by local banks and merchants, arrive at the Forgery Squad each and every working day of the month.

Of course, check forgeries are only one part, although an extremely important part, of the total forgery picture in the United States. Forgers hold no particular positive prejudice toward checks. In fact, they don't discriminate between any document which will produce hard currency. In this respect we should recognize that 95% of the hundreds of billions of dollars of business contracted each year, is represented not by money but by documents. These documents may be checks, but they may also be money orders, credit cards, stock exchange certificates, warehouse receipts, etc. All of these documents, as we shall see later, have been the subject of increasing interest to the forger.

The United States Government is probably one of the single largest issuers of checks in the whole world. Quite naturally, they are often the target of forgers. Each working day of the year more than one million checks spew out of the Disbursing Offices of the United States Treasury. These checks represent payment for services rendered to the government, salaries, pensions, Social Security payments, medical payments, veterans payments, payments for goods, loans, etc. Social Security checks probably represent one of the largest categories issued each year. In 1967 the Treasury issued more than 549 billion checks. Of this total 45,000 individual checks were in some manner or other forged. These checks were intercepted before they reached their rightful owner, were forged, and negotiated. The dollar amount in forgeries thus involved came to some $4,500,000. As a result of these forgeries, 2,431 persons were arrested for government check forgeries. Most of those arrested had forged one or more checks. U. S. Secret Service agents estimate that 60 to 70% of all forgeries of U. S. Treasury checks are eventually traced to a particular forger. In addition to Treasury checks, the Secret Service also investigated 6,415 cases involving the forgery and subsequent fraudulent negotiation of U. S. Savings Bonds. These bonds had a maturity value of over $700,000. As a result of the latter investigation a total of 113 persons were arrested. The U. S. Secret Service has an enviable record for pre-trial preparation. Of the 4,117 persons arrested for forgery and counterfeiting offenses, 97.2% of these were subsequently brought to trial.

As we shall see, the widespread availability of high quality printing equipment has been an important factor in the increased activity of both counterfeiters and forgers. Many of the checks now being passed by the professional forger are facsimile or counterfeits of legitimate company checks. Frequently the same persons are involved in printing counterfeit currency and counterfeit checks. Any substantial increase in counterfeit currency production is almost certainly accompanied by an increase in counterfeit check production.

In the decade 1956 to 1965, 5,029 persons were arrested for counterfeiting offenses. These counterfeiters were estimated to have produced 26 million dollars worth of counterfeit currency during that time period. Eighty-two percent of this currency ($22 million) was seized before it could be passed.

Now we take a look at a more recent year, 1967. In this single year 1,072 persons were arrested for counterfeiting violations. This is double the average for the previous ten year period. In addition, almost $10 million worth of counterfeit currency was seized, an amount equal to almost 50% of all the counterfeit currency produced during the previous ten years. Thus, we can see that there has been a dramatic increase within the past few years in both the number of counterfeiters and the number and value of counterfeit currency produced. The author cites these available statistics on counterfeit currency production as an indication of what is occurring in counterfeit or facsimile checks. We have no precise statistics on the increase in the number of counterfeit checks, but neither do we have any reason to believe, based on the research performed, that there has not been a rise at least equalling and perhaps exceeding, that rise experienced in counterfeit currency production.

The U. S. Secret Service credits the rise of production to improved methods in photography and printing which have simplified the techniques of counterfeiting. This improved technical equipment has made it possible for relatively unskilled persons to manufacture passable notes. In addition, a jet age transportation system has permitted nearly instantaneous widespread distribution of counterfeit currency. The loss to the public from counterfeit currency in 1965 was $1,658,000. The amount lost from counterfeit check production, if accurately known, would make the latter figure appear paltry. Yet it is ironic that the public is more aware of the potential of forged or counterfeit currency than it is of counterfeit checks. In a curious way this awareness is a tribute to the investigative skills of a relatively small law enforcement agency, the U. S. Secret Service. The latter agency through its public efforts has alerted the business and general community to the existence of counterfeit currency where it appeared.

The U.S. Secret Service Report of 1964 is perhaps a portent of things to come. This report revealed a developing trend where employees of printing shops, many of whom have costly and refined equipment available, take advantage of this equipment to print bogus currency and counterfeit checks. Frequently this production is done after hours and without the knowledge of their legitimate employers. In addition, of course, there is also the reported growth of the pseudo-legitimate printing concern. Such a concern is specifically set up for the production of counterfeit currency or checks. This type of shop goes through a normal business incorporation or registration procedure and provides a front, by maintaining a small volume of legitimate business, while it actively engages in counterfeiting operations.

One of the strangest facets of the crime of forgery is the reaction of the merchant and the general public. This reaction, in the vast majority, is characterized by an attitude which is more concerned with restitution than with prosecution. Therein lies the heart of the present day enforcement problem. This is a factor which plagues and bedevils the life of law enforcement agents throughout the country. One can only imagine the frustration of a police officer who has conducted a successful investigation, apprehended the forger and then discovers that the merchant affected could be bought off by the forger for the sum involved in the forgery itself. In fact, the whole attitude of the business community toward forgery is paradoxical.

Surveys conducted by the University of Michigan, under a grant by the Office of Law Enforcement Assistance, revealed some interesting statistics with regard to merchant reaction to bad check cashing problems. This particular report notes that "36% of all those who have check cashing customers say that they honor almost *all* requests for check cashing." More than 50% of the merchants interviewed in this survey indicated that they did have a problem with bad check passing. In fact, about 12% of the sample reported that they had accepted 20 or more bad checks during the 1965 period. When one estimates the average value for such a check is probably about $65, we can see that these merchants were victimized for sums exceeding $1600 a piece. In some cases, the value is naturally much higher.

One of the strange facets of this survey lies in the merchants reaction to receiving a bad check. While he might obviously alert police officers to even a minor breaking and entering case, he is not similarly disposed to report forgery cases. In fact this survey concluded "the volume of bad check passing that goes unreported to the police is substantial". Less than one-third of the merchants interviewed reported that they called the police under any circumstances regarding forged checks or bad check losses. This is an astounding percentage and seems almost to provide a license to

REGIONAL VARIATIONS IN FORGERY AND FRAUD
(incidents per 100,000 population)

	NORTHEAST	NORTH CENTRAL	SOUTH	WEST
COUNTERFEITING OR FORGERY	38	32	38	76
FRAUD—GENERAL	139	202	298	418
CONSUMER FRAUDS	114	85	96	247

SOURCE: TASK FORCE REPORT – CRIMINAL VICTIMIZATION IN
THE U.S.: A Report of a National Survey, Field Survey II,
Table 10, pg. 22 (Washington, D. C. – U.S. Government
Printing Office)

steal, and is certainly one of the factors accounting for the major rise in forgeries. Forgers are well aware that the merchant is primarily interested in restitution rather than prosecution.

The University of Michigan survey completely confirms this fact. The existence of this tendency explains why many professional forgers, even though occasionally detected and apprehended, are able to avoid prosecution. They quite literally buy themselves out of the situation through immediate cash restitution. In fact, the Michigan study notes that "quite clearly then business and organizations do not rely primarily on law enforcement agents to deal with their bad check problems".

One might expect that forgery losses would be rather uniformily spread out across the nation. However this is not the case. The Far West, including primarily the State of California, seems to suffer a far higher incidence of all kinds of fraud, including forgery. The above chart illustrates this differential. The author has questioned California police officials on this point, but no definitive explanation exists for this difference. Some authorities have stated that the variance is due to better police reporting on the West Coast. But even in those crimes were police reporting across the nation is absolutely uniform, such as in bank robberies, we find that an area like Los Angeles holds the dubious distinction of being "the bank robbery capital of the world". Perhaps, the forger and con man just naturally gravitates to California because of the anonymity created by an exploding population.

CREDIT CARDS
THE FORGER'S FRIEND

The credit card is to the forger what the jet engine was to the airline transport industry. It is, in essence, the means to faster and higher flights of profit. To some forgers, perhaps discouraged by the bankers, the credit card has provided a rejuvenation that we are only just beginning to measure.

We may well be moving away from checks and towards a "check-less" society. But in many respects it would appear that the economy is first going through a "card society" interim stage. Credit cards are now a major factor in the American financial system. Current estimates indicate that there are between 150 and 200 million credit cards in use within the United States. These include credit cards for department stores, restaurants, oil companies, airlines, universal shopping cards and the established general credit cards of the major card companies themselves.

As credit cards have blossomed in the economy, so also has credit card fraud. Fraud operators prefer to swim in a sea of anonymity provided by widespread activity. Credit cards have provided such activity, and in turn the anonymity vital to successful fraud operations. Credit card fraud, utilizing forgery, has increased 400% in the last year according to statistics now available from the U. S. Postal Inspector's Office. This increase is based on the increased case load for inspectors within that law enforcement agency. Credit card frauds, it would appear, is an important portion of the total increase in fraud activity within the last year or so. The Post Office Department notes that there was an 15% increase in mail fraud complaints in the first half of fiscal 1968. In fiscal 1967 there were a total of 135,000 separate complaints by businessmen and others who felt that they had been cheated on various transactions involving the use of the mail. The Enforcement Report covering that period goes on to state "the most significant increases involved credit cards and fake accident swindles against insurance companies."

All agencies, both Federal, local and private, report sharp increases in credit card fraud during the past two years. The essense of this fraud is forgery. The American Petroleum Credit Association, a cooperative association for 300 oil companies,

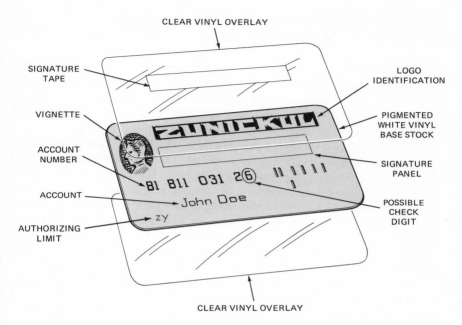

Fig. 1 The typical component parts for a credit card.

reports that in their sector alone more than 30,000 cases of credit card fraud were perpetrated during 1967. This is double the 1966 total.

Credit card plans are popping up all over the country. Excluding banks, over 1000 separate card companies handled, a billing volume of over $5 billion during 1967. The losses to these companies, due to theft and subsequent forgery, was estimated at between $20 and $50 million dollars. This is probably a conservative estimate. More precise estimates are not possible because credit card companies themselves are deliberately secretive about their losses. They are secretive not only to inquiring journalists, but also to legitimate law enforcement agencies. There may be a justified belief that revealing the extent of their losses would impair their financial position and that this in turn would have an adverse psychological impact on the firm's security rating. Despite this reluctance, we have been able to obtain some data which provides an estimate of some typical losses.

For example, the First National Bank of Chicago, one of the banks involved in the Chicago Credit Card case reported later in this volume, listed bad debts in 1967 at $5,680,000. This is double the previous year's losses, and one may reasonably estimate that the major portion was due to credit card forgery.

In 1967, Diners Club, Inc. had a single loss of $350,000 involving the theft of legitimate cards and their subsequent use as "doubles". This theft involved the taking of some 2000 Diners Club cards from a plant in Queens County in New York. A well organized ring was involved and this ring managed to charge the $350,000 in a four month period. 800 of the 2000 cards originally stolen were recovered as of November 13, 1967. Thirty persons have been arrested for various activities connected with this particular fraud operation.

During the Chicago credit card case, one bank, in a single business day, was hit for $46,000 in forgery losses through its credit card. This bank subsequently recalled its credit cards and issued new ones. But not until it had over 5000 cards on its "hot list".

Hot lists frequently become so long as to be nearly unmanageable. By the close of 1967 the Diners Club had nearly 12,000 cards on its hot list. Each of these cards in the capable hands of a skilled forger had the potential for generating $5 to $10,000 worth of forgery losses within a single month. One writer, H. J. Maidenberg, writing in the Sept. 18, 1967 edition of the New York Times, estimates that 10% of the 200 million cards in use during 1968 will be lost or stolen. He estimates that American Express Cards accounted for 46,000 cards which were either lost or stolen. The same writer puts the fraud loss for credit card forgery at $40 million for 1967.

There have been widely placed estimates on the number of cards which are stolen and used fraudulently each year. In truth, no one knows exactly how many cards are lost and fraudulently used. One of the recurring statistics in this area reports that 300,000 cards are lost, stolen, or misplaced. However, it is this writer's opinion, based on my own research, that a majority of the cards in this 300,000 figure are never used directly in forgery operations. Nonetheless, there is very little doubt that a huge volume of financial loss is regularly incurred due to credit card forgeries. One analyst, Arthur T. Ross, Chairman of the Franklin National Bank of Long Island, commenting in the March 15, 1968 issue of the Wall Street Journal, notes that "five credit card programs (banks) had combined losses of $80 million in their early years. Two of them are no longer in business". Losses for the Midwest Bank Card System, the system involved in the Chicago credit card case, have been put 3 to 4% of the total sales volume handled by these banks.

One might think that with losses of the magnitude previously noted, banks and credit card companies would be reticent about expanding their operations. However, nothing could be further from the truth. Despite all these losses credit card companies continue to flourish and expand. California, which often leads the nation in this type of movement, reports that 81 banks have succeeded in signing up 85,000 individual merchants in a state-wide credit card system. It is now estimated that 22% of the merchants in California honor this type of credit card. The national percentage for retail merchants honoring credit cards is about 11% as of 1968.

As of September, 1968, it is estimated that there were more than 2000 American banks which were utilizing general purpose credit cards. These credit cards are sometimes referred to as "revolving credit" cards and are primarily used by housewives, homeowners, etc. The issuers of the bank type of cards derive their income primarily from discounts they receive from merchant establishments plus the service charges that they render against the unpaid balance of the card holders. Participation in bank credit card plans has extended far beyond the national boundaries of the United States. For example, the Bank of America with its Bankamericard, which was first introduced in 1959, now has 8,300,000 persons enrolled through agent banks in 34 American States, plus Japan, Ireland, Great Britain and Canada. The Diners Club which is now expanding into Soviet Russia, has its card in use in over 134 countries outside the United States. The company's card has already penetrated the Iron Curtain to the extent that it has been in use in Czechoslovakia, and Yugoslavia for nearly a year.

The First National City Bank of New York, which began its "Everything Card" in 1967, already has 1,500,000 cards in circulation in the metropolitan New York area. The American Banker (November 9, 1967) reports that bank card credit rose 39% during the first 23 weeks of 1967. There is little doubt but that many of the banks involved now receive an appreciable portion of their income through bank credit card operations. The Bank of America estimates that 5% of its total net income is derived from operations of its Credit Card Division. The credit card is actually administered through Bank of America Service Corporation which is a wholly owned subsidiary of the nation's largest bank.

The American Express Company, with a current list of more than 2 1/4 million card holders is receiving applications in mid-1968 at a rate of 30,000 per month. A good portion of these new applications will be added to the roll of the nation's largest credit card company. Diners Club, Inc., although their new application rate is unreported, is probably experiencing a similar rate of growth. American Express notes that they only have 14% of the total available market. This market consists of individuals or families with incomes in excess of $10,000. It is not inconceivable that they will eventually garner 50% of this particular market and thus have a total card list exceeding 7 million members.

It should also be remembered that many of these card holding members are multiple card holders. They have memberships in Diners Club, Carte Blanche, American Express, Inc., etc. The same is true of the oil company credit cards. Oil companies are one of the major segments of the credit card picture. They have over 50 million cards issued. The oil company credit card activity is particularly noteworthy in that recently they have expanded their range of services into motels, restaurants, etc. Thus, many more items other than simple gas and oil charges can be run up against the oil company credit card. At the same time you may have noticed that many oil company credit cards do not even contain a signature panel. Whoever has the credit card is in theoretical full possession of the cardholders credit. Many people believe that oil company credit cards are of minor significance. They believe that relatively little could be charged against an oil company credit card. This is not always the case. In one recent case, reported by the Queens County, New York District Attorney's Office, a gas station operator, functioning with stolen credit cards, obtained over $30,000 within a 90 day period. Meanwhile, in the Bronx, New York, a ring of 24 men utilized stolen oil company credit cards to ring up $35,000 in non-existent gasoline charges at cooperative gas stations. Still another ring utilized a "front" company's scheme to charge truck tires and similar items from four major oil companies. The loss in this case is reported to be over $1 million.

THE FORGERS

In many cases of oil company credit card frauds, involving the theft of the cards and their subsequent forgery, the amount is so small that the companies are hesitant to incur the costs of prosecution. In still other cases, they actually buy back their own cards. Recently Sales Management Magazine reported how one company bought back 69 of its own cards for the sum of $1600.

The Gulf Oil Company with over 1,200,000 credit card accounts, and a credit card business of $500 million a year, reportedly lost $200,000 in credit card misuse. Martin Pollner, former Assistant U. S. Attorney, has been faced with this type of problem for the past six or seven years. Mr. Pollner estimates that unless all of the credit card companies pool their enforcement and investigative resources, their losses will probably increase 400% over the next couple of years.

Many of the credit card companies have very well trained and able investigative forces. Increasingly these forces are headed by or staffed with former FBI, Secret Service or Postal Inspector personnel. The American Express Company is alleged to maintain a security force of some 250 investigators spread throughout the world. In 1965 the American Express security personnel were reportedly responsible for more than 200 separate arrests. The previous year there had been 131 credit card arrests. The American Express security organization has a particularly difficult task. Not only is the volume of credit cards increasing drastically, with the consequent fraud effect, but the company has also been extremely successful in the sale of travelers checks. As we shall see later, these are also a source of forgery material. Traveler's checks have grown at a compound annual rate of more than 8% per year during the last decade according to estimates by Leslie Goldstein of Abraham & Company. It is now estimated that the sales of traveler's checks during 1968 came to more than $5 billion. American Express probably accounted for about 2/3 of that market. American Express is also active in the shopping type credit card through its ownership of Uni-Serv Corporation which operates the Uni-Card Retail Shopping Credit Card in northeastern United States.

Any discussion of credit card forgery and loss inevitably involves statistics on loss resulted from unsolicited credit card operation. There is no doubt in this writer's mind but that the wholesale mailing and pilfering of credit cards has weakened the value of the card and contributed to the nationwide rise in forgery crimes. In recent testimony before Representative Wright Patman's Banking Committee, one witness graphically illustrated the economics of unsolicited credit cards. It was reported that unsolicited cards, when mailed to a large population of potential users, provided a 19% pick-up ratio. This is 19% of the total number of cards mailed. By contrast, when the same or a similar population was mailed credit card applications, which required initiative on the part of the person receiving the application, only 3% of the population applied for cards and subsequently purchased the company's product. The result is obvious. Credit card companies know full well that unsolicited mailing technique is up to 600% more effective than the mailing of credit card applications alone.

The potential for sales growth is obvious and immediate. One oil company is reported to have experienced a dramatic 50% increase in its credit sales following a large unsolicited credit card mailing. With this type of business increase potential, it is evident that the credit card operators are willing to absorb certain theft and forgery losses arising directly from their unsolicited card technique.

Despite this acceptance there are some responsible voices in the business community who take a cautious view. Mr. Charles A. Agemain, Executive Vice President of the Chase Manhattan Bank of New York, notes that "a bank has a responsibility to lend only after determining that the borrower will not become financially overburdened by the loan". Mr. Agemain's reference is to that provision of credit cards which provides an immediate loan capacity to the card holder. The card holder has the discretion to initiate charges which he knows himself to be quite incapable of paying. This often results in some interesting cases.

One credit card forger, a 19 year old Bronx, New York youth named Robert Miraglia, is alleged to have acquired a set of credit cards by applying for them in a name pattern which caused the card issuing company to confuse him with a relative who had a good credit standing. The cards were mailed to Miraglia and then it is alleged that he departed on a world-wide five week trip during which he ran up some $15,000 in fraudulent charges. These charges included such miscellaneous items as a mink stole for one of the girlfriends he met during his odyssey. Miraglia's adventure may have in turn provided the inspiration for two other New York forgers who managed to maintain five separate Miami Beach hotel suites through the use of a single stolen credit card. These suites provided a base of operations for a wild round of parties thrown by the forgers.

Credit card companies, despite their reluctance to talk to inquiring journalists about their losses, nonetheless are only too well aware of the depth and expense of the problem. Some interesting insights into this problem can be gained through an investigation of the credit index services provided to these companies. A unique service is that provided by the old established Hooper-Holmes Bureau, Inc. of Morristown, New Jersey. Hooper-Holmes does most of its business with major credit card issuing companies such as airline, auto rental, petroleum companies and general credit card companies. The latter firm maintains a computer bank of derogatory credit information. This derogatory credit information consists of both fraudulent and simple failure-to-pay situations. As of January, 1968 the Hooper-Holmes file contained some 9,285,390 items. This derogatory credit information represented over $469 million in delinquent accounts supplied by subscriber companies. Credit card items amounted to 1,882,211 individual items for a value of $294,668,548.00. Credit card credit problems generally follow the national population patterns. The State of California was the first with the largest number of items on file. New York was next, followed by Texas. The total number of items reported in these three States alone represented over 25% of the master index file.

One of the foremost problems in credit card forgery involves the very complexity of the law itself. At least a dozen States have no applicable legislation at all dealing with credit card forgeries. In still other States the possession of a stolen or fraudulently obtained credit card is a relatively minor offense. The credit card companies themselves have been actively lobbying for the issuance of both federal and state legislation which would put more bite into the enforcement machinery. The State of Virginia, for example, has recently enacted a bill which specifically defines credit card theft, card forgeries and fraud. Similar laws, based on recommendations provided by the credit card companies, have also been enacted in Florida, California, North Carolina and New York.

The Illinois legislature, reacting to the Chicago credit card debacle, has also recently passed legislation specifically dealing with this problem. On a federal level, bills have been introduced in Congress that would specifically deal with credit card forgery and fraud. The attempt of most of these bills is to make such operations a federal offense and to bring the FBI directly into this area of jurisdiction.

The author's personal impression is that the FBI would rather be left out of some areas of credit card fraud. Conversations with former FBI agents are revealing in that they point out that the case loads generated by granting jurisdiction to the FBI would be so voluminous as to be self-defeating. Rather, it would make more sense to set a dollar limit, of say $500.00 or more, and to apply FBI jurisdiction to these cases only. This would bring the Bureau into those cases where organized crime or large scale interstate operations were involved. It would save them from the burden of the numerous 5 and 10 dollar type forgeries which can be more properly handled by a local police personnel and credit card security personnel.

Of course, in any enforcement mechanism, the wholesale cooperation of the credit card companies themselves is a vital factor. There is still much work to be done in this area. Some credit card companies are not noted for their cooperation. In fact, their lack of cooperation prompted one credit card official, Joseph Tilem, of the then Hilton Credit Corporation to note that "the lack of cooperation in this competitive industry is fantastic! The card companies must learn they have to cooperate to cutdown misuse." (Business Week September 10, 1960, Page 49). In the case history section of this report some specific cases involving credit card fraud will be more closely examined. However, as an introduction to this subject area, we might consider some of the following vignettes of credit card forgery in operation.

Manhattan District Attorney, Frank S. Hogan, announced the arrest of a 7 man ring operating on the newly established "Everything Card" of the First National City Bank of New York. The credit losses on this credit card fraud are alleged to be approximately $50,000. The charges on this particular ring involved possession of forged instruments, third degree grand larcency, possession of stolen goods and petty larcency. Conviction resulting from these charges would result in a 1 to 7 year term. Cards in this particular case were obtained during the commission of burglaries, theft, pick-pocketing, etc.

Bronx, New York forgers, not to be outdone by their Manhattan contemporaries, also took an interested look at the First National City Bank's card. District Attorney, Burton B. Roberts of Bronx County recently announced the arrest of a separate group of forgers also operating on the "Everything Card". This seprate ring is said to have defrauded the First National City Bank of approximately $100,000.

This particular case was the third major credit card fraud ring broken up by the Bronx County District Attorneys Office. The two previous rings involved oil companies credit cards. The nature of these rings is such that they always involve multiple count indictments and present a tremendous workload to the District Attorney's Office involved. In the First National City Case just described, the 11 indictments produced over 1700 separate counts.

The ubiquitous telephone credit card does not seem to be capable of producing any grand amounts of forgery deception. Yet, a 51 year old exporter from Babylon, Long Island, is alleged to have defrauded the New York Telephone Company of some $146,000 in phone charges. Richard S. Fincke was indicted in 1968 for wire fraud through the fraudulent use of a telephone credit card. He alleged ran up a $146,000 bill through the placement of long distance and international calls connected with this import and export business. The calls were placed over a five year period. The Assistant U.S. Attorney handling the case, James B. Zirin, said that Mr. Fincke began use of the card in early 1962. It is alleged that Fincke had no intention of paying the bill and the telephone company eventually cancelled his service in June of 1967. Despite this cancellation, the exporter was able to run up an additional $2,000 in charges. It is also alleged that Mr. Fincke lent his telephone credit card to certain creditors in partial satisfaction of his debt. At the time of this writing this case is still under investigation and has not come to trial. The United States Attorney in charge of the Criminal Division has refused to comment on how the exporter had been able to evade payment of his bills for such a long time. However, he did note that this was probably the largest telephone bill ever run up through such a telephone credit card scheme.

Miss Ann Ayleen Foley, a 25 year old San Francisco secretary, participated in a credit card promotion arranged by the Bank of

America in San Francisco. Miss Foley was supplied with a Bank Americard and told to spend no cash at all for a period of 31 days. For 31 days, Miss Foley lived completely, in the San Francisco area, by using the credit card. She had some difficulty with things like buses and taxis but the card, of course, provided car rentals which made such unnecessary. This card promotion while obviously a publicity stunt, shows the extent to which a credit card, in the metropolitan area, can be used as a substitute for cash. The more extensive the credit card is recognized, the more closely it approximates money. The obvious moral drawn from this comparison, is well documented by history's experience with currency, counterfeiters and forgers. (Forbes Magazine, September 5, 1966, Page 39)

Thus far we have been talking solely about the forgery of credit cards. The forgers either steal or in some other fraudulent manner obtain the credit card and places his signature on it. He utilizes the name on the credit card but makes no particular attempt to disguise his handwriting or to match the known handwriting of the legitimate cardholder. The forger prefers of course to receive the card without anyone's signature on it. The cards that he intercepts in the mail or steals from card producing plants are in such a condition. However, other cards which are obtained by prostitutes, pickpockets, burglary, etc. usually have a signature already on the signature panel section of the card. The forger has a variety of methods for removing this signature without damaging the erasure-sensitive panel itself. For security reasons, the author cannot reveal these exact techniques although they are well known to law enforcement officials and, unfortunately, to organized crime. It suffices to say that the erasure prevention techniques which the card allegedly has are worth relatively little in the hands of a skilled forger.

One of the most amazing things about credit cards concerns the fact that they have not been more extensively counterfeited. There are relatively few cases thus far where the card itself has been completely fabricated from start to finish. One of these cases, which is currently pending in the Southern District of New York does involve organized crime figures in the alleged counterfeiting of American Express Cards. However, in most cases, the extent of counterfeiting involves manipulation of card blanks which are obtained from the theft of credit card manufacturing plants, etc. I have questioned many credit card security personnel about the potential for counterfeiting credit card. Almost all feel that at the present time we probably won't see too much large scale counterfeiting of the credit cards. The reason for this is quite simple. The cards are just too easy to obtain through less imaginative and expensive means. It is far easier to steal the cards as they progress through the mails or to obtain them from normal criminal sources.

Technically, the credit card is perhaps 100 times easier to counterfeit than ordinary U. S. currency. The card itself is usually a three-ply plastic laminate. The front and back plies are clear vinyl film. The center ply is a pigmented vinyl film which has printing on the face and back. This center ply is imprinted and is then laminated to the protective clear front and back ply. The impression of the customer's name is done later. All of the principal printing techniques are utilized in the production of credit cards. From a counterfeiting standpoint, a credit card could be counterfeited with printing equipment which would cost no more than $20 to $30. When one considers the value of certain of these cards, such as the American Express, Diners or Universal Air Travel Plan Card, it is quite frankly amazing that they have not been cunterfeited. Industry security personnel are well aware of the counterfeiting potential of the cards and are holding their breath against the day when this potential is realized by some enterprising counterfeiter-forger.

Bibliography

Adams, Thomas F., FIELD INTERROGATION-POLICE (March, April 1963)

Banton, Michael, THE POLICEMAN AND THE COMMUNITY (London; Tavistock, 1964)

Bell, Daniel, THE END OF IDEOLOGY (New York; Free Press, 1960) Chapter 7 "Crime As An American Way of Life"

Black, Hillel, BUY NOW, PAY LATER (New York; William Morrow & Co., 1961)

Bordua, David J., Editor, THE POLICE (New York; John Wiley & Sons, 1967)

Cameron, Mary Owen, THE BOOSTER AND THE SNITCH (Glencoe, Ill.; Free Press, 1964)

Cressey, Donald R., **OTHER PEOPLE'S MONEY; A STUDY IN THE SOCIAL PSYCHOLOGY OF EMBEZZLEMENT**(Glencoe, Ill.; Free Press, 1953)

Fuller, John G., **THE GENTLEMEN CONSPIRATORS** (New York; Grove Press, Inc., 1962)

Gordon, Wayne, C. and Pittman, David J., **REVOLVING DOOR;** A study of the chronic police case inebriate. (New York; Free Press 1958)

Hancock, Ralph, **THE COMPLETE SWINDLER** (New York; Macmillan Co., 1968)

Jaspan, Norman with Black, Hillel, **THIEF IN THE WHITE COLLAR** (Philadelphia; J. P. Lippincott Co., 1960)

Jentry, Curt, **THE VULNERABLE AMERICAN** (Garden City, Doubleday & Co., Inc., 1966)

LaFave, Wayne R., **ARREST** (Boston; Little Brown & Co., 1965)

Matza, **DELINQUENCY AND DRIFT** (New York; John Wiley & Son, Inc. 1964)

Niederhofer, Arthur, **BEHIND THE SHIELD; THE POLICE IN URBAN SOCIETY** (Garden City; Doubleday & Co., 1967)

O'Connor, George W. and Watson, Nelson A., **JUVENILE DELINQUENCY AND YOUTH CRIME; THE POLICE ROLE,** (Washington, D. C.; International Association of Chiefs of Police, 1964)

Sagi, Philip C. and Wellford, Charles F., **"AGE COMPOSITION AND PATTERNS OF CHANGE IN CRIMINAL STATISTICS"** - special paper prepared for the President's commission on law enforcement and the Administration of Justice.

Skolnick, Jerome H., **JUSTICE WITHOUT TRIAL** (New York; John Wiley & Sons, 1966)

Sparrow, Gerald, **THE GREAT SWINDLERS** (London, John Long, 1959)

Sutherland, Edwin H., **WHITE COLLAR CRIME** (New York; Dryden Press, 1949)

Sykes, Gresham N., **THE SOCIETY OF CAPTIVES** (Princeton; Princeton University Press, 1958)

Weil, Joseph and Brann, W. T., **YELLOW KID WEIL; THE AUTOBIOGRAPHY OF AMERICA'S MASTER SWINDLER** (Chicago, Ziff Davis Publishing Co., 1948)

Westley, William A., **THE POLICE;** A Sociological Study of Law, Custom and Morality. (Unpublished Ph.D. dissertation, Dept. of Sociology, University of Chicago, 1951)

Wheeler, Stanton, Editor, **CONTROLLING DELINQUENTS** (New York, John Wiley & Sons, 1968)

CRIME AND ITS IMPACT-AN ASSESSMENT (Washington, Government Printing Office 1967)

MODUS OPERANDI

Con games — and forgery is in essence a confidence-type criminal scheme, are immortal. They may disappear for awhile, because of local or national social climates, but they soon reappear, even if in modified form. Some of the forgery M.O.'s in use today date directly to the birth of widespread banking during the growth of the Industrial Revolution. On the surface they often appear quite different. They have been plated and polished by 20th century artisans. But beneath the plating the skeleton of the scheme is unchanged. They prey on the same human gullibility and employ a financial sleight of hand which dates directly to a mideastern bazaar.

Recording and classifying forgery M.O.'s is a confounding task. First, there are literally hundreds of con schemes of which forgery is an essential ingredient. Second, many of these schemes are but minor variations of other schemes, while still others overlap in a manner which defies orderly classification.

What the author has presented in this chapter is a grouping of the most common types of check, document and credit card M.O.'s This is a sampling from hundreds of cases researched during the past several years. There are no absolutes here. The only certainty is that we have probably missed some M.O.'s and that still others are evolving as we write.

The Split Deposit

The split deposit is one of the oldest and still one of the most successful bank forgery methods in use today. It is safe to say that it has been in use against American banks for over one hundred years. Some of the earliest bank journals caution against this forgery method. Yet it remains one of the simplest and most trusted ways of parting a bank from its assets. There are several dozen minor variations of this method. Here are but a few of them.

The essential element of the split deposit method involves the alleged "deposit" of a portion of a check being cashed at a bank. The check is forged or fraudulent. There are a number of ways this technique works. For example, the forger may "legitimately" open an account with the bank and deposit a modest amount of cash. Later he will make additional small deposits. Then he will appear with a large value check, say for $1,000. He will deposit three or four hundred dollars of the check to his account and will ask for the balance in cash. Thus he has "split" his deposit. The check may be counterfeit, stolen, etc. In any event it is worthless. He has partially allayed any suspicion the bank teller might have had by "depositing" part of the check in his account. He has depositor status and this lends credibility to the transaction.

Depositor status is not even needed for this type scheme, and in fact in the majority of cases the forger doesn't bother to set up such a front. All that is required is the appearance of depositor status. The forger may learn the names of some of the principal depositors, then, representing himself as the depositor, make the split deposit. In smaller towns and cities there are a limited number of banks and the forger can usually assume that the town's more prominent citizens have accounts in the major banks.

There are still other variations of the split deposit method involving messengers, secretaries or part-time help who are set up to act as unwitting accomplices for the forger. Sometimes the forger will set up a dummy business operation and use temporary help as dupes in a split deposit scheme. In these cases the forger has usually also set up an account in the bank as part of his front operation.

Within the past few years many banks have gone over to printed deposit slips. These slips contain the name of the depositor and sometimes the magnetically encoded depositor number identification. This step may discourage the amateur forger, but it actually works to the professional's advantage. To the forger with the facility to counterfeit actual checks, the counterfeiting of a deposit slip is a snap. The fact that the slip is imprinted often gives the bank teller a completely false sense of confidence in the legitimacy of the operation. He might hesitate at a split deposit transaction in which a counter-type deposit slip is being presented. But when confronted with a split deposit in which the deposit slip is custom printed with the depositor's name, he loses much of his caution and occasionally much of his bank's money.

Check thief-forgers also use the printed deposit slip to their advantage. In the course of a robbery where they pick up checks, usually lifted from the back or center of a checkbook, they will also be certain to take along some printed deposit slips. Check printers obligingly bind the deposit slips into the back of the check book.

Merchandise Frauds

Straight merchandise frauds, accomplished through forged checks, are among the time-honored M.O.'s of forgers throughout the world. These methods have lately been neglected by the American "pros", but they are still popular among the garden-variety forger. Here are but a few of these schemes.

Used car sales are one profitable outlet for the forger's handiwork. In one recent case, which the writer is personally familiar with, a late model Mustang was for sale by a Long Island, New York family. The car was advertised in local papers and a prospective "buyer" arranged to see the car on a Thursday evening. He was "thrilled" with the condition of the car and readily agreed to purchase it. The buyer said that he would return the following evening, Friday night, with a certified check for the full purchase price of the car. He did return the following night with a certified check. The check bore a rubber stamp certification seal, the bank signature, and was made out to a bank in Glen Cove, Long Island. The bank, as it turned out later, was nonexistent. Police finally located the car some months later in a small Ohio city where it had been subsequently "sold". The operator of this swindle is a young, personable looking forger who arrived with his "fiancee" to inspect the car. At the date of this writing this couple is still at large.

One forger, dubbed "Willie the Whiz" cashed "certified checks" and received merchandise and cash. Willie would hit 50 or more banks per day. He obtained credentials and signature samples from pick-pockets who originally were only concerned with cash. (Since that time they have come to sell packages of stolen checks and matching credentials). Before arriving in town Willie would send registered letters to fictitious names which he intended to later impersonate. This mail would be sent to a downtown hotel to be held pending his arrival. He would register at each hotel using the appropriate alias. Later he would purchase a valuable item, using a forged certified check and would display the stolen ID credentials and invite the store owner to call the hotel and check the registration. He would also display the envelope indicating that it had been mailed to him at that particular hotel from out of town.

Still another merchandise-check fraud swindle involves the utilization of the "social event" calendar of the daily newspaper. In this case the writer uses the term "social event" to encompass all events ranging from births, marriages, deaths, etc. The swindler in this technique will visit a retail establishment and order a gift, flowers or some other appropriate item, to be sent to the party mentioned in the newspaper. For example, the proud mother of a set of twins may discover that she receives a dual set of cribs. What has actually occurred is that a confidence man has visited a local furniture store and, representing himself as the uncle of the new twins, ordered two cribs to be sent to the mother. He pays for the cribs with a check which usually amounts to $75 or $100 more than the purchase price. He explains to the furniture dealer that he needs some additional cash for minor additional purchases that he wishes to make for the new set of twins. The furniture dealer, if he is suspicious, can easily check the local birth announcements and discover that, in fact, a set of twins has been born to a particular family. The check is usually drawn on a local bank where the con man may have just opened an account. This technique is also referred to as the "overpurchase technique."

The same con man can visit flower shops, clothing stores, etc. and pull this technique a dozen or more times within a single day, sometimes escaping with several thousand dollars before either the bank, the retailer, or the mother of the twins is aware of what is going on. The same technique can be used for weddings and wedding gifts and may even be employed for funerals where flowers or similar items are ordered for the funeral itself.

Sometimes the con man uses stolen merchandise as a front for a bad check operation. For example, a forger might steal an automobile and deliberately cause it to need some minor repair. He would then take the auto to a repair shop and receive an estimate. When he has been given an estimate for the job he would request that he be allowed to pay for it in advance since he was going to be away for a few days. He would then write a check for a sum larger than the amount of the bill, collect the difference in cash and be on his way. The garage mechanic believes that he has plenty of security in that the vehicle is in his possession, but does not realize that the vehicle has been stolen for the occasion. There are dozens of variations of this particular type of merchandise M.O. with merchandise ranging from stolen television sets, hollow watches, etc. used as "security" in the course of passing a bad check as previously described.

The C.O.D. Switch

C.O.D., as every schoolboy knows, stands for cash-on-delivery. In the C.O.D. switch, it is the forger who ends up with the cash. There are two principal methods involved in this type of forgery. The first involves the actual counterfeiting of C.O.D. delivery slips, while the second is based on the mechanics of a C.O.D. transaction coupled with a fraudulent check.

Penny ante fraud continues to be employed in the counterfeiting or forging of C.O.D. slips. The forger fabricates a package which appears to originate from some gift store or similar well known location, forges a C.O.D. slip attached to it and arrives at a prosperous home owner's residence. He utilizes a local delivery service uniform and perhaps even a false truck. A member of the family accepts it, believing it was ordered by someone else, and pays the C.O.D. charge.

Forged checks can also be used as part of the C.O.D. switch. One of the M.O.'s typical to this operation involves the individual who opens a legitimate account with a large chain store. He orders and pays on time for several major items. Following this repeat pattern the forger then sets up a switch operation. He orders a large quantity of merchandise such as appliances, etc. and specifies that they should be delivered to a particular address. When the delivery man arrives at the address he is greeted by the "good customer" who advises him that he is moving his apartment or home and that the delivery man arrived "just in time". The newly ordered merchandise is transferred from the delivery van to a "moving truck" and the forger pays for the delivery which, like the previous deliveries, has been on a C.O.D. basis, with a check. This time the check is worthless. The forger then proceeds to fence the merchandise, more than offsetting his initial cost in purchases at the store.

The Non-Forgery

The furor about check forgery creates a built in opportunity for another type of "forgery" swindle. In this particular case, no actual forgery occurs, but the fraud depends on the illusion of forgery. A seedy-looking character walks into a jewelry shop, gift shop, automobile showroom, photographic equipment store, etc. He selects a well known brand product. This could range from a Leica camera to a Cadillac automobile. He offers to pay for the item with a check. Naturally, the management is very suspicious but the "buyer" persists. He asks them to call and check with the bank where he maintains his account. A check with the bank reveals that the "buyer" does in fact have an account there and that the balance is more than sufficient to cover the purchase. The forger has seen to this particular eventuality way ahead of time, and in fact he has counted on it.

The purchase is consummated and the buyer leaves with his purchase. This usually occurs in early afternoon a few hours before bank closing time. The "buyer" then proceeds directly to another dealer where he attempts to sell the item he has just purchased. The new dealer is also suspicious and calls back the original vendor. The original vendor now thinks that he may still have been the victim of a forgery. He envisions the man drawing out the bank account and demands that the "buyer" be held. The police are called and the indignant original seller arrives on the scene. The suspect is maintained under guard until the following day when the bank opens.

During all this time the suspect maintains his innocence. He has been "convicted" by circumstantial evidence. The following day when the bank opens the seller discovers to his chagrin that the check is in fact good and that he can get full payment on the check presented to him. Now he is faced with a false arrest suit by the "buyer." A settlement out of court occurs and these settlements have ranged from $10 to $50,000 in some cases.

The Swiss Transfer

Foreign depositors in American banks are often "protecting" their funds by maintaining them in a stable currency and a "stable" banking climate. Unfortunately, they are sometimes in for a rude awakening. The sanctity of the mail in some countries does not approach that of the United States and it is quite feasible to intercept bank statements and cancelled checks sent by American banks to their foreign depositors. Utilizing these samples, plus a knowledge of the bank balance, foreign forgers have been able to open accounts in Switzerland and then forge "letters of authorization" advising the American banks to transfer large quantities of funds to these Swiss accounts. The Swiss accounts were, of course, those of the forger and the monies were in turn transferred out of these accounts as soon as they became available. In this particular case the forgers did not in fact forge the true depositor's signature to a check, money order, etc. This is a fine point, but it is important in that the forgery of signatures to *authorizing* documents is sometimes more profitable than the forging of a signature to an actual fiscal document. The authorizing document may be one step removed from the fiscal document itself, but it is no less effective in prying open the depositor's account.

Another example of this type fraud is contained in the case history section in the case entitled "The Twelve Million Dollar Wire". This case illustrates the use of the authorization forgery as practiced by organized crime within the U.S.

The Innocent Passer

The utilization of third parties for the obvious purpose of cashing checks is a well known M.O. In this case the forger is utilizing someone else who had a valid ID. For example, he may draw up a series of worthless checks payable to a particular messenger, chauffeur, secretary, etc. which seem to be from his "company". The dupe has been hired that week for this particular operation. After one or two days employment in miscellaneous tasks, he is sent down to the bank to cash a check from the "corporation" drawn to himself. The dupe can supply valid ID and is usually asked to cash it at his local bank. In some cases these "dupes" are shadowed by the forgers to determine whether or not the check has been successfully cashed and whether any police suspicion has been aroused. This is usually an operation that begins and concludes within a few days.

Organized forgery rings are particularly anxious to obtain "fresh faces". Summer college students often become the innocents in this type of scheme. They are hired as messengers and clerks for a front operation. They don't look like forgers because they aren't. In some recent cases forgery rings in the northeast have even been able to use coeds from other parts of the country as passers.

The Telephone Decoy

The ubiquitous black box, the telephone, can be amongst the forger's best friends. Forgers operate on public gullibility. They rely on creating an essential aura of confidence. The telephone is often the instrument best equipped to do this job. Take a look at some of the ways that the forger uses a telephone.

The first M.O. utilizes the telephone to provide an identity verification that does not exist. An accomplice working with the forger telephones a particular bank and represents himself as an executive of one of the local respected companies. He says that one of his assistants, Mr. John Doe (the forger), will be arriving at the bank shortly and he would appreciate it if they would ask Mr. Doe to call him when he arrives. The forger arrives shortly after this call and is given the message. In the presence of the banker he returns the call to a front or pay phone number and proceeds to have a short conversation with the "executive." Following this he presents a check for several hundred dollars. The check has been counterfeited with the name of the local company, but is usually drawn on another bank in town. With this type of verification the bank affected is most likely to accept the check forgetting that anyone can make a telephone call and represent himself as an executive of a local company. This procedure links the man with the company and the check and provides an extra bit of identity. The forger is doubly prepared. He probably has additional "identity documents" on his person. This may include a letter, envelope packing slip, etc. from the company in town.

A further development of the telephone M.O. technique involves the use of a local lawyer. In one case the forger and his accomplice had made some actual studies of the lawyer's voice and had remarkable success in imitating it. Now the forger will arrive at a bank with a large check, from the local well known law firm and present it for payment. The banker, if he is hesitant, will then be advised by the forger to call the lawyer. At this point timing is of the essence since an incoming call from the "lawyer" (actually the accomplice) is made to the banker. This call, in the imitated voice of the lawyer, advises the banker that he should expedite the handling of the check and request the "client" to return immediately to the lawyer's office for the completion of a real estate transaction. The banker later discovers that the lawyer knew nothing of any of this. Sometimes, to guarantee that the true lawyer will not be present, he may be drawn out of his office by a decoy telephone call from a client who is "at the local jail" or at the scene of an "automobile accident," etc. This guarantees that the true lawyer will be unable to answer a further call back by the banker to verify any further information on the check, etc.

Purchases of durable goods and the subsequent credit applications for installment buying provide an additional mechanism for the telephone decoy scheme. In this particular M.O. the forger first approaches a car dealer, home furnishing supplier, etc. He proposes to purchase the item but advises that he will have to get a bank loan in order to complete the purchase. Usually he puts down a small deposit, say $25.00 or $50.00 and then proceeds to a bank. At the bank he makes out a credit application listing his "employer" and the employer's telephone number. The latter telephone is a front number tended by an accomplice. When the bank calls to confirm the credit applicant's employment, the accomplice answers and "confirms" that the forger does work there and that he makes a good salary and is a long-term employee. With this "assurance" the bank writes an installment loan and makes out a check to the car dealer, home furnisher, etc. Usually the bank also checks by phone with the dealer and confirms that the individual has been in and has put down a deposit pending his successful credit application and that he has placed an order for the goods in question. The bank now issues a check. The check is drawn to the attention of the dealer to be used in the purchase.

The forger, once he gains possession of the check, forges the dealer's endorsement and follows with a second disguised endorsement which he uses to deposit the check, usually for several thousand dollars, into a previously prepared bank account. Within a day or so he withdraws the balance of that account in cash and flees. The bank usually becomes apprised of the forgery and fraud when the dealer calls a few days later to inquire why they haven't approved credit on the "loan".

The Duplicate Deposit Slip

The deposit slip is an innocent enough looking piece of paper. In simpler times it was solely used to aid bank bookkeeping, and to provide the depositor with a record of his deposit. The deposit slip can also be a signal to the bank teller that a depositor does have sufficient funds to cover a newly drawn check. In some cases this signal is jammed by the forger.

The duplicate deposit slip M.O. has been used countless times with a number of variations. The basic premise is that the forger, who either has acquired, or represents himself to have acquired, depositor status, makes a cash deposit of a large sum and receives a stamped duplicate deposit slip. He may choose to utilize a legitimate U.S. Treasury check, corporation check, legitimate certified check from another bank, etc. in establishing the duplicate deposit slip. Later, with this duplicate deposit slip he will return to the bank and, selecting another teller, will present his own check drawn to an amount almost equal to the deposit he has made. He will repeat this process to two or three different tellers, thus making a 400% profit on his initial investment and regaining his initial investment. In one recent instance, four separate tellers were hit with the same duplicate deposit slip. The forger often acquires a working knowledge of the lunch hours, coffee breaks, etc. of various tellers and times his visit to take advantage of their absences. The stamped duplicate deposit slip is shown as evidence that he has a certain amount in his account. If he has set up a legitimate account, the first teller will discover nothing amiss, even if he checks. Perhaps before this withdrawal can be posted to the forger's account, he will have hit a second or third teller.

The O.K. System

Most people like to pass the buck. And when you're a bank teller and can pass it to the Vice President, you're usually in good hands. Unless, of course, the hands happen to be that of a skilled forger.

Most banks utilize an "okay" system in which an officer's initials are jotted down on a check to indicate clearance to the teller. Various initial designs, monograms, etc. are commonly utilized. The trick in this M.O. is for the forger to obtain a copy of the bank officer's clearance initials on a legitimate check. He will either then raise the check or create a completely counterfeit check and forge the "O.K." initials. One of the methods utilized here is for a forger to go in and purchase, for cash, a certified or bank check. Later he will return declaring that he doesn't need the check anymore and that he wishes to cash it. The officer will apply his initials to the check and the forger will supposedly "cash it". In some cases he will palm the check and simply ask the teller for change.

In other cases, he may have had two checks drawn, will later request refunding, and will palm one and cash the other. This gives him a check with the correct authorizing initials and perhaps even an opportunity to raise the check. Tellers have been instructed never to cash initialed checks except when presented by a bank employee. But in the rush of business, frequently the executive cannot walk to the teller's window or find a messenger or bank clerk, or guard to transfer the check to the window. If such a transfer occurs, the only thing the forger loses is a little time since he has purchased the check for cash and it has been redeemed for nearly the same amount less a small service charge.

Sometimes you will see the "refund check" variation of the O.K. System. In this variation the forger manages to overpay a local business concern and to obtain a refund check made out to his attention. He first takes the check to a teller and is referred to the authorizing bank officer. He gets the O.K. initials by any of the methods described previously. On the way back to the teller he palms the small refund check and substitutes a much larger one, procured from counterfeit or stolen check sources. The fraudulent check has the forged executive's initials. The teller has observed his contact with the bank officer, and he cashes the "O.K." check.

There are dozens of variations to the "O.K." M.O. All of them operate on the basic principle that the O.K. System has been initiated as a countermeasure to forgery. As such a counter-measure, it engenders in the bank teller a degree of confidence and security which it really does not deserve.

In more human terms it also shifts the responsibility for accepting the check to the officer whose initials appear on the check. To show how this system works, we might consider the case of William Hamilton Harkins who allegedly was one of the most skilled practitioners of this particular M.O. Harkins might purchase one or two legitimate checks from a bank and combine them with forged checks of much greater amounts in setting up his scheme. Harkins would obtain the initialling characteristics of the bank officers by the scheme previously described. He would then prepare two identical checks for a larger sum, say two or three thousand dollars. Next he would approach the victim bank and present to the teller one of the uninitialed checks for the larger amount. The teller would refer him to the bank officer for clearance. The forger would then go to the bank officer and produce the much smaller check which he had purchased, pretending to be in need of refund, and receive the bank officer's initials.

A conversation would ensue between Harkins and the bank officer. Harkins would advise the officer that he had purchased the check, later decided to return it and had it initialed the previous day but because he was in a hurry did not have a chance to wait in line to cash it. The bank officer would tell him that it was still all right and no further initials were required and Harkins would then return to the teller. During his return trip he would palm the small check and produce the second large amount check which had the officer's initials forged. The teller, observing the conversation, would now accept the "initialed" check.

The Banker's Friend

Friendship with forgers can be fatal — especially for bank tellers. Forgers are known to deliberately "work on" the personal vanity, friendliness, or curiosity of a particular teller. There are many ways they can accomplish this. The female teller may be complimented on her appearance, her resemblance to some celebrity, a fictitious relative, etc. A male teller can be similarly conned by a female member of a forgery team.

Some forgers will take this technique a step further and learn some personal details about the teller through local newspapers, school records, city registration lists, etc. This information will be casually inserted in a conversation with the teller distracting his or her attention away from the real transaction — the cashing of a fraudulent check.

Forgers frequently operate on the gullibility of bank tellers, store clerks, etc. An alert forger can quickly discover whether or not a particular teller pays much attention to what the closest bank officers do. At certain times of the day, when the action is slow at the teller's window, the teller naturally observes what occurs in other departments in the bank. In this situation a forger will time his entrance for a slack period and will stop by at a bank officers desk to exchange a few pleasantries. The bank officer may be somewhat taken aback by the unprovoked familiarity, but he will usually reciprocate believing that he has met the "customer" some time previous and does not recall his acquaintanceship. This little vignette is witnessed by the target teller. The forger then proceeds to the teller's station where he cashes a fraudulent check on the basis of his "familiarity" with the bank officer.

A slight variation of the latter technique takes place when the forger visits the bank during a period when he knows that a particular bank officer will be absent. Again, in view of the subject teller he asks for a particular bank officer by first name and intimates a friendship with the subject officer. He may also stop by a second officer and relate how they have been previously introduced by his "friend". When this act is witnessed by the teller, he obtains a favorable impression of the "customer" and subsequently accepts the forger's check.

The "Uniform" Dodge

Uniforms work wonders. Military uniforms are particularly appropriate as the dress for a check forger. The higher the military rank the better. What some store clerks and bank tellers seem oblivious to is that military insignia from a general on down are readily available for a modest sum and that uniforms can be purchased or rented to fit a particular occasion. The teller, faced with a major general presenting a check, may be slightly swayed and intimidated by his own previous lowly military experience. Other favorite uniforms of check passers are those of priests, ministers, nuns, nurses, doctors, airline pilots, police officers, etc.

Recently in New England a forger dressed in a Coca-Cola deliveryman's uniform. Typically, he would drive into a drive-in bank, in a panel truck decorated to look like a company service truck, and present a company "payroll" check for cashing. The checks were counterfeit.

The William J. Burns Agency reports on the escapades of one "doctor" forger who ran up some big scores in and around New York City. This operator would use the names of legitimate doctors in the area, and would sometimes rush in at noon garbed in a doctors white coat, stethoscope and all. Although he always ran the risk that some teller might know the real doctor, he nonetheless seemed to practice this routine for quite awhile before being apprehended.

Religious garb also gets its share of attention from professional forgers. One forger is known to have travelled throughout the U.S. employing the credentials and clothing of a legitimate priest. This operator even managed to defraud churches he visited and which he asked to cash a check.

A forger, dressed in a priest's garb, also visited a series of Chicago catering firms. He provided each catering firm with a purchase order for several hundred dollars worth of supplies to be delivered within a few weeks to a "church party". He inquired about a deposit and was usually told that a $30 or $40 deposit is necessary. He would then make out a check for a $100.00 sum commenting that he needed the cash for "some additional shopping while downtown". The $60 balance would be paid to the "priest" in cash. Of course, the check was fraudulent.

The uniform impersonation method serves other types of criminals equally well. Willie Sutton popularized this M.O. in bank robbery. The FBI now reports that this technique has spread to South America, where it was recently used to rob a major industrial plant of its payroll. The uniform dodge is completely within the character of the forger and indeed some forgers are probably using it when they don't even have to. The sense of triumph they obtain through a successful impersonation fits exactly into the personality profile described elsewhere in this report.

Still other variations employ less formal "uniforms". For example, one forger who counterfeited the checks of a casualty claim insurance company, would regularly appear in banks with his arm in a cast and a bandage about his head. There is also the "widow" dressed in mourning black who shows up in a local bank, after having previously set up an account there, and deposits a counterfeit insurance company check for $10,000 to her account. The next day the check balance is withdrawn in cash and travelers checks and the "widow" travels on.

The Doubles Game

The game of "doubles" is often played by the more sophisticated check artist. In this scheme, the forger actually becomes the "double" of a respected and well-known business or professional man. He either acquires or counterfeits identity credentials in order to represent himself as a sound business man. He learns of the businessman's banking operations and proceeds to a bank where the businessman regularly deals. Representing himself as this businessman (this is quite possible because in larger urban banks the better customer may not even be personally recognized by many bank officers), he advises the bank that he is going to open up a second account at this bank. He opens this second account, providing an additional signature card, and then during the next few days proceeds to transfer most of the funds out of the true depositor's account into this second account. From the second account he then withdraws cash completing the fraud.

Another of the ways in which depositor status is effectively utilized in the *Doubles Game* is in the establishment of an account with a name very similar or identical to a prosperous and legitimate firm. For example, suppose the Smith Company (fictitious) is a reputable and well known stock brokerage firm. Forgers might visit a nearby city or community and set up a bank account with an identical name. Then, using a dishonest employee or direct mail theft methods, they would procure checks drawn to the favor of the Smith Company. They would take these to their "own" bank and deposit them to the newly opened account. Once the account had been built up into what they consider a desirable figure, they would draw it out in cash or convert the account in some circuitous method and depart before the legitimate Smith Company discovered that a major portion of their checks, over a one or two-week period, had been intercepted. A La Cosa Nostra family recently utilized this exact technique.

Depositor Switches

As previously noted, depositor status is highly prized by the
check forger. In one recent case reported by the ABA, a gang of
three men individually opened accounts under assumed names
and provided as references each other's names. They arranged to
receive the bank's letters of reference inquiry and of course replied
in glowing terms. Their forgeries on banks located in major cities
yielded nearly $100,000.

In one of their operations, they opened accounts at more than
30 separate banks and created a pattern of repeated deposits and
withdrawals. In some cases they let the account age for many
months. Some of these banks were selected for target operations.
Tellers at these particular banks were cultivated so that they were
familiar with the forger and his deposits and withdrawals. The
forgers then proceeded to present forged checks in amounts
between $4 and $5,000. They neatly withdrew their own balance
plus defrauding the banks out of over $100,000.

The Company That Never Was

There are many varieties of the phony company-type scheme.
Philadelphia police report one designated "The Ajax Construction Company Case". In this case two forgers set up a typical front
with an answering service, stationery, etc. They then arranged to
have a quantity of payroll checks printed. They opened a local
bank account with a $500 deposit. A secretary is engaged, she
proves to be an innocent dupe, and is provided with a list of
"employees" who are authorized to cash the construction company check. Thus, if anyone phoned in asking for a confirmation,
the secretary confirms the fact that the person is authorized to
cash the checks.

Now, with the scheme set up, the forgers go into operation.
They make out a large number of payroll checks and take them to
local merchants, banks, check cashing company, etc. They suggest
in many cases that the merchant or bank call the office and verify
their employment. All of these checks proved to be good because
the forgers are setting up the merchants for a kill later on. They
repeat this pattern making out checks and allowing them to be
legally passed through their account where they have deposited

sufficient money to cover the checks. They follow the same routine and visit the same merchants and banks each Friday depositing what appears to be weekly paychecks. Since all of the checks have passed the banks previously, the merchants or banks are lulled into a false sense of security. On the fourth Friday in the sequence, the forgers now write checks totalling $5,000.00 and take them to the places where they are now established. Besides their own checks they also have some checks from "fellow employees" each of which is scrupulously endorsed. At this point every single one of the checks for both the forgers and their "fellow employees" is cashed. The forgers now return to their bank and shortly before closing, draw out most of their initial deposit which has been used to cover the previous checks. Within hours, they have left the city to begin their scheme somewhere else and are $5,000 richer for one month's work.

The set-up of phony companies is integral to dozens of forgery M.O.'s. It is nearly always the trademark of a professional forger. In the case history section of this report the reader will see further evidence of how this M.O. is employed by the pros.

The Honest Depositor

The forger is constantly impressing people with his innate honesty. For example, he will walk into a small town bank and politely ask the teller for change of two twenty dollar bills. When the correct change is handed back to him he will begin to walk away, while palming a separate five dollar bill into the stack of bills. Suddenly he will "discover" that the teller has given him too much change and will return to the teller. The teller is both flustered by his "mistake" and impressed by the man's honesty. The forger will turn as if to walk away again and then will decide that "he better have a little more cash handy". He will present the teller with a fraudulent check for $100. The chances are good that the teller will cash it. The net profit to the forger is $95.

The Big Spender

Some forgers have found that they can best gain the bank teller's confidence with a display of personal wealth. Expensive clothing doesn't do the whole job. Sometimes the desired effect is obtained by having the forger present three or four large bills, for example $100 bills, and then ask for change in smaller bills. This establishes a climate of financial security and the forger then passes a bad check for less than $100.00. He might also pass a legitimate travellers check which has been raised or which has been stolen and endorsed.

A further refinement of this technique finds the forger purchasing two or three large value certified checks from another branch of the same bank system. These are "salt" for the worthless check that he cashes at the same time that he presents the legitimate checks.

The Illiterate Forgers

As reported previously, the forgery of welfare and social security checks is fast becoming a major problem. Ironically, since this type of forgery is often committed by criminals with relatively little education ... a new forgery M.O. evolved to fit the talents and needs of this type of criminal.

In this operation, twelve or more persons may be involved in the forgery. The check will be filled out by a number of different persons. For example, the date may be filled in by one gang member, the amount by another, the first name of the signer by one gang member and the last name by another, the endorsement by still another member and the last name by another, the endorsement by still another member and finally the check itself will be passed by one or more of the remaining members of the gang. In some cases a single gang member has been found to have the task of filling in only the middle initial in a check maker's signature. This procedure complicates the life of the document examiner, but does not make detection and prosecution impossible by any means.

The Benefactor Routine

Chicago police recently uncovered a forgery operation involving a typical con man scheme. One of the local voluntary religious hospitals was visited by a well dressed man of Spanish origin. The man provided a story indicating that he was greatly impressed with the hospital's good work, and being very wealthy, planned to leave them a large sum in his will. He was taken on an extensive tour of the hospital's facilities and provided engaging conversation through the entire tour. The tour took place in late afternoon and the forger, feigning ignorance of local banking customs, "discovered" that the banks were closed and he was unable to cash a $500.00 check. He told hospital authorities that he was flying back to Mexico and needed cash before he boarded the plane. He even displayed a valid airline ticket. Obligingly, the hospital's treasury office cashed a $500.00 check which of course proved to be a forgery and worthless.

The Autoforger

There is one forger type who is extremely rare on the American scene, but who deserves special attention because of his intimate knowledge of the very science used to apprehend him. This man is known as the autoforger. Here is how he works.

The forger, sometimes with impressive credentials, opens an account in an urban bank. He may open additional accounts in other banks and transfer amounts from one account to another to create the impression of activity in the account. He maintains a very healthy balance in the target account. Next, either using an accomplice or a very professional disguise, he draws out his balance by cashing a check with his own signature against his own account. The key here is the signature. The forger, and this variety is fortunately very rare, is able to produce a signature that, while it looks a great deal like the signature he has been using, must nonetheless be honestly classified by a document examiner as a "forgery". The bank is forced to make good the amount "forged" from this individuals account.

As shown elsewhere in this report, handwriting disguise *is* possible, particularly by an extremely skilled individual. Where the document examiner is provided with insufficient standards of the suspect's handwriting he may be unable to detect disguise.

The Proud Father

One forger, Walter Mitler by name, popularized a distraction routine dubbed the Proud Father Method. Mitler would burst upon a small bank lobby with a handful of cigars and stop by at a number of the bank officers to proclaim himself the proud father of a new baby boy. He would pass out cigars and finally get around to the tellers, who had watched with interest, and cash a check to buy his new boy a complete set of toys.

Somewhat the reverse of this routine was used by an East Coast husband and wife team. The wife would enter the bank lobby with a bawling infant, actually one of her own, and with complete fluster produce a batch of checks set up in a split deposit routine. The teller was anxious to restore the bank to its normal peace and quiet and would only give perfunctory attention to the check cashing operation that he was performing.

The Printed Signature

Printed maker signatures are routinely used by leading business firms. Forgers, in counterfeiting the checks, also routinely print the signature. But you seldom see this technique used on personal checks.

Chicago police recently discovered a new twist on fraudulent checks and forgery methods. Ironically, the victim of the forgery was a Chicago police sergeant. Apparently, one of his checks had been stolen. Instead of a simulation or tracing type forgery, the forger made an offset plate of the sergeant's true signature and printed the signature onto the blank check. The register, alignment, ink deposit, etc. were excellent. However, under microscopic examination, it was possible to determine that the line had been printed rather than written. Police investigation subsequently uncovered a messenger within the precinct house who had formerly been taught offset printing and who later admitted to the forgery.

Raising One's Standards

The "raising" technique has been utilized by thousands of forgers in an attempt to raise their own personal standard of living. Simply stated "raising" is the practice of taking a legitimate check and increasing the face value of the check by manipulating or altering the writing in the numerical value section of the check.

This technique is obviously more suited to handwritten checks than it is to either typewritten or machine imprinted or "protected" checks. However, even the latter class of checks is not completely immune.

Once a forger comes into possession of a legitimate check issued to his account he can utilize a variety of raising techniques. Among those not generally employed, but occasionally seen, is the "cutout" technique. This technique requires two or more checks from the same victim company. In this technique the forger cuts out portions of one check, that is the check-writer numeral amounts, rearranges them, and reinserts them into a new check. Such a technique was employed within the past few years by a South American forger who procured a check from a South American stockbroker with an account in a New York bank. The check was raised from $6.00 to $6,000.00 and successfully cashed.

Forgers utilize a variety of means to obtain bonafide checks which are available for raising. The refund device is typical of these. A forger purchases an item through the mails and deliberately overpays the purchase price of the item. The company in question often cashes the forger's check which may or may not be legitimate, but usually is, and then issues their own check for the overpayment. The forger thus comes into the possession of a check which is capable of being cleverly altered for an increased amount.

Some check-raisers work a particularly vicious racket against the ill and the elderly. This type of technique is often discovered in retirement communities and in cities such as Fort Lauderdale, Florida. In this particular technique the salesman, selling a relatively simple item or perhaps a magazine subscription, gives the customer a particularly good "buy". He then "helps" the victim fill out a check, specifying that payment must be made in check. In helping his victim fill out the check he is careful to space the volume portion of the check form to provide for subsequent "raising" of the check. The forger — con man — also will utilize numerical amounts, in payment for the goods he alleges to sell, which lend themselves to ready "raising". The victim is defrauded two ways. His check is fraudulently raised and subsequently cashed and the goods or services that he purchases is rarely provided.

Kite Flying

Check kiting, in its simplest form, involves the practice of pyramiding a series of worthless checks. In a true technical sense, the checks may not be forgeries since they could contain the true name of the con artist and his true handwriting. The term "kiting" is also sometimes erroneously used to describe the raising of a check from its established amount. Some references find this applied to what is obviously a "raising" technique whereas others more generally apply it to the process of pyramiding accounts through the issuance of a series of checks drawn on accounts which do not have sufficient balances to sustain them. In this case the con artist is usually intimately familiar with the number of days it takes for a check to pass from the receiving bank to the clearing house to the bank being drawn upon and back to the original bank. Professional check kiting schemes, operated by organized crime artists, can become quite complicated and involve multiple transfer of funds from banks throughout the country in order to cover checks that are pyramided from one account to another. However, it is not uncommon for these operators to clear up to $100,000 in their operations.

In practice, the swindle usually involves setting up ten or more separate bank accounts in ten separate banks. These accounts are opened with a minimal deposit. Now the operation begins. A check for a larger amount is drawn on a completely separate bank. Money is transferred from one account to another, in gradually increasing amounts, and always in sufficient time to cover the checks, until checks are being issued for $25,000 or more at a clip. When these large amounts are reached, depending upon circumstances, the professionals may decide to get out before the banks can begin to compare notes and become suspicious of the activity. In reality, the check kiter may begin his operation with little more than a couple of hundred dollars in deposit and within weeks pyramid this into upwards of $100,000, through a series of skillful manipulations. The professionals in this area naturally employ aliases, but usually do not attempt to disguise their true handwriting characteristics.

The Misdirected Deposit Slip

There is a popular folk tale that circulates in banking circles about those electronically encoded deposit slips. It claims that one forger took his own deposit slips and surreptiously substituted them for the uncoded counter deposit slips in a major urban bank. For days the accounting machine dutifully credited his account with other peoples deposits. He then withdrew the balance and was never seen again. The author can't vouch for this tale, but with the other experiences in forgery, it's quite possible it did happen.

In addition, there is the possibility that a forger could counterfeit a deposit slip with the correct magnetic ink characters and arrange to have some wealthy depositor's account credited to his own account. To accomplish this he would have to gain access to the legitimate account holders supply of deposit slips and substitute the counterfeits.

The Scam or Bust Out

In the familiar Scam or Bust-Out operation a hoodlum may buy into or gain control of a legitimate business operation. He will inherit the credit rating of the legitimate business. He will then issue a series of checks, utilizing the validating equipment and signature stamp of the business. Next he will issue a whole series of forged and fraudulent checks which in fact rely on the former business owner's reputation and standing in the business community.

This method is particularly the province of organized crime and is discussed in more detail in the section dealing with organized crime.

The Overpurchase Technique

The purchase process brings understandable joy to the heart of any merchant. This balloon of joy is sometimes punctured by a forger employing the Overpurchase Technique. The method is fairly simple and amongst the most widespread forgery techniques in use.

A smartly dressed, distinguished looking man approaches the counter of a camera store. He asks to see a particular camera. The camera sells for $100. He examines the camera closely, asking a long list of questions. He is hesitant about buying, but the salesman finally "sells" him on the camera. The man writes a check for $175 and asks for the difference in cash explaining he has to make some additional purchases while downtown. The salesman is happy to cash the check. The man is a forger and he has just made at least a $75 profit for fifteen minutes work.

The overpurchase technique is often combined with other forgery M.O.'s such as the Uniform Dodge, etc. It does not individually produce large scores, but in aggregate it can be very profitable. One of the most famous practitioners of this technique was a forger from Indiana known as the "Traveler". The Traveler hung paper all over the midwestern United States. When he was finally apprehended, the arresting officers found a whole barn full of cameras and related articles acquired during the overpurchase technique.

Contact with the New York Police indicates that this technique is among the most widespread used in New York. Camera stores incidentally are still being hit with this technique despite repeated warnings.

The Inside Man

In relating the M.O.'s used in professional forgery schemes forgery squad detectives often refer to the "inside man". The term is self-explanatory. In many complex forgery schemes, especially those involving banking operations, you will come to suspect the presence of an inside man. In many cases this individual may be a bank teller a minor officer of the bank or perhaps the operator of a check cashing service.

In the War on Poverty Case the reader will note how inside men were allegedly used both within the payroll department of the Neighborhood Youth Corp and within the two check cashing establishments implicated in the conspiracy. The involvement of such firms in forgery schemes is far from unknown. It has happened in New York before, and the writer is fairly certain that there have been similar cases in other cities.

The existence of, and the importance of, the inside man is seldom recognized by the general public. One New York detective told the writer that the inside man exists in far more cases than is ever revealed by news accounts of forgery schemes. In one such case in New York, recently investigated by the latter detective, a teller was directly connected to a bad check passing scheme.

Private investigations conducted by both bank security personnel and by the police showed the individual in question to be linked to the forgery scheme. Yet the evidence obtained was never hard enough to present in court or to obtain a conviction.

In many cases, particularly where dishonest employees are linked with the forgers, the employee will offer the perfectly plausible excuse that "he was too busy to notice the irregularities in the check" or "I thought that the check was O.K., the man looked like one of our regular depositors". Since these are the same excuses that completely honest employees also offer, it is hard to establish conspiracy. Even in those cases where private investigation of the employee reveals good cause for suspicion, the evidence tends to be highly circumstantial. Without the arrest and testimony of the other conspirators it is difficult for law enforcement agents to build a case.

The Romantic Paperhanger

Forgers are certainly not averse to using a little romance to further their operations. One such scheme involves the forger seeking out an innocent partner who is romanced and set up for a particular type of passing scheme. Typical of these "romantic paperhangers" was a forger known as J. Stanley Weinberger.

Weinberger would seek out a likely girl, romance her, and gain her confidence. He would tell her that he had access to a large amount of money but that Internal Revenue Service agents had him under close surveillance. He would relate that he had a check worth $5,000, but that he couldn't deposit it to his account because of the surveillance. Weinberger was careful to select a mark with a healthy bank account. He would endorse the check to the girl and ask that she give him one of her own checks drawn on her account. He would then cash that good check and flee before the girl became aware that his check was worthless.

Weinberger was detained in Tucson, Arizona on a minor traffic violation. He was escorted to the courthouse. Once there, he panicked and attempted to pull a gun. He was shot dead by a courthouse guard.

Flying Under A Flag

The term "flying under a flag" is sometimes used to describe forgery schemes involving the setup of false payroll records. The War on Poverty Case is a beautiful example of this technique but actually the M.O. itself is well known in fraud investigation circles. In fact the technique was probably acquired from a study of the manipulations of some former politicians who were past masters at creating phantom payrolls.

This technique involves the creation of fictitious persons who are put on the payroll, and to whom payroll checks are issued. The checks are then forged and cashed. A variation of this scheme also involves the issuance of duplicate payroll checks. One is cashed by the legitimate employee and the second is forged and cashed by the conspirators. One also finds separate "overtime" payroll checks being made out in the name of legitimate employees, forged and cashed.

Companies such as construction firms, who set up operations far from their home base and establish a local payroll, are particularly susceptible to this type of fraud. Ironically, a number of these frauds have been uncovered when a cross check by the Internal Revenue Service showed that the "employee", whose withholdings had been forwarded to the IRS, did not file a tax return. Inquiries by the IRS showed the person or persons to be non-existent.

The Welfare Check Forger

The exploding welfare case load, which is now nearing one million persons in New York alone, has spawned a whole new breed of forgers. This new breed doesn't look like or act like the forgers you will meet in other sections of this book. These forgers are ghetto residents, often recipients of welfare themselves. Many of them are narcotic addicts with prior arrest records for petty theft, auto boosting, etc.

New York City, because it is the city where the welfare abuse was invented and brought to its pinnacle of artistic perfection, provides the best case study in welfare check forgeries.

Each month the Department of Social Services spews 800,000 checks, worth some $80 million into the New York postal system. The checks are, for the thieves' purposes, conveniently mailed on the same days each month and contained in easily identifiable brown envelopes. The checks are distributed by urban mail carriers who ordinarily travel by themselves and utilize a golf cart-like device to move the postal sack about their routes.

The mail carrier approaches each tenement and sorts out all the mail for the designated address. He leaves the mail cart in front of the building, walks into the building and deposits the mail in the vestibule mail boxes. The carrier is equipped with a master key which opens the individual mail boxes.

The mail thief-forger hits the system in two ways. First he may steal the check from the vestibule mail box by prying open the box and removing the check. Secondly, he may openly remove the welfare check envelope from the carrier's sack as it stands unattended outside the apartment building. He may also steal the check directly from the welfare recipient when he or she comes to the mailbox to pick up the check. Apparently, even these devices are not satisfactory for some thieves. These individuals will actually hold up the letter carrier and relieve him of the welfare checks he is carrying. Such thieves have been known to methodically sort out the junk mail and lift only the welfare checks.

By December of 1968 check thieves were stealing 2% of all the checks mailed, or an estimated 15,000 checks per month. Postal authorities noted some 80 separate assaults on postal carriers during 1968. The postal union claimed more than 200 assaults took place. The 15,000 checks stolen each month are alleged to produce some one million dollars worth of loss each month according to the estimates released by the Department of Social Services. It is further estimated that approximately $670,000 of this amount is absorbed by banks, check cashing services, merchants, etc. The remaining portion is absorbed by the city through the "replacement device", i.e.: the city replaces some 3,000 checks a month which are allegedly "lost" or "stolen". In reality, an undetermined number of these checks have been negotiated with the complicity of the person from whom the check was "stolen".

The loss has now reached the point where a private insurance company, dismayed by the astronomical rise in thefts, has cancelled the city's insurance coverage on such thefts and forgeries. There apparently has been a substantial rise in thefts of this type within the past two years. The author was shown a report for 1966 which estimated the loss at 1.2 million dollars. If the loss is now 12 million dollars annually, then there has been a 1,000% increase within two years. This writer tends to be somewhat sceptical of the one-million-dollar-a-month loss figure. It may be higher and it may be much lower. One knowledgeable Federal law enforcement official told this writer that the city was up to a year and a half behind in investigating suspicious welfare check cases. Previous experience with the New York welfare organization, in connection with other forgery cases, convinces the author that anything is possible.

The forgers operating on welfare checks vary in experience and M.O.'s. In general they are becoming more "street wise" in the past year or so. There is also an increase in the number of organized groups using the welfare check forgery racket as a principal source of revenue. Some of these same gangs previously worked as shoplifting groups, car thieves, etc. Forgery has now become a more lucrative outlet for their energies, although in some cases they have not given up their past criminal pursuits. The Postal Inspectors have racked up a 6.2% increase in arrests for this type violation during fiscal 1968.

The lone thief and forger represents the biggest problem in welfare check forgery. Most of these thieves are narcotic addicts, some of them supporting a 30-40 dollar-a-day habit. Their effort towards signature disguise are either crude or non-existent. The very volume of thievery and forgery that occurs is their best disguise.

Traveler's Check M.O.'s

The banks and credit card companies that issue travelers checks have tried to make them as good as cash. For forgers they frequently are just that good. The case history section of this report relates what forgers have recently done to one million dollars worth of American Express Travelers Checks.

There are at least four basic M.O.'s used in traveler check frauds. The checks may be, and are being, completely counterfeited, endorsed and cashed. They may also be stolen, in blank form, endorsed and cashed. Or they may be stolen from travelers and the second endorsements forged and cashed.

In addition, you also find some interesting M.O.'s involving the legitimate purchase of the checks and their later manipulation. A

21 year old Massachusetts man applied to the State Department for a visa under his true name; he received the visa and applied again under a false name and also received a visa. He then began to purchase travelers checks and to "lose them". He would sign affidavits attesting to their loss and be reimbursed. Later the "lost" checks would be cashed using the identity credentials of the second visa. This young man traveled throughout the world using this technique before being arrested in San Juan, Puerto Rico.

There are a wide variety of traveller check forgery M.O.s. As noted, most of these involve a falsified affidavit whereby the person who "lost" the travellers checks swears that the checks have been lost and is refunded their value. Subsequently, he or an accomplice attempts to forge the "lost" checks and cash them. The FBI reports one actual case which is cited here as illustrative of this type of modus operandi. On July 9, 1957, Wayne Leroy Peters showed up at a travellers check agency and claimed that he had lost three travellers checks worth a total of $150.00. After signing an affidavit, the agency manager delayed Peters because of irregularities in his story. The check apparently had been "lost" out of numerical order. Facing this delay, Peters wired the traveler's check agency's home office complaining. As a result of his wire, the local office was directed to make immediate payment. However, because of the circumstance of the case, further investigation was called for. When the three forged traveler's checks were later obtained by the agency, they were forwarded to the FBI Laboratory. The FBI Laboratory confirmed that the signatures and counter-signatures were in fact those of the subject Wayne Leroy Peters. Peters was charged, indicted and convicted of fraud by wire.

Document Forgeries

The primary emphasis of this report has been on checks and credit cards. However, modern forgers are not oblivious to the potentials of other types of "cash authorizing" documents.

Bills of lading, invoices, delivery receipts, etc., all lend themselves to forgery. In fact, some of these are more easily forged than checks or credit cards. The "false trucker" is among the favorites in this category. A group either steals or fabricates the truck of a legitimate trucking company. It also counterfeits the "authorizing" documents needed for the pick up of goods. It arrives an hour or so prior to the legitimate pickup vehicle. The forged documents are presented, the goods loaded onto the truck and away they go. This technique was recently used to pick up nearly $400,000 worth of rare metals at a metropolitan airport. It was also used when a gang impersonating an armored car service calmly removed several hundred thousand dollars in cash from a New York area bank.

Other documents such as mortgages have also been forged to temporary good advantage. One recent case in Miami, uncovered by Postal Inspectors, employed a fraudulent mortgage scheme to milk millions of dollars from unsuspecting mortgage lenders. The M.O. in this particular swindle involved the setting up of a local company which would research the property of local citizens to determine whether or not they owned their homes without a mortgage. This research resulted in a list of individuals with good credit standards and who owned their homes without encumbrance.

The forgers, then purporting to represent the home owner, would apply for mortgages on the home owner's property. These forgeries were free hand forgers without any attempt at simulation of the actual home owner's signature. The mortgage companies apparently did not have access to legitimate samples of the home owner's signature. The forgers would prepare a fraudulent application and, when the mortgage sum was granted, they would arrange to either intercept it in the mail or to have it diverted to their office as the "agent" for the unsuspecting home owner. In order to keep the scheme going for awhile, they would make the first two or three payments on the mortgage so that the home owner was unaware that a mortgage was pending against his property. The bubble burst when home owners were advised by the "mortgagee" to make payment on the mortgages "they" had negotiated.

An insurance agent also went into business for himself utilizing a novel forgery technique. He would mail to known policy holders a letter stating that their policies were being revamped and that new, wider coverage policies were to be issued by the company. He would request that the policy holder's policy be mailed to a certain P.O. Box number in his name and the name of the company. Then, with an example of the policy holder's signature, he would forge their signature to the policy and request a cancellation and refund. Within a relatively short period this agent was able to fraudulently collect nearly $13,000.00.

CREDIT CARD M.O.'S

Some of the M.O.'s utilized by credit card forgers stem directly from prior historical experience in check forgery and fraud operations. However, because of the new procedures and techniques, coincident to the use of credit cards, we now see some forgery and fraud methods which are unique to credit cards themselves. In general, there are three major areas of operation with regard to the fraudulent use of credit cards.

A. Direct Merchandise or Service Charges

The simplest, and one of the most frequently employed methods, is simply the use of a stolen, counterfeit, or fraudulently obtained card to obtain goods or services which are used directly by the forger. We find the credit card forger using the card itself to obtain food, clothing, air travel, etc. which he himself consumes rather than attempts to convert into a more negotiable currency. This type of operation is more frequently the province of a smaller operator, the juvenile, the amateur thief, etc. The well publicized excesses of juveniles who have come into their parents' travel cards or general purpose credit cards, are good examples of this type of operation. What characterizes this particular category is that the forger, while he fraudulently obtains goods and services, makes no direct attempt to convert these goods or services into cash, credit allowances, etc.

Sometimes this method also involves the forger who may utilize the card for direct charges which benefit his business, which incidentally may also be fraudulent. In this category, we find con men who would use telephone credit cards to finance "boiler room" operations. Gamblers would use credit cards for travel purposes, hotel accommodations, etc. In the latter cases, the forger is employing the card as a financing mechanism for his other business operations, but still is not attempting to directly convert the card's purchasing power into cash. Incidentally, the use by La Cosa Nostra members of credit cards, as documented in the Organized Crime Section of this report, is also one example of the direct use method.

B. Goods or Services Into Cash

There are literally dozens of methods by which credit cards can be turned into cash. These range from such a simple method as the $100 "loan" of cash obtainable through certain credit cards, to much more complex schemes. Summarized below are some of the principal methods by which credit cards are converted into hard currency.

(1) Acquisition of hard goods or tickets and sale to "innocent" third parties. One of the most popular methods of turning a credit card into cash is simply using the card to obtain merchandise, air line tickets, etc. and then in turn selling these items to a third party. The author has used the term "innocent" to describe the third parties because in many instances there must be some doubt that the parties who bought airline tickets at half price or cameras at one third of their listed retail value were "unaware" that there was a tinge of fraud to the transaction. In this operation the forger obtains either an all-purpose card or even a department charge plate and purchases a select group of items such as jewelry, cameras, perfume, portable TVs, etc. The forger simply walks into a store or ticket agency, purchases the item with the fraudulent card, walks out with the item and them proceeds to a sale point. This sale point may be a local bar, factory, social club, etc. He then disposes of the item either directly to the purchaser or operates through a fence.

(2) Acquisition of goods or services for refund purposes. A number of M.O.'s have evolved in which credit cards are first used to charge the purchase of merchandise or travel tickets, or some similar commodity, and the item is then later turned back to the seller and a cash refund obtained. This method was particularly widespread in the New York and Los Angeles area in connection with the refunding of airline tickets. The way it worked was relatively simple. Using a forged or fraudulent credit card, the thief would purchase an airline ticket worth several hundred dollars for a transcontinental trip. He would then take the ticket to another airline agency and turn it in for a new ticket on the second airline agency's service. He would continue changing airlines until along the way the purchase identity, that is the fact that the ticket had been purchased through a credit card, was inadvertently missed by a hasty clerk.

Fig. 2 The "cut-out" technique is sometimes used to rearrange the code numbers on a credit card with the resultant effect of charging the wrong account for a purchase or of escaping the hot list of the card company. At times these numerals are also "pressed out" and new numerals pressed in.

Now, having a bona fide ticket which appeared to have been purchased for cash or check, he would turn it in at a separate ticketing location and receive a cash refund. Thieves operating in this manner frequently would hit several major metropolitan ticket agencies and then retrace their steps in a complex rerouting system, exchanging tickets and cashing tickets as they went. One thief is known to have netted several thousand dollars within a single operating day using this technique.

It is also possible to use this technique in certain merchandise transfers. For example, the thief may use the credit card to purchase a $400 camera. Later he will return with the camera, unused in its original container, and state that he has had second thoughts and wishes to exchange it for a much lower price camera, say a $100 model. The store may not be aware of the ruse and refund him the difference between the camera that he is turning in and the $100 camera in a cash refund. In still other cases, the operating procedure of the store may be such that it will be possible to purchase an item through a credit card, bring it in for an exchange for a second item or third item and then finally to obtain a cash refund. Ironically, the higher class or better grade of department stores are more susceptible to this type of con than the middle class stores.

(3) **Auto theft through credit cards.** The advent of the all-purpose credit card has made the life of the professional auto thief immeasurably smoother. In the past, should a thief steal an auto and attempt to transfer it to a distant state for resale, he always ran the risk of being stopped on a routine charge and being discovered because of his lack of proper registration and identity credentials. Not only that, the license plates of the car were frequently teletyped on an interstate basis within hours after its theft. The credit card has removed much of this type of risk for the professional auto thief. He can now, using a forged or fraudulent credit card, walk into a Hertz or Avis rental agency and rent one of the best cars they have for a two or three week period. In the course of obtaining the rental he will probably utilize a forged or counterfeit driver's license which is easily obtained through "identity package pools". He will then proceed to take the car to another state or city where its identity will be changed and where it will be sold. The credit card company and the rental agency will not have a "want" out on the particular car for at least a month. In the meantime, if in the course of transporting the car, the thief is routinely stopped, he is in perfectly safe position since it is a rental car and he does not need to have the registration certificate, etc.

In actual practice this is exactly what has occurred. The author was briefed on an operation by one group which took place in Queens County, New York; Dade County, Florida; and Los Angeles County, California within a four or five week period. In fact, when this group was apprehended in California and placed on recognizance bond, they moved to Florida and then to New York with the same scheme.

Organized crime groups have also used this technique to obtain late model cars which were then exported out of the United States.

(4) **Non-existent charge schemes.** One facet of fraudulent credit card operations that is frequently underestimated involves the complicity of dishonest merchants with credit card forgers. The Chicago credit card case, described in the case history section of this report, illustrates this method. The credit card thief or forger can work with a fraudulent merchant in a scheme in which the merchant agrees to fraudulently ring up purchases which are completely non-existent. Thus, the merchant rings up a purchase of several hundred dollars worth of merchandise and splits the charge with the thief. No goods ever change hands. The bank, or credit card company pays the merchant and his portion of the 50/50 split is complete profit.

There have been a number of cases involving this type of operation in New York, Chicago and Los Angeles. Bank credit cards, all-purpose cards such as Diners, American Express, and a number of other varieties have been employed in this scheme. The same technique can be utilized where personal services are chargeable on credit cards. The person alleging to provide the service, such as a specialty air charter service, can testify that they provided the service without having actually done so and split the charge with the forger. These types of frauds are even more difficult to obtain evidence against than the non-existent merchandise charge fraud.

(5) **Credit cards in "Scam or Bust-Out" Operations.** Some of the "Soldati" of organized crime have been involved in "Scam or Bust-Out" operations involving credit cards. This scheme involves the LCN group and their takeover of a legitimate business operation. Once they have gained control of a going business organization, with an established credit line, they are frequently able to obtain company credit cards. Then, using these credit cards they will proceed to charge vast amounts of goods and services which the company is theoretically liable for. However, since they have no intention of the company continuing in business, they have no worry about paying its debts; in fact, the debts sometimes become applicable in later bankruptcy proceedings. Individuals utilizing this technique may be employing the cards for direct charges, but more likely are utilizing cash refunds or resale techniques for the goods and services acquired through the use of the cards.

A typical example of this technique is when an old line import-export firm falls into the hands of the local "button" men of a nearby "family". The control of the company may have been gained through loansharking or some similar device. Now, using this company's reputation, and previous credit line, new air travel cards and general purpose credit cards will be issued to the new "executives" of the concern. These executives will use the cards as described previously. A prominent New York garment manufacturing firm recently provided the front for this type of operation.

(6) **The credit card as a bogus "reference or identity" credential.** Occasionally, one runs across a case where the M.O.'s of check forgery and credit cards frauds cross. This is such an instance. The forger fraudulently obtains a high value credit card such as an Air Travel Card or American Express card. He then proceeds to use this as an "identity credential" in papering a local resort with a series of rubber checks. Although nothing has been charged against the card itself, it nonetheless has been the touchstone to a successful check forgery operation.

(7) **Sale of fraudulently obtained cards.** As might be expected, there are methods for fraudulently obtaining a credit card. Another means of converting the card into cash is the simple "rental" or sale of the card to a similarly dishonest operative. Prostitutes, bellhops, waiters, etc. may acquire cards by theft or deception and convert them into cash simply by the direct sale of the card to another party.

C. Illegal Charges Against Legitimate Cards

Even valid credit cards, used by legitimate parties, can sometimes be the subject of fraud through forgery. There are three principal methods involved here.

(1) **"Raising" charge slips.** In much the same manner that a forger raises a check, from a lower amount to a larger amount, it is also possible for a dishonest merchant, waiter, etc. to insert additional numerals and thus raise the value of the charge to a particular card account number after the customer has signed the charge slip. This type of fraud is most likely to occur in charge

slips involving credit cards to company accounts, etc. Ordinarily, the customer maintains his tissue copy of the charge slip and is thus aware of what the legitimate charge should be and conversely aware of any discrepancy that might occur. However, charges made to company accounts are frequently paid almost automatically, without a consistent effort to compare the employee's charge slip against the value charged by the credit card company. This is an area of petty larceny and we do not have any statistics on any major fraud committed through this technique.

(2) **Preparation of duplicate charge slips.** There have been a number of sizable cases in which dishonest gas station operators, restauranteurs, etc. used the customer's credit card to register a complete duplicate charge slip. In practice what may take place here is that a gas station operator, when given the oil company credit card, will walk back to the station and ring up two or three slips. He will only bring one out for the customer's signature. Later he will forge the customer's signature to additional slips putting in non-existent sales for batteries, tires, etc. One might think that this could only amount to petty larceny, yet one New York station operator managed to fraudulently obtain nearly $30,000 over a three-month period, utilizing the duplicate charge slip method. Another restauranteur was known to have fraudulently charged nearly $900 in dining expenses against a single credit card number within a thirty day period.

In the oil company credit card case cited above, the gas station operator managed to intercept the credit card company mail to the principal patrons affected by his operation. Coincidentally, they lived within the same apartment house.

(3) **The "double charge" method.** The so-called "double charge" method of credit card manipulation begins with the theft of legitimate credit card blanks. These blanks are imprinted, using the same type of imprinting equipment as the credit card company employs, with the legitimate names and account numbers of patrons of the credit card company. The names can be acquired easily enough through the purchase of lists from the credit card companies. There are a variety of methods for accumulating the credit card number of the patron. The name and number are imprinted onto a card thus creating a situation where there are two cards, one legitimate and one fraudulent, for a particular

person. The patron becomes unaware that a second card is being
used until, usually some four to six weeks later, he receives a host
of fraudulent billings against his name and account number. This
method is particularly devastating because the name and account
number of the legitimate card has not been hot listed and there is
no way of knowing that the card is being fraudulently used until
the patron complains.

Theoretically, computor facilities at some of the credit card
companies are capable of "kicking out" charges which are suspi-
ciously high against a single card number. However, even this
practice does not guarantee against a certain minimal misuse of
the card.

The credit card itself may be physically manipulated in such a
manner as to provide a M.O. in itself. One of these manipulations
is the so-called "press-out" method. In this system, a stolen credit
card which has probably been hot listed by the card company, is
manipulated to keep it off the hot list. The numerals have been
impressed into the card and there apparently exists a technique
for pressing out a specific numeral and then reimpressing a second
numeral. It may also be that certain numerical designs lend
themselves to "raising" techniques by the completion of a line, the
pressing out of a portion of the numeral, etc. This new number,
which of course is either completely fictitious or which applies to a
wrong name, provides the forger with an additional two to three
weeks of grace prior to the new number being hot listed. Because of
physical considerations in the manufacture of the card, this press
out method is probably limited to one or two attempts. It might
also be noted that this technique could be utilized, as the "cut-
out" technique is utilized, that is with the complicity of dishonest
merchants.

Forgery and Airline Operations

In recent years the forgery fraternity has paid special attention
to the airline transport industry. Forgery thrives in a growing,
sometimes disorganized, industry. The M.O.'s used here are based
on the same principles of deception used in other forgery schemes,
but there have been some special techniques developed which are
worthy of study by law enforcement officials.

Airline security personnel note that they have picked up numerous travellers who have shown up at airline terminals with such tickets. Usually, when such a traveller is intercepted, the investigative agent is more interested in tracing the sale of the ticket than he is in prosecuting the person who attempted to use the ticket. In many cases these people are relatively innocent dupes who have been infected by the "I can get it for you wholesale" syndrome and honestly believe that airline tickets can be bought at a discount.

Recently, a number of innocent travellers have been conned into believing that the reason they could obtain "discounted" tickets was because of a practice known as *due bills*. This practice, which is used in the advertising business, involves a business or industry giving an ad agency, radio station, etc. a *due bill* in exchange for a free "plug". This bill is then presented in payment for goods or service rendered by the business getting the free plug. Forgers sometimes explain their possession of stolen tickets by explaining that the tickets were obtained through the *due bill* device. Actually, the airline industry is prohibited by law from issuing such *due bills*.

In an effort to cut down on these types of fraud, the airlines encourage their ticket agents to look closely at all credit cards. However, it is known that during peak rush hours the ticket agents are under extreme pressure and frequently do not consult the hot sheets provided by the various credit card companies. The latter sheets can become quite voluminous and sometimes it is difficult to pick out the number. The latter sheets are coded with an asterisk alongside of a card which has been reported stolen. When such a card is obtained the ticket agent is instructed to retain possession of the card. Usually this represents no problem since the forger, once he observes the ticket agent going to check on the hot card list, departs the terminal in a blaze of speed. The ticket agents are provided with a $25.00 reward by the credit card company for each card that they turn in.

A few years ago the writer ran across rumors that a European group was counterfeiting and selling airline tickets. However, the author has never been able to obtain a positive confirmation of this operation from among the many airline security personnel interviewed. It would appear that if such an operation did exist it had little effect on American forgery operations.

Forgers who do obtain stolen credit cards are not presented with too many real difficulties in forging the card. To begin with they do not actually attempt to forge the card holder's signature. Instead, they remove the signature and write in the cardholder's name in their own natural handwriting. While this is technically a forgery, it is not a forgery in the sense of trying to match a specific person's handwriting. There are a variety of methods normally employed to remove or obliterate the card holder's legitimate signature. For example, they may simply mask the card with masking tape, except for the signature panel, and overspray it with a flat white paint. Still other forgers have found ways to lift the signature, without destroying the safety signature panel coating, by the use of two simple household chemicals, which for security reasons are not described here. The latter materials may lift the signature without creating an erasure "void" pattern. The forger then writes in the card holder's name using his own hand.

Stolen airline tickets, which are fraudulently filled in and validated, are an equally serious problem to airline security personnel. There is incontrovertible evidence that organized crime is involved in this aspect of airline fraud operations. It would seem that certain burglars are commissioned to steal airline tickets from various travel agencies, ticket agencies, etc. Recent cases show that tickets stolen from several different travel agencies located in widely different parts of the United States showed up on the person of a single fraudulent ticket vendor. This person, who occupies the position of a "runner" in the organized crime hierarchy, obviously had access to stolen tickets from a variety of sources. As further evidence of organized crime's position in this field, investigators report that airline tickets stolen on one coast of America appear, sometimes within hours, on the opposite coast. Such diverse movements require preplanning and a degree of organization which is clearly indicative of organized crime. In the latter case, the author does not necessarily imply that the organized crime involved here is a direct operation of the La Cosa Nostra. However, it would be naive to believe that they do not have an interest in this area.

Stolen tickets frequently involve a validation and a "raising" of the ticket which requires alterations or erasures on the face of the ticket. In August 1968 the airline industry introduced a new type of ticket stock which drastically reduces such possibilities. As

Fig. 3   Credit card forgers sometimes seek to use the stolen card by erasing the
legitimate card holders signature with detergent materials.

an example of the type of M.O. that evolves around such alterations, we might consider what was happening on the West Coast
about a year and a half ago. A group in Los Angeles was
purchasing airline tickets from Los Angeles to San Diego to Los
Angeles. This trip which hardly involves getting on or off a plane
provides a ticket with a round trip value of about $15.00. The
forgers managed to remove the San Diego imprint on the ticket
and substitute New York. They also changed the fare portion of
the ticket to reflect the higher fare. Thus a $15.00 ticket in-
vestment was now worth $336.00. A series of these tickets were
used or refunded before the accounting departments and investigators joined to uncover the fraud.

Some companies also have what are known as "flight checks".
These are tickets that the company themselves can make out. The
airline subsequently bills the company when the ticket is turned
in. Recently, a Queens, New York firm was robbed of a supply of
these, some 200 in fact, and they have now begun to appear in the
New York area. Interestingly enough, they all seemed to be used
for flights to Las Vegas. Las Vegas is a favorite destination for
organized crime figures departing from New York.

The vast majority of forgers involved with airline depradations are native Americans. Some of these forgers feel the heat occasionally and leave the country. In the past these American nationals could be traced through the I-94 form that they filled out when leaving the country. Recently this form was discontinued and this has greatly complicated the tracing process as far as locating persons who leave the country on stolen or forged tickets.

CASE HISTORIES

Introduction

In the following pages the reader will have an opportunity to review some of the principal case histories of forgery that have occurred during the past several years. There are two parts to this chapter. In the first part we shall examine some of major recent forgery conspiracies. We shall then look at some individual forgers and review their particular case histories with an emphasis on their modus operandi.

In the course of interviewing law enforcement agencies we naturally ran into literally hundreds of forgery conspiracies that have taken place during the past five years. Space does not allow inclusion of but a fraction of these. The cases presented have been selected on the basis of both the dollar loss incurred and also on the basis of the unique M.O.'s employed.

The individual forgers were selected on the basis of their national scope of operations and the individuality of their methods. The latter case histories were largely compiled from file data made available by the Federal Bureau of Investigation and from available court records.

It is hoped that the reader will pay close attention to the modus operandi revealed by both the forgery conspiracies and by the individual case histories. The total number of forgery schemes is not unlimited. As surely as dawn follows night, these schemes will be repeated with minor variations by a new generation of forgers. A recognition of these patterns is the first step in the detection and prevention of forgery.

The J.W. Mays Case

In 1964, an indictment, which was followed by a trial and subsequent conviction of seven individuals, led to the disclosure of a massive check counterfeiting and forgery operation within Kings County, New York. Seven individuals were indicted. These were Herman Witt, Louis Quentin Leone, Salvatore Agro, Raymond Leone, Stephen Hirschorn (alias Bertram Williams), Frederick Gruebert and Abe Levine (alias Mal Reif and Morris Reif).

The story begins with a meeting which was held early in 1964. The ring leaders for the counterfeiting and forgery conspiracy were present at this meeting and were looking for someone with financial background who could provide the necessary know-how for a major operation. They found a neighbor of Leone, one Frederick Gruebert, who worked in the Comptrollers Office of J.W. Mays, Inc., a major Brooklyn Department Store.

Gruebert appeared to be the inside man in the case. He allegedly was familiar with the form of checks used by J.W. Mays and with the fact that Max Shulman, an officer of J.W. Mays, Inc. was the only individual authorized to sign for checks in excess of $10,000.00. He also knew that the bank maintained two hard goods bank account balances on which they issued checks. These balances were maintained in the First National City Bank and Underwriters Trust Company. Gruebert was also familiar with the dates when checks were issued (each Saturday) and he knew the counter approval that was necessary for the check. Sometime early in 1964, Gruebert surreptiously obtained two legitimate checks before they were mailed to the invoicing vendors. These checks provided samples of both the Underwriters Trust and First National City Bank checks. They also showed the form of paper used and its coloration. From these samples, photo-offset plates were produced duplicating the two different types of checks.

The check plates were produced by a known counterfeiter. Stephen Hirschorn then formed a company which represented itself as a national automotive claim-adjusting firm. Then, going to an upstate check and business form manufacturer, he ordered a series of "Claim Adjustment" forms which were printed on safety bank paper which closely matched the stock used by J.W. Mays for its own checks. The "Claim Adjustment" form was specifically designed so that it had a large blank area in the center of the form. This design permitted counterfeiters to cut out the center portion and obtain the necessary blank stock required for their counterfeits.

Next the checks were counterfeited. It is interesting to note that the signature section of the check was printed on to the check along with the remaining portion. No attempt was made to forge Mr. Shulman's signature by tracing or simulation forgery technique. The counter approval signature was apparently forged. The check was printed in a single black color on top of the pink or green safety paper as required by the particular bank on which it was drawn.

Following this operation, Raymond Leone and Stephen Hirschorn began to open bank accounts and to set up a series of fictitious companies. By July, 1964, they had established 17 separate companies and had registered these companies with the County Clerk. Beginning in July, the forgers made out a series of checks drawn on First National City and Underwriters Trust and payable to these fictitious companies for sums exceeding $10,000.00. These checks were issued every Saturday so that they coincided with the dates of legitimate check issuance.

In the particular MO of this operation, Raymond Leone would first deposit the forged check. Three or four days later, he would obtain a bank teller's check from the bank holding the account of the fictitious company. Then, with the bank teller's check he would proceed to a stock brokerage firm, open up an account and buy and sell during the day with the proceeds of the bank teller's check. At the close of the day he would ask for a broker's check for all but $2,000 or $3,000 of the balance in his account. He would also arrange to have the broker's bank prepare cash for the broker's check. He would proceed to the bank and pick up the cash for the broker's check and then turn the money over to one of the ring leaders. The operation blew apart when the forgers negligently overdrew the Underwriters Trust Company account. Each of the two accounts had approximately a $500,000 balance but the forgers in their eagerness had overdrawn the one account. The executives of J.W. Mays quickly determined from First National City that they were also receiving counterfeit checks and that their balance had been nearly depleted in that particular account. They notified the Kings County District Attorney's office and that office placed police officers in all banks where Raymond Leone had opened accounts. When Leone returned to one of the banks to obtain a bank teller's check, he was arrested. Subsequently, the District Attorney's Office was able to recover over $300,000 of the original sum, but at the time of this writing nearly $600,000 is still missing.

As a footnote to the J.W. Mays, Inc. case, it is interesting to note that the District Attorney's Office feels, probably with good reason, that the principals in this case had professional legal counsel in the setup and operation of the case. In this respect, there is a very distinct possibility that some principal members of the case have escaped official prosecution and conviction. There is also some basis to theorize that the setup costs for the operation may have been bank-rolled by members of organized crime. One member of the gang, who was indicted and convicted had known organized crime links in the Buffalo, New York area.

The Chicago Credit Card Case

In October of 1871 the city of Chicago was engulfed in a conflagration reported to be one of the greatest fires ever to destroy an American City. Ninety-five years later Chicago was once again the scene of a conflagration. This time it became the site of one of the most widespread forgery operations reported in the annals of American crime. What distinguised this particular forgery operation was not the value of money defrauded, although that amount was substantial, but rather the number, variety and diversity of persons involved in the case.

During the Fall of 1966 Chicago area bankers began to hear some rather disquieting rumors. It was alleged that the giant, San Francisco-based, Bank of America was about to introduce its Bankamericard to the Chicago area. Chicago banking is primarily dominated by two banks, The First National and the Continental of Illinois Banks. These two giants are fairly evenly matched and are known throughout the country for their alert and aggressive marketing techniques. If the rumors about the Bankamericard were true, these banks stood to loose a very profitable market for their own potential bank credit card. Apparently, they had no intention of allowing the Bank of America to gain a foothold in the Chicago market without a battle. Bank credit cards were in a period of explosive growth and the time was right for a major bank credit card move in the Chicago area.

Shortly before Christmas of 1966, Chicago's already overburdened mailmen found their sacks a bit heavier than usual. The added weight wasn't merely early Christmas cards. It was part of a gigantic, unsolicited bank credit card mailing. It is estimated, by knowledgable postal authorities, that several million bank credit cards, all of them *unsolicited,* were mailed to patrons in the Chicago area.

In organization, five Chicago banks. operating under the Midwest Bank Card System, Inc., had joined together in a non-profit cooperative corporation to market the bank credit card. The two principal credit cards involved were the *"First"* card from First National Bank and the *"Town and Country Card"* of Continental of Illinois. Within a week or so the mail boxes of Chicago were quite literally flooded with unsolicited credit cards. These cards, ostensibly sent to bank patrons who were equipped to use them, could be used to purchase all kinds of assorted merchandise and services. This mailing had been preceded by a cooperative marketing effort intended to enroll the majority of Chicago area merchants in the credit card plan.

For the first few weeks the credit card plan seemed to be off to a fast start. Then, it seemed that something had gone radically wrong. This avalanche of unsolicited credit cards had produced a flood of forgery and fraud on a scale seldom experienced in America before. It didn't take Postal Inspectors long to determine what had gone wrong with this effort. Preliminary investigation disclosed that multiple mailing lists had been used and that some of the lists were substantially outdated. Personal acquaintences in Chicago revealed to this writer that they had received as many as fifteen different bank credit cards within a period of a few months. Some of these cards showed addresses that were more than five years old. Apparently, in preparing the mailing lists, the banks had utilized their depositor records as one of the prime sources for addresses. There was an inherent fault in this research technique. Many people had multiple accounts and, in addition, their dormant accounts produced special address problems. For example, a depositor might have a savings account which laid relatively unused for five or ten years. During that time the person may well have made two or three address changes within the city. The depositor knew where his bank was, had possession of the bank pass book, and frequently made no effort to advise the bank of his new mailing address. There was no way for the bank to know that these addresses were obsolete. In addition, the author suspects that many different lists were employed and that mailing list management left something to be desired.

As soon as the mail began to be delivered certain well known problems arose. To understand the implications of these problems, let us take a look at how mail is typically distributed in a metropolitan area such as Chicago. Much of the first class mail goes to apartment houses. Mail carriers, because of personnel changes, vacations, illnesses, etc. change routes and are sometime oblivious as to whether or not a particular person or family lives at a designated street address. Faced with an unfamiliar name at a particular address, the mail route carrier might well distribute the mail to the apartment house and hope for delivery. Persons in the apartment house, such as the superintendent, will usually return undeliverable mail to the carrier the next day. In the interim, this misdirected mail lies in front lobby or in a variety of locations where little or no security exists. These initial mailings were by first class mail. Registered mail was not used. Many of the cover envelopes provided little or no camouflage as to what was contained in the envelope, and the envelope could also be manually examined to determine that a credit card was inside.

From a mail distribution standpoint, very large quantities of these cards were poured into the mail system within a relatively short period of time. Inside postal workers who were faced with this flood of unsolicited cards, and with equally large flood of returning cards noted "Addressee Unknown", "Addressee Moved", etc. could well have regarded this mailing as a nuisance. However, the latter evaluation is that of the author and is not attributed to postal authorities. In any event, there were an awful lot of credit cards being returned to the Post Office.

As mentioned previously, fraud and forgery soon became a massive problem. Fraudulent charges began pouring into the banks. Initially the banks were ill-equipped to meet this massive new security problem. With few exceptions they had not secured the services of forgery experts and in fact did not do so until several months after the problem was in full swing. Even here they ran into some problems. Two of the newly hired investigators were subsequently charged with alleged wrongdoing in connection with the credit card operation.

The banks had gone on the assumption that their credit losses would approximate the national average on bank credit cards which is approximately 1%. This reliance on previous experience proved to be quite erroneous. In estimating their losses the banking community had completely failed to take into account the effects of an unholy alliance between larcenous merchants and forgers. Bank financial statements released the following year showed a noticeable drop in earnings. How much of this reduction is due to forgery losses is difficult to ascertain since the banks certainly aren't broadcasting this type of data. One estimate of loss puts the value at between 2 and 3 million dollars, although it quite conceivably could have been greater than this. An article in the Congressional Record notes that a single day's loss at one bank amounted to $56,000.

The forger-dishonest retailer alliance provided for several different types of M.O.'s. One of the most frequent involved the forger utilizing the card to charge-up fictitious purchases. In connivance with the merchant, the forger would charge a series of purchases. Often these were for items which had a value of less than $50.00. This technique avoided the necessity for the merchant cross-checking with the bank to determine whether or not the card was hot. After the charge had been made and paid by the bank, a split would be made between the forger and the merchant based on the amount drawn up on the fictitious purchase. No goods ever changed hands in these transactions. There was no change in inventory because the merchant never really "sold" anything. For many retail merchants, who are characteristically in trouble with their credit, this new scheme was a bonanza.

Postal Inspectors confirmed that organized crime groups were also utilizing the bank credit card in a special operation all their own. For some years previous, Chicago Postal Inspectors had been extremely successful in breaking up what has come to be known as *scam* or *bust-out* frauds. These schemes work this way. A local hood, who may be a *Soldati* or *Button Man*, buys into a legitimate business operation. Then, using the name of a legitimate company and its credit rating, he orders a large quantity of saleable merchandise from out-of-town suppliers. He then proceeds to sell out the merchandise and pockets the cash without any intention of paying for any of the goods purchased. Often, the business subsequently goes into bankruptcy. Organized crime thus infiltrates a good many businesses, makes a quick killing and gets out. In the two or three year period prior to the beginning of the credit card battles, Chicago Postal Inspectors had racked up more than 50 arrests stemming from the scam or bust-out type fraud.

Obviously, the heat was on and these operators were squirming and looking for a "safer" occupation.

Postal Inspectors now noticed that some of the same people involved in the scam and bust-out operations were moving into the bank credit card fraud field. It was theorized that some of these individuals moved into, or setup business fronts, in order to take advantage of this specific situation. They apparently had little trouble in procuring a number of misaddressed cards and immediately began to make massive billings against the credit of these cards. As soon as payment was made by the bank, the operators would disappear. At the time of this writing, some of these persons are still under investigation. It is probable that the financing of these operations was provided by local organized crime capital and it proved to be a lucrative short-term investment.

The Chicago credit card forgers utilized manipulation techniques which have since appeared in other parts of the country. One of these is the *cut-out* technique. In this technique the credit card thief takes a razor blade or similar sharp instrument and cuts out the individual numbers on the credit card. He interchanges them and thus changes the billing identity of the card. This technique provides additional working time and keeps the new "number" off the hot list for a little bit longer period. Obviously in cutting these numbers out and reinserting them he creates a card which is visually apparent as a forgery. Such a card could only be used with the cooperation of a dishonest merchant. Such cooperation was apparently available on a wide scale and it is this factor that produced one of the principal problems in the bank credit card operation.

When we analyze the background of the credit card thieves, we find that they came from both ghetto and middle-class neighborhoods. Some of the regular groups that work U.S. Treasury check thefts and frauds were also involved in the credit card scheme. Unfortunately, there were also some postal employees involved in the theft. Considering the magnitude of the mailing, and the frailty of human nature, it is amazing that there were not more postal employees involved. Interestingly, postal employees who were subsequently apprehended and indicted, revealed that other persons had requested that they obtain the cards for them. One might theorize that the employees themselves placed very little value on the cards. Considering the volume of cards that were mailed, and the number of incorrect addresses, one can almost sympathize with their attitude.

The Chicago credit card problem produced reverbations felt round the country. Bills have subsequently been introduced in Congress to prevent the unsolicited mailing of credit cards. Penalties for credit card misuse were subsequently codified and reinforced through a bill passed by the Illinois legislature.

By the Fall of 1968, things in Chicago had stablized quite a bit. The banks had learned their lesson well and security had tightened up to minimize losses. Postal Inspectors were busy preparing a batch of new indictments and apparently another chapter in American forgery had been closed.

American Express Travelers Check Cases

During the summer months New York's Kennedy International Airport is a beehive of activity. The tourist season is in full swing and the airport is jammed with vehicles and travelers. The Kennedy Air Freight Terminal is busy year around. August of 1966 was no exception. Early in August a truck entered the Air Freight terminal area and drove slowly towards one of the loading docks. Somewhere along the way, while the truck was making its rounds of the terminal, a package was kicked off the back of the truck. This package was quickly retrieved and taken to Brooklyn.

A few days later, a meeting was held in a small Brooklyn bar. Four men attended this meeting. They inspected a small portion of the "package." The portion consisted of $10,000 worth of American Express Travelers Checks. The men were enthusiastic and they were well prepared. Within hours after this meeting, the quartet had booked a flight to San Juan, Puerto Rico. The following day they were in San Juan and became what must be one of the most industrious forgery operations in recent years. Within four hours after their touch-down in San Juan, they had passed a total of $10,000 worth of American Express Travelers Checks. The forgers were literally passing the checks on the run. The maximum value of any individual check was $20. The four men had come to San Juan well prepared. In Manhattan, probably from an identify "pool", they had purchased a series of stolen identification credentials. These identification credentials included such materials as credit cards, (American Express) driver's licenses, Social Security cards, etc. These credentials were liberally displayed during their San Juan visit. The $10,000 "consignment" that the four had taken on proved to be a profitable inspiration for other members of the gang.

Within days, the scene shifted to Las Vegas, Nevada. Members of the gang moved into Las Vegas and again working at fantastic speed, passed a total of approximately $20,000 worth of checks in a 6-7 hour period. While in Las Vegas there was some rumble between the gang members over an alleged "holdout" by one of the members of the gang.

The check passing sprees in San Juan and Las Vegas had proven the ready marketability of the American Express Travelers Checks, but gang members were anxious to dispose of the checks in even larger lots. In Baltimore, Maryland, there reportedly is a fence who is capable of buying large quantities of this type of merchandise. The gang moved on to Baltimore. But for some reason this deal apparently fell through. Now, taking a leaf from their San Juan book, the group proceeded to New Orleans, Louisiana, and passed an additional $10,000 within one day.

Other resort areas and business districts fell prey to the depredations of this group, and a total of $325,000 of the original $400,000 "package" was cashed before the ring was apprehended.

The prompt issuance of warnings to banks, hotels, etc., was partially responsible for the apprehension of the gang. Some of the members were arrested as they passed checks at points that had been alerted to the operation. Other members were apprehended through intelligence gained through informers.

An analysis of this particular operation indicates that most of the forgers were experienced and had extensive prior arrest records. One defendant in this case had a list of over 50 arrests dating from the age of 12. Another of the principle defendants had been arrested previously for an armed holdup and kidnapping at Kennedy Airport. He had served a five year sentence on the latter conviction.

An analysis of this case, considering the method by which the checks were obtained and the speed and precision with which they were negotiated, leads U.S. Attorneys to believe that there was a definite link between the operation and operations of organized crime. This belief is reinforced by the fact that some of the parties arrested had been previously reported as Cosa Nostra "Button-

Men" and have well established links to Cosa Nostra families. It is further believed that the arrest and conviction in this particular case of the passers and dealers, while it broke up the major portion of the ring, probably failed to get the brains behind the operation. The party or parties who planned the theft and the rapid distribution of these checks, have never been apprehended. It is quite likely that they have definite organized crime links.

Check forgers in the New York area were not content to let American Express Travellers Checks rest with the August, 1966 loss of $400,000.00. In a separate case, but also involving American Express Travelers Checks, approximately $600,000.00 worth of checks were obtained during the armed robbery of a Holland-American Line pier on the North River of New York. These checks were rapidly disseminated throughout the United States and some of them have recently appeared in the Seattle, Washington area.

At the time of this writing, thirty-four persons have been arrested in connection with the passing of these checks. However, most of the parties arrested have been passers or lower echelon criminals and there is no evidence at this time to indicate that the organizers of this theft and forgery have been apprehended. Much of the $600,000.00 has never been recovered. There have been no federal indictments returned in the North River pier case, but many local city and state indictments have been obtained. The checks in this case were passed by typical confidence men types. They were successful in passing them in hotels, restaurants, large resort areas and particularly at casinos.

The details of the planning of this robbery and the subsequent massive forgery are as yet unavailable. But initial evidence would certainly seem to indicate extensive planning. One also wonders about the relative security involved in the transfer and holding of these checks on the pier in question. Once again, we see that particular mental quirk of both the public and business community in which they zealously guard printed currency but are nonchalant about other readily negotiable instruments which can be converted into currency.

The $12 Million Wire

When you talk of forgery, you naturally think of the forging of documents such as checks, stamps, credit cards, etc. which have financial value by their very existence. What the public often overlooks is the fact that other documents have considerable value not in and of themselves, but by reason of the "authorization power" that they confer. Such is the case of Wills, Bills of Lading, identification credentials, etc. Perhaps one of the most bizarre and revealing incidents of "authorization" forgery began in early 1967.

In a case, presently pending before the Southern District of New York, it is alleged that five men entered into an embezzlement scheme designed to defraud the Chase Manhattan Bank out of nearly $12 million. Since the case is still pending, this review of the case must be based on the evidence released by the U.S. Attorneys Office and by the allegations contained in the Federal Grand Jury indictment. However, other aspects of the case by inference provide the real background for the event.

On January 16, 1967, 33 year old Carmen Giambola walked into the downtown Manhattan headquarters of the Chase Manhattan Bank. Giambola may have been nervous that particular day. He was accompanied by one Anthony Statile. Statile was rumored to have been an "enforcer" for organized bookies in the New York area. Statile was a specialist in debt collection and it is theorized that Giambola may have been in debt to one or more underworld gamblers.

Carmen Giambola belonged in the bank. He was a bonafide employee in the cable department at Chase Manhattan. Chase Manhattan estimates that it transfers about 6.5 billion dollars in funds by wire each working day. These transfers occur throughout the world. A number of them occur between New York and international banking headquarters in Switzerland. On this particular day, January 16th, a routine wire requesting the transfer of $11,870,924.00 was dispatched from Chase Manhattan headquarters to the Union Bank of Switzerland. The Union Bank is one of Chase's corresponding banks in Zurich, Switzerland. The wire requested that the nearly $12 million be transferred from the Union Bank to a bank in Geneva, Switzerland identified as the Exchange and Investment Bank. The latter bank is reportedly controlled by an unidentified group of Americans. The wire itself was routine enough except for one fact. The request indicated the sum in "dollars" rather than in "francs". Cable personnel at the Union Bank were well aware that the Chase Manhattan Bank normally requested the transfer in the currency of Switzerland, which is of course Swiss Francs. Their suspicions were aroused and a confirmation was requested from the Chase Manhattan Office in New York. Chase security personnel in New York, which incidentally are among the very best in the banking community, immediately became suspicious. A rapid investigation disclosed that the wire was a complete forgery and the field office for the Federal Bureau of Investigation in New York was immediately notified.

In the meantime, it is alleged that an Alfred Brawer, 48 years old, and described as a self-employed real estate man from North Bergen, New Jersey, was on his way to Switzerland. Brawer apparently was to collect the money being transferred out of the Union Bank in Zurich to the Exchange and Investment Bank in Geneva. At this point the Government has declined to describe how Brawer was to pick up the money from the Exchange and Investment Bank in Geneva. However, and this may be coincidental, at the time of this writing a federal grand jury is also investigating allegedly unlawful activities of a small group of Swiss Banks.

The FBI and Chase security personnel managed to round up the conspirators and on March 4, 1968, they were indicted by a federal grand jury meeting in Manhattan Federal Court. Among those indicted was an accountant, a restaurant supply dealer, and a woman public relations consultant who was named as a co-conspirator but not as a defendent. A few weeks prior to the indictment, in March, 1968, Anthony Statile, who was named as a co-conspirator in the plot, was found dead in Greenwich Village. His death convenienty eliminated a direct link between the conspiracy and known organized crime groups that Statile was employed by.

The Florida Withdrawal

The extent and detail of some forgers' operations are illustrated by the case of a particular postal clerk in a large Florida city. Apparently, this clerk had become intrigued with the possibility of committing a major forgery against the U.S. Government. For a two year period the postal clerk in question planned to steal a blank U.S. Treasury check and convert this into a large cash fund. One day his chance arrived. He succeeded in stealing a check and utilized the necessary instruments to forge the check to the value of $98,600.00.

Now, proceeding with the second stage of his plan, he phoned a local bank where postal funds were deposited for business purposes. He informed the bank vice president that the local bank would have to have a sum of $98,600 in cash available for pick-up by a representative of the Post Office Department. During his conversation, the clerk represented himself to the vice president as the Postmaster of the local post office and explained that the funds were to be used in a special business arrangement requested by the Washington office of the Post Office Department. He informed the vice president that this was an extremely confidential matter and asked for his cooperation in keeping the withdrawal quiet. The vice president agreed.

Next, the clerk gained access to a General Services Adminstration car and drove to the front door of the bank. Without getting out of the car, he motioned to a bank guard stationed inside the front door. When the guard came to the car the clerk gave him the forged check in an envelope and instructed the guard to seek out the vice president of the bank and obtain the money in a deposit, pouch. The bank had been alerted to the withdrawal and the cash was ready. Within a few moments the guard returned with $98,600 in cash within a deposit pouch.

The following day, realizing that he would have to convert the cash into other forms in order to avoid detection, the clerk went to another bank and purchased two U.S. Savings Bonds worth $15,000. He attempted to disguise himself during this transaction by shaving off his mustache and using dark glasses. However, the bank clerk who sold these bonds recognized the clerk from previous transactions at that bank. By this time postal inspectors had become alerted to the transaction and were in hot pursuit. An investigation of the clerk's activities revealed that he had a small boat at a local yacht club. One of the local inspectors discovered that the clerk had a duffle bag of "marine fittings" stored in the attic of the yacht club. The inspector procured the duffle bag and found $38,500 of the original funds concealed within the bag. By this time the postal clerk was in custody and, when advised of the discovery of his yacht club cache confessed to the crime. He was subsequently indicted and convicted and is now serving a five year term.

The Everything Card

In August of 1967, the First National City Bank of New York sent out to its customers and depositors the "Everything" Charge Credit Card. This credit card was good for purchases up to $400.00 total. The procedure for use indicated that when purchases in excess of $40.00 were to be charged, the merchant involved was to check back with the bank and determine that the card was being properly used, and not stolen or similarly fraudulently obtained, and that the credit of the card holder was sufficient for the purchase, etc.

Sometime, apparently in the Fall of 1967, a group of persons, who had fraudulently obtained the "Everything" cards, began to utilize them and make extensive purchases and to obtain cash credits. At least 40 separate cards were involved. The forgers obtained the cards and forged the card-holder's name under the signature panel of the card. They then proceeded to make purchases and in turn to fence the goods for cash. In some cases they made purchases and then returned the goods for a cash refund.

The cards may have been obtained through mail theft, through theft from personal belongings, or may actually have been given to the forgers by the original recipient of the cards. There is no specific evidence at this point to indicate the method by which all of these cards were obtained. In any event the forgers did not use fictitious names, nor apparently was there any attempt to consciously match the known signature pattern of the card holder. Rather, the forgers merely signed "John Doe" or whatever the card-holder's name was in their own handwriting pattern.

On Friday, June 14, 1968 indictments were returned against 11 people. These were multiple count indictments charging amongst other things, forgery in the second degree, criminal possession of stolen goods, grand larceny and petit larceny. It is alleged that this part of the ring was successful in defrauding the First National City Bank of approximately $100,000.00. Five separate store owners were also indicted on the charge of criminal facilitation in the second degree. These store owners apparently cooperated, it is alleged, with the forgers and made out multiple sales slips, managing to keep each slip below the $40.00 critical limit in order that large quantities of merchandise might be purchased.

This particular case is the third major credit card fraud ring broken up by the Bronx County District Attorney's Office. The two previous rings involved oil company credit cards. The nature of these rings is such that they always involve multiple count indictments and they present a tremendous work load to the District Attorney's Office involved. In the First National City case, the 11 indictments produced over 1700 separate counts. This creates a terrific investigatory problem as well as a very large paper work problem.

D.A. Burton Roberts notes that their problem, in connection with the credit card fraud, is certainly compounded by the indiscriminate mass mailing of credit cards. In some cases these cards have been thrown away or discarded in a manner that potential forgers were able to obtain them and subsequently perpetrate the forgery.

There is also some feeling that the possession of the stolen card should constitute presumptive evidence of intent to defraud. Apparently, as Mr. Seymour Rotker, head of the Frauds Division, points out, the credit card companies are willing to accept a certain amount of fraudulent loss because of the large increased sales volume that accrues from these indiscriminate mass mailings. He cites one oil company who reportedly, following a mass mailing, experienced a 40% increase in credit sales.

The original release of data on this case, it appeared that the original eight persons arrested were part of a ring of 35 persons. Subsequent investigation produced evidence sufficient for the indictment of 16 persons.

The War On *Poverty*

The summer of 1968 was a warm one in New York City. By late August much of the energy and zip had been drained from most of the city employees. But New York City Police were still very much on the job when they stopped a late model sedan on a Manhattan street. The sedan contained four men, all employees of the Neighborhood Youth Corps, a Division of the Human Resources Administration. The sedan had been leased from a New York automotive leasing firm to the Neighborhood Youth Corps. Its lease was over a month past due and the car should have been returned to the leasing agency. Perhaps that is how the police came to stop the vehicle. For whatever reason, the police thoroughly searched the leased auto. This routine search was to uncover one of the largest check forgery operations of 1968.

Secreted within the car were 105 checks. Each check was made out for $38.82. All of the checks were official payroll checks of the Neighborhood Youth Corps. They were all made out to different individuals and, as was later shown, each of these individuals was fictitious.

Within a few days the case began to break in several directions. It was first discovered that some 7,290 checks worth $282,997.80 had been issued to fictitious persons, then forged, and subsequently cashed. The chance arrest by New York City Police gave the city time to stop payment on 1200 checks. At first it was believed that the $282,000 loss covered the principal amount of the forgery and embezzlement. But this belief was soon to be dashed by local and federal investigators who began a minute inspection of the payroll records of the Neighborhood Youth Corps, one of the many operations of the New York City Human Resources Administration. The latter administration expends some $1.36 billion a year on welfare and poverty operations. The Neighborhood Youth Corps had some 50,000 slum youths on its payroll the previous summer. At the time of this writing they have approximately 9,000 year around members.

As the investigation proceeded, it discovered that at least one out of five or 20% of all of the checks issued by this agency were fraudulent. The estimate on the amount of loss climbed astronomically. Where estimates had once put the loss at $490,000, including frauds in both 1967 and 1968, it now climbed to $1.5 million by official estimate of the city. Meantime, investigators on the case noted privately that the amount could well climb to some $6 million.

The investigations were conducted by auditors from the Human Resources Administration, detectives of the City Department of Investigation, investigators from the United States Department of Labor, FBI agents from the U.S. Attorneys Office, and investigators from District Attorney's Frank S. Hogan's office. These investigations produced an initial arrest of some 7 persons.

In this particular forgery operation we can detect the existence of several different M.O's. The basic plan involved the creation of both fictitious "work sites" as well as phantom payrolls. The investigators uncovered the fact that some of the projects and work sites were complete dummies and that fictitious persons had been added to the payroll to perform the "work" at these sites. One investigation showed that some 7,000 separate time cards for non-existent persons had been created. It was also discovered that duplicate paychecks were being issued. For example, a legitimate employee would receive his paycheck and then later the same week a duplicate check would be issued. The second check would be forged with the legitimate employee's name and subsequently cashed. This particular case also involved the use of the so called "inside man" M.O. The latter technique utilizes a confederate located in the bank or check cashing establishment. This investigation revealed the alleged collusion of two check cashing corporations.

After the checks had been prepared they were cashed in bulk amounts of about 800 checks at a time at these check cashing services. Investigations Commissioner Arnold Fraiman noted that some 5,751 checks were deposited at one check cashing operation and 1,503 checks at another.

As the case began to unfold city investigators became very interested in Mrs. Helynn R. Lewis, a $19,000-a-year Director of Fiscal Affairs for the New York City Human Resources Administration. Mrs. Lewis was originally called in to Investigation Commission Fraiman's office for a preliminary discussion. She later appeared for an additional discussion, but this time was accompanied by her lawyer. No charges were filed against Mrs. Lewis at that time. But by September 28th Mrs. Lewis had a good idea about what the future held in store for her.

On Saturday morning, September 28th, Mrs. Lewis departed her exclusive Central Park West apartment house and caught a cab to Newark Airport. At Newark she boarded a plane for Los Angeles. Once in Los Angeles, she went to the Olympian Hotel and checked in.

On Monday, September 30th, two FBI agents arrived at 444 Central Park West and began a stake-out on the apartment. It was known that Mrs. Lewis had fled and a warrant had been issued for her arrest. The FBI continued the stake-out until the following Friday when it was discovered that Mrs. Lewis had been arrested in Los Angeles at the Olympian Hotel. She was subsequently returned to New York by federal agents. The warrant for Mrs. Lewis' arrest reveals that she was allegedly involved in a check operation of her own. The warrant charges that Mrs. Lewis did "embezzle and appropriate to her own use sums belonging to the Employees Emergency Imprest Funds of the Human Resources Administration of the City of New York". The sums, which were allegedly obtained through fraudulent check operations amounted to some $4,300 taken from the Chemical Bank New York Trust Company on August 13, $14,500 on August 15th and $4,112.69 on August 26th. The Imprest Fund is a revolving loan fund setup in the early days of an agency's operation in order to provide monies for payroll prior to official funding.

Mrs. Helynn R. Lewis is an interesting example of New York City employment practices. In examining her case, and perhaps considering some of the aspects of the Marcus Case, one is struck by the fact that apparently all that was needed to obtain a very responsible job in fiscal administration was to know the proper parties. It is hard to believe that any extensive pre-employment check was made on Mrs. Lewis. In fact it is difficult to know whether Mrs. Lewis is in fact Mrs. Lewis. Police investigators revealed that she had used at least five different names in California. She was alledgedly known by the names of Lewis, Henderson, Garcia, Holloway and Clemmens. All of these names were reputedly names of ex-husbands, although Mrs. Lewis also maintained that she had never married prior to meeting Ernest Lewis in 1955. Some other interesting facts about this "fiscal administrator" were uncovered. Mrs. Lewis reported that she had a law degree from Los Angeles State College in 1954. Los Angeles State, now designated California State College, Los Angeles, does not award law degrees. Mrs. Lewis also claimed that she had worked as an engineer at Radio Station KVCA-FM from 1956 to 1959. KVCA did not come on the air until 1959. Mrs. Lewis also reported having worked for station KTRS in Kansas City from 1961 to 1963. But checks with the latter radio station revealed that the only person working there fitting Mrs. Lewis' description, had worked for six months as a typist. Mrs. Lewis also reportedly worked for the National Jewish Welfare Board in Denver, Colorado in 1964. There is no present telephone listing for the National Jewish Welfare Board in Denver, Colorado.

As this report goes to press there are further details unfolding about the War on Poverty check fraud case. For example, one New

York councilman, Councilman Joseph Modugno has charged that money obtained in this fraud was utilized to subsidize a radical left wing spokesman on a $40 a day consultant basis and that money through the Human Resources Administration was utilized to pay the transport for Yippies going from New York to Chicago, and subsequently employed for the disruption of the Democratic National Convention.

While the War on Poverty scandal involving check frauds was in progress in New York, somewhat similar details were evolving halfway across the country in Chicago, Illinois. A United States Senate Permanent Subcommittee on Investigation had found a large scale forgery of signatures on time records and checks ostensively issued to the notorious "Blackstone Rangers" in the Woodlawn Poverty Organization of Chicago. The latter poverty program began in 1967 and was abandoned in May of 1968. A United States Internal Revenue Service handwriting expert, Mr. Howard C. Doulder, testified that his examination, conducted over a five week period, had shown that more than $50,000 was paid to members of two gangs through fraudulent check operations. These payments had been made for supposed attendance at training sessions. The Senate Committee then continued its investigation of some $927,241.00 granted by the Office of Economic Opportunity to this particular Chicago "War on Poverty" Program.

Hardin-Sonnier — U.S. Treasury Checks

The following case is presented through the cooperation of the United States Secret Service. Data presented herein is based on Secret Service files and from the court records publicly available on the case.

U.S. Treasury Checks have always been a particularly attractive subject for forgery. They are recognized throughout the business community. Many merchants believe that they are just as good as money and pay little attention to identification and endorsements. While most forgers rely on mail thefts and similar devices to gain access to U.S. Treasury checks, one particular ring took a short cut and began both counterfeiting and forging U.S. Treasury checks.

Early in May of 1959, four counterfeit U.S. Treasury checks appeared through a Florida clearinghouse. Within a week, a trail of similar counterfeit checks appeared in Georgia, Mississippi, Louisiana and Texas. The counterfeiters usually forged checks for $100 or less and worked supermarkets, liquor stores, and clothing stores. By the middle of May, 1959, the U.S. Secret Service had circulated warnings to banks and storeowners to be on the alert for these phony checks.

On May 23rd, one of the principals in the ring walked into a Baton Rouge, Louisiana supermarket and attempted to pass a counterfeit Treasury check. The clerk had been alerted by the Secret Service bulletin and refused to cash the check. In addition, he provided a description of the passer and his auto. This description was passed onto Louisiana State Police who broadcast a pick up order on interstate police teletype. The passer fled southwest over the Louisiana border into Texas. However, two days later, the suspect now identified as Arphy Justin Sonnier, was found in Beaumont, Texas and identified as the Baton Rouge passer. Sonnier had a previous contact with the Louisiana State Police on a narcotics conviction and this conviction provided information on some of his associates.

The Secret Service now began a carefully planned undercover operation which would eventually result in the detection and apprehension of the counterfeit ring leader plus 15 other persons connected with the manufacture and passing of the counterfeit checks. A review of Arphy Justin Sonnier's associates provided two additional names; that of James Douglas Simmons and Carl Jay Schaaphok. Simmons was identified as cashing one of the checks in an Atlanta liquor store and it is believed that he and Schaaphok worked the southwest with Sonnier. However, the most interesting acquaintance of Sonnier's was a girl friend identified as Jo Ann. The Secret Service believed that this girl had access to the other members of the ring and perhaps to the source of the checks themselves.

An undercover agent, purporting to be a New York gangster, was brought into Louisiana. This agent made contact with one of Jo Ann's associates through a local Louisiana Bar. The undercover agent spread stories about his inexhaustible source of funds and let it be suspected that he was cooling off in Louisiana after an escapade in the New York area. The agent made contact with the small time hood who was Jo Ann's friend and eventually made contact with Jo Ann herself. After some haggling, the agent purchased 11 counterfeit U.S. Treasury checks. The agent, then feigning disinterest, moved back to New York to set the bait for a larger trap.

Through an interstate telephone contact, a larger buy was set up. Jo Ann turned negotiations over to Joseph Lovely Sonnier and Louis Emory Roger. Arrangements were made for a large delivery of checks to be made to the Washington, D.C. area. The deal at Washington involved the delivery of 1,000 counterfeit checks at a price of $20,000. The agent had previously purchased the 11 checks for a price of $275.00.

July 8th, 1959, was a warm muggy day in Washington, D.C. On the balcony overlooking the ticket counter of Washington National Airport, two Secret Service agents waited for a rendezvous with the counterfeiters. Late in the afternoon, the New Orleans flight arrived and two men, identified as Joseph Lovely Sonnier and Louis Emory Roger, made contact with the agents and were subsequently arrested and then removed to Alexandria, Virginia for arraignment. In their possession were 755 counterfeit checks along with counterfeit military identification cards, U.S. Social Security cards, and counterfeit Alabama driver's licenses. The following morning, Jo Ann was arrested at the residence of Joseph Lovely Sonnier at Duson, Louisiana.

Subsequent interrogation of Joseph Sonnier and Louis Roger disclosed that they had made trips to the Texas border and particularly to Durango, Mexico. A team of bilingual Secret Service agents moved into the area and alerted Mexican authorities. In a joint effort, all printing plants in the area capable of producing the Treasury checks were carefully screened. This screening eventually narrowed down the potential points of production to a single plant. The Spanish-speaking Secret Service agent worked his way into the confidence of one of the printing plant's employees who told of a strange occurrence. The employee related that he had seen the printing plant owner's sons, identified as Rosalio and Ponciano Salas, working late on a secret printing job. This job turned out to be the counterfeiting operation. The Salas brothers were arrested and a subsequent search of the Salas plant disclosed parts of a printing plate as well as materials used to counterfeit social security cards, government checks, drivers licenses, etc.

Meanwhile, immediately following the arrest of Jo Ann in Duson, Louisiana, Secret Service agents searched her personal belongings and found a lead to a Rufus Howard Hardin. Hardin was known to Birmingham, Alabama Secret Service agents although he had never been convicted on previous charges of bank robbery, murder, and a Mexican timber fraud swindle. The Mexican connection again pointed to the Salas plant and further intensive interrogation of the Salas brothers revealed the Hardin link. Subsequently, on October 13, 1959, in Gulf Shores, Alabama, Rufus Howard Hardin, the alleged mastermind of the operation, was arrested and charged with the manufacture of counterfeit U.S. Treasury Checks. The following day his brother, Will Max Hardin, was arrested in Birmingham, Alabama as an accomplice in the conspiracy. Fifteen other persons were subsequently arrested. In a round-up of the 15, nine American nationals and 6 Mexican nationals were arrested and subsequently convicted.

PART 2 — CASE HISTORIES

The following cases on Courtney Townsend Taylor, Frederick Douglas George, and George Lester Belew are derived from files and court records provided through the courtesy and cooperation of the Federal Bureau of Investigation.

COURTNEY TOWNSEND TAYLOR

The case of Courtney Townsend Taylor is important to the study of forgery because in many ways he is the prototype of the 20th Century check forger. His unique methods have earned him the FBI's description as "perhaps the most ingeniuous check passer ever to operate in this country". It is the opinion of many law enforcement agents that the checks Taylor passed were amongst the best ever distributed. By the time Taylor was apprehended, in Mobile, Alabama, on February 16, 1951, he had left a trail of checks covering nearly every State in the Union.

The Taylor case begins in East Hartford, Connecticut. Taylor was born there on June 22, 1908. His early education was meager and limited to a grade school attendance. We know relatively little about his early childhood except for the fact that his father died when he was four years of age and his mother when he was 23.

Taylor himself provides an interesting psychological side light in that he himself describes his conduct as a child as "not normal". One incident in this early childhood period is recalled by Taylor and provides a kind of perverse rationale for his later career. Taylor tells of attempting to buy a clock for his mother's birthday. He approached a Buffalo, New York credit jewelry store and made a $5.00 deposit on the clock. In filling out the credit application he stated that he had been working at his present job for a six-month period. In reality he had actually only been working two weeks. When Taylor returned one week later to claim the clock, he found that the credit manager for the store had discovered the misrepresentation and now refused to give Taylor either the clock or the $5.00 deposit. This action proved to be a costly error. Taylor would later relate how he had cashed checks of more than $600 in the same store, all of which were fraudulent and approved by this same credit manager.

In Taylor's first recorded brush with the law, he was apprehended and convicted for a breaking and entering offense. At age 16 he was committed to the Cheshire, Connecticut State Reformatory. By the time he was 20, Taylor had been released from Cheshire and had begun to feel the travel itch. With two local acquaintances he decided to make a trip to California. In casting about for a source of funds, Taylor discovered a letter addressed to a neighbor from Sears, Roebuck and Company. This particular neighbor was using the same mail box as Taylor's mother. Taylor lifted the letter from the mail box and quietly returned to his own room. There he steamed open the letter and removed the check. At age 20 Courtney Townsend Taylor copies the neighbor's name and forges his first check.

The following year on January 7, 1929 Taylor is arrested at Xenia, Ohio for auto theft, convicted and sentenced to the reformatory at Mansfield, Ohio. By 1931 Taylor had been released from Mansfield and was reverting to the mail theft and forgery pattern established during the 1928 forgery of the Sears-Roebuck & Company check. From the period 1931 to 1941 Taylor continued his mail theft and forgery activities and was arrested several times, serving three terms in Federal penitentiaries. His last period of incarceration was at the United States Penitentiary at Atlanta, Georgia where he was released on April 19, 1941 to the custody of Milwaukee, Wisconsin Authorities who sought him on local forgery charges. He was tried, convicted and sentenced to a State Prison at Waupun, Wisconsin.

The period from April, 1941 to January 23, 1943 is an important part of Courtney Townsend Taylor's history. During these two years at the Waupun State Prison, he abandoned his haphazard crime career and decided to become a specialist. During those months in prison he obtained and read all of the available literature that he could get his hands on in the fields of printing, inks, etc. He may even have had access to the prison print shop to improve his new found interests. By the time Taylor was released in January, 1943 he had acquired a good background in the field of printing and was ready for some practical experimentation. One of his first moves was to purchase a small hand printing press, miscellaneous fonts of type, safety papers, inks, etc.

Taylor took a good look at an industrial register and proceeded to print hundreds of checks with the imprint titles of such internationally known corporations as The Campbell Soup Company, H.J. Heinz Company, Noxema Chemical Company, Parker Pen Company, E.R. Squibb Company, Hershey Chocolate Company, New York, New Haven and Hartford Railroad Company, and included for good measure checks of the Commonwealth of Pennsylvania and the State of New York. By carefully researching his subject Taylor was able to select not only the names of principal American corporations but also the names of banks where these firms might logically do business.

From the period of February, 1943 to June, 1944 Taylor ranged through 28 States leaving a trail of startled and angry check cashers. His modus operandi in this period was to act as a salesman, buyer, etc. of one of the nationally known firms. In addition to the checks Taylor also prepared a series of identifications to match the aliases he would utilize. These included auto registrations, driver's licenses, etc. In a typical operation, Taylor would enter a store and select a minor purchase. He would offer one of the bogus checks representing it as a salary or commission check to the store owner. He would then display the false identity papers to substantiate the validity of the endorsement. Taylor even reinforced his identity by going to the trouble of obtaining samples of the company's products he was reported to represent. He would pass out these samples and promotional literature in the store that was cashing his check. With moves like this Taylor had advanced beyond the simple mail thief-forger combination to the pro league of forger and con artist.

On June 6, 1944, FBI agents in Seattle, Washington caught up with Taylor and arrested him for cashing fraudulent checks and the interstate transportation of securities known to be fraudulent. At the time of his arrest Taylor admitted to passing $55,000.00 in fraudulent checks during the 18 month period. Taylor had averaged nearly $800.00 a week during this 18 month attack on the American economy.

FBI agents searching Taylor's apartment found an additional 172 checks valued at over $16,000.00. They also found 57 individual Selective Serivce Cards, an uncounted number of fraudulent identification cards, and an assortment of railroad and airplane ticket stubs. In total Taylor was prepared to use over 102 different aliases, and the equipment found by the FBI agents offered the potential for creating hundreds of additional aliases. At this point in his operations Taylor had established a documentation mill in Philadelphia, Pennsylvania. He had a range of printing equipment, rubber stamp production equipment, cutters, etc. Apparently Taylor would return to Philadelphia to replenish his stock of checks and to create any identity documents.

Following his arrest by the FBI in Seattle, Taylor was transferred to the United States District Court in Philadelphia and on September 18, 1944 pleaded guilty to the interstate transportation of fraudulent checks. He was sentenced to two years imprisonment starting October, 1944. He was released early but on February 23, 1945 Taylor was again in court in Utica, New York on identical charges and was sentenced to an additional two years. He was now transferred to the United States Penitentiary in Atlanta and by February, 1944 an additional six detainers had been placed against him. For the next several years Taylor was shuttled between various states and jails on forgery charges ending up in the Onondaga County Penitentiary, Jamestown, New York on August 10, 1949. He served a term there and was released April 14, 1950. This stretch of alternating jail sentences may have satisfied the penal requirements of the several States involved, but it did little to dampen Taylor's ardor as a forger. Within six days after his release from Onondaga Taylor was back in business and had passed his first check in what was to be his last major check spree.

Taylor may have reviewed his previous method of operation and decided that it was no longer necessary for him to be in the printing business. He devised what has been referred to as "the voucher system." In this system Taylor enlisted the help and facilities of many of the country's printers. They unwittingly provided him with a ready source of blank checks printed with the best of equipment.

To make his voucher system work Taylor would first obtain a photographic cut of a well known brand name; for example, he might obtain the trademark and logo of the Smith Brothers Cough Drop Company. Then, utilizing this cut, he would represent himself as a sales promotion executive of the company. He would contact a legitimate printer and provide him with prepared artwork for the printing of a "promotional piece". This artwork was cleverly designed so that it did not appear to be a check. a retailer. However, by cutting away portions of this "agreement" a section was left which could be readily utilized as a check. The check portion of the agreement was usually contained in the upper portion of the form with a center dividing line. Below this dividing line was the "agreement".

This particular method of operation is particularly dangerous in the hands of any experienced con man. Undoubtedly Taylor utilized the various identification cards he was capable of making and probably even used samples of the company's products as he approached these printers. In addition, he never ordered small quantities of the "agreement" and would purchase in lots of 500 pieces or more. He often impressed on the printer the need for haste telling him that he was in town and had run short of these forms which were ordinarily printed by the company's major printing supplier. Unfortunately, many of the country's small print shops, hungry for business and inattentive to the details of the document, continue to be a potential source of check counterfeiter's production.

Taylor, recognizing that a few printers might have some second thoughts after they had accepted his order, planned for this eventuality. Using an accomplice, Taylor would make arrangements to pick up the form at a specific time. Realizing that the print shop might be staked out, Taylor worked with an accomplice who would go in to the shop ten or fifteen minutes prior to the designated pick-up time. The accomplice would time his entry into the shop in such a manner that he would be there as Taylor telephoned the printer. The accomplice would observe the printer during this telephone conversation and attempt to detect if there was any suspicion on his part or if police officers may have been in or around the premises. If there was nothing suspicious, and there seldom was, then Taylor would stop by and pick up the forms. The next step in the voucher system involved the conversion of these forms to what appeared to be legitimate checks. Cutting off the agreement portion of the form posed no difficulty and Taylor then proceeded to utilize a check-writer, a numbering machine, typewriter, etc. to create a fictitious check.

Taylor would construct fictitious executive names as the signer for these corporation checks. It is alleged that one of the methods he used to produce a signature which appeared to be a "machine" signature involved writing the signature through a multicolored ribbon with a stylus. The ribbon, similar to that used in check signing machines, was layed over the signature portion of the check. He then impressed the stylus in a casual signature pattern and was able to successfully simulate the impression gained by a signature machine. The signature machines, as related elsewhere, utilize a cast metal signature plate which is impressed on a multicolored ribbon to form the facsimile signature. Taylor also embellished certain checks with rubber stamps where such embellishment created a further chink in the armour of legitimacy which he was attempting to build around the check.

On April 20, 1950 Taylor was in Baltimore, Maryland. He had prepared his first check utilizing the voucher system. The check was a facsimile of a Bristol-Myers Company check. The travel from Onondaga and the cost of having the facsimile checks printed had eaten deeply into Taylor's finances. At this point, he had only $1.15 left. Taylor selected a likely Baltimore store, made a small purchase, and attempted to pass his first check. The clerk delayed in cashing the check and Taylor, only six days out of prison, became naturally apprehensive. He must have had a vision of being immediately carted off to a penitentiary again. His fears were ill founded. The store had just made its daily deposit and was short of cash. In a rare quirk of fate the store issued Taylor a check for the balance of his payment. Taylor hurried out of the store and passed the good check in a local men's furnishing shop. This may be one of the only good checks that Taylor ever passed.

During the next day Taylor managed to pass four more fraudulent checks in the City of Baltimore. He then began a route which took him through Pittsburgh, Toledo, Detroit, Chicago, St. Louis, Kansas City and Minneapolis, then returning to Philadelphia. During his route, which covered the next eight days, he continued to utilize the voucher system to supply him with checks reportedly issued by major corporations. Returning to Philadelphia, he destroyed the remaining Bristol-Myers checks and produced new sets reportedly issued by Miles Laboratories, Mars Candy, Inc. and Smith Brothers. Taylor's next route took him through New York, Boston and Providence, Rhode Island.

At this point, Taylor, perhaps aware that the new batch of fraudulent checks would be soon identified by the FBI Laboratory, took a step which he believed would complicate his detection. Taylor acquired the servics of a junior partner.

This junior partner was a former prison friend who had helped dispose of some of the merchandise that Taylor "bought", in the check passing activities of the past. This "fence" became friendly with Taylor and joined him in his check passing forays. The new partner made all the arrangements for rented automobiles used during the check passing trips and in effect became a chauffeur for Taylor. He was also the bookkeeper during these trips and proceeded to split the net gains on a 50-50 share basis.

An interesting sidelight to the junior partner reveals that he was on parole in Philadelphia when he began his chauffeuring activities for Taylor. Parolees must stay close to their probation officer and his extensive travels with Taylor threatened to pose a problem. Taylor met this problem by creating a fraudulent identification card and stationery from an established New York leather company. Taylor also prepared a letter reported to be from the leather company requesting that the parolee be given permission to travel about the United States as a company salesman. The parole officer was fooled by the forged letter and identification card and did actually grant permission for Taylor's chauffeur to travel about the country.

Courtney Townsend Taylor was a student of police detection methods as well as the technicalities of printing and check passing. He was well aware that check passers are often identified through the personal description provided by check cashers to investigating officers. He sought, unsuccessfully, to use his new junior partner to pass checks. The chauffeur stalled Taylor on the grounds that his daughter was being married and didn't want to jeopardize her social standing by risking the passing of checks. He procrastinated telling Taylor that he would pass them after her marriage. However, after his daughter was married, he again procrastinated and as far as can be determined never did pass a check during the entire time he was Taylor's chauffeur and accomplice.

Following Taylor's initial success he began a well organized route plan which took him through 26 different cities during the month of May, 1950. During this time Philadelphia was the headquarters for his operation and he returned here to replenish his supply of identification cards and checks. Taylor now had to move so quickly that the voucher system often proved to be too cumbersome and slow. He went back into the printing business. In June, 1950 he once again began printing his own checks and identification cards. As his headquarters he found a former poolroom on the second floor of a clubhouse in Philadelphia and set up his press.

During June he slacked off his check passing activities and concentrated his energies on printing. During the four weeks of

June, he must have printed thousands of different checks and identification cards. It is known that he and his accomplice printed check forms for 32 well known corporations and divisions of state and city government. In addition to these checks he also produced state automobile license and registration forms, bonded employee identification cards, club membership cards, credit cards and Social Security cards. Apparently, Taylor had access to some legitimate cards in order to form models for these creations. These cards may have been available through the underworld since Philadelphia also has a ready market to fence stolen credit cards or identity credentials. Taylor must also have scoured the Philadelphia area for the various types of paper stocks needed in his operation. Significantly, his purchases did not arouse suspicion among the graphic art suppliers in the Philadelphia area. This is a problem, that is the failure of recognition, that comes up again and again in forgery and counterfeiting cases. In the case of Courtney Townsend Taylor we have relatively simple printing operations involved and the chances of detection through the tracing of equipment, supplies, etc. are relatively poor. It is also possible that Taylor may have purchased these materials out of state or through the mails.

After four weeks of operation Taylor and his accomplice closed up shop in Philadelphia and put their equipment in storage. Before leaving the poolroom they made a thorough search of the premises to remove any incriminating evidence. During a final check out Taylor found a forged identification card which had fallen into the pocket of the pool table. This chance discovery provided Taylor with an extended lease on his liberty. Two days later, neighborhood vandals broke some windows in the building during an attempted break-in. The Philadelphia Police completely searched the second floor in the course of checking out the attempted burglary. They failed to find anything suspicious and lady-luck had once again bowed in Taylor's direction.

Early in July, Taylor, with a girlfriend, left Philadelphia for the South. They first swung through Chicago, then Iowa and finally the deep south states before heading for the Gulf Coast. Their foray in the Gulf Coast took them through Gulfport, New Orleans, Mobile, Panama City, St. Petersburg, Tampa, Ft. Lauderdale and finally Miami Beach. Then they swung North through Daytona Beach, Charleston, Wilmington, North Carolina and Pocono City, Maryland, returning to Philadelphia at the end of the month.

Taylor was moving in high gear now. He purchased a car and drove to the West Coast. Setting up Long Beach, California as his headquarters, he moved up and down the West Coast cashing checks in Long Beach, San Diego, and Los Angeles. Moving inland from Long Beach, Taylor drove to Reno, Nevada where he passed a number of fictitious travellers checks reported to be on the Chase National Bank of New York. He then swung back north passing through Bakersfield on to Fresno, Oakland and San Francisco. Once again reversing his field, he drove to Oklahoma City. By this time his girlfriend, who had accompanied him from Philadelphia, was feeling the pressure. Taylor could stand the pace but she couldn't. At Oklahoma City she deserted Taylor. Taylor returned to Philadelphia distributing bogus checks in Indiana, Missouri, Ohio and Michigan as he moved North again. He rested for a period in Philadelphia and then returned to Tucson, Arizona. In Tucson he linked up with a former cellmate, one David Edward Loveless. Loveless joined the chauffeur and Taylor in a three-way partnership. The trio moved south during the fall, of 1950 distributing checks throughout Tennessee, Georgia, etc.

During this period, Taylor and Loveless would pose as salesmen cashing expense checks and would characteristically purchase small items and offer a check, usually for under $100.00 to the store owner. By passing small checks in large quantities, they were quite able to make several hundred dollars per day in profit. Taylor was anxious to add members to his ring since he recognized that his description was now well circulated to various law enforcement agents and to banking and business officials. The addition of David Edward Loveless was an attempt to provide additional "hands" for the distribution of his checks. By October 23, 1950, Taylor was back in Philadelphia and had recruited a new member for his gang. Andrew J. Newhouse had alledgedly been part of a 40 man hold-up and burglary ring which operated in Philadelphia during early part 1949. Newhouse liked the look of Taylor's operation and joined with Taylor, Loveless and their chauffeur on a trip which took them to Providence, Rhode Island. They headquartered in Providence and proceeded north to Boston to scout out some prospective stores for their paper hanging operation. Loveless and Newhouse had been fitted out with new identities. Newhouse was fictitiously identified as David A. King a "bonded representative" of the Pittsburgh Steel Company. Loveless was identified as Jacob D. Reese a representative of Johnson & Johnson, Inc., New Brunswick, New Jersey. Newhouse and Loveless operated in Providence passing checks in supermarkets and bars. On October 26, the quartet moved from Providence to Newport, Rhode Island. Taylor once had lived in Newport and was familiar with the names and characteristics of the people. Now Taylor joined the operation.

Assuming the identity of a "Rodney S. Hickson" of the Phillies Cigar Company, Taylor visited two of the best men's stores in town. Taylor, balding, heavy set with a neatly trimmed mustache, was the picture of affluence and credibility. He talked easily of some of the town's principal citizens and of the old school he had attended there. Meanwhile, his two new associates were working the supermarkets of Newport. Loveless made one successful pass in a supermarket but Newhouse, in his first attempt made a unavoidable serious error. When asked by the store manager for a local street number and address he furnished a number and address on the same street as the store manager. The manager passed the check but had some second thoughts. The number Newhouse had given him didn't sound right. Quickly, he referred to a city directory, and confirmed his suspicions. Newhouse was just leaving the store and one of the store clerks was detailed to tail him. Newhouse returned to the confederates car and was spotted by the clerk. A local Newport police officer was in the store at the time and as the clerk returned to report on where Newhouse had gone, the manager related his suspicions. The officer reported the manager's suspicions to headquarters and within minutes Loveless and Newhouse had been apprehended.

Once again, Taylor had been plain lucky. He happened to be out of the car and down the street a short distance when the two passers and the chauffeur were apprehended. Taylor recognized the arrest at once and quickly began a circuitous route which would return him to New York City. Loveless and Newhouse were interrogated by local police and FBI agents. However, it wasn't until the next day that they admitted Taylor's existence and by this time he had escaped to New York after back-tracking to Boston momentarily.

Once again, as in the Seattle arrest, FBI agents were able to obtain many of the "working papers" of Courtney Townsend Taylor. A briefcase in the 1951 Kaiser auto revealed nearly 400 checks from thirty different major business corporations. The usual stock of employee identification cards, credit cards, licenses, etc. were also enclosed. As related previously, it had been theorized that Taylor was forming his facsimile signatures through the use of a stylus and an inked ribbon. The briefcase contained a number of postcards which were used as stencil frames for this type of operation. A center section of the postal card is cut out and a strip of ribbon layed across the opening. The ribbon is in turn fixed and covered on one side with a piece of cellophane tape. The stylus is impressed on the cellophane tape pressing the inked ribbon on to the check surface to form a very good replica of a stamped or machine impressed signature. The arrested trio were released by Newport, Rhode Island authorities to federal custody and charged under the Federal Interstate Transportation of Stolen Property Act.

Taylor was now back in New York but all of his equipment and supplies had gone down the drain in the Newport, Rhode Island arrest. He did have several thousand dollars in cash and travellers checks with him. With this capital he renewed his "voucher system" and had several hundred R.J. Reynolds Tobacco Company checks produced. He proceeded to Chicago in the early part of November, 1950 and then on to Los Angeles and San Francisco; moving north along the Pacific Coast, he obtained a hotel suite in Seattle and concealed 265 of the R.J. Reynolds checks in a cubbard in the kitchenette of the suite. The concealment was excellent and these checks were not recovered until May of 1951, by searching FBI agents.

As November, 1950 came to a close, Taylor began an eastward trek which would take him through St. Paul, Chicago, Nashville, Chattanooga, Atlanta, back-tracking to Miami and then on to New York. During the early part of December, 1950 Taylor worked out of the New York area. His check passing activity was slowed during Christmas of 1950 but immediately after Christmas he reverted again to the voucher system and he prepared a batch of checks representing the Louisville and Nashville Railroad.

Taylor had been moving quickly throughout the United States and had been primarily relying on air and railroad transport during the past two months. Now he was sure that airline and rail terminals might be staked out and that wanted notices were posted for him. In Philadelphia, he arranged for a new driver and staged a reunion with the girlfriend who had deserted him in Oklahoma City. He moved south again stopping in Miami, Florida to pass additional checks and finally arriving on February 16, 1951 in Mobile, Alabama. Taylor was tired and cautious. His instinct told him it was time to stop, but his obsession for work drove him on. He discussed going fishing that bright February morning in Mobile. But he deferred plans for one day to pass some checks in the downtown area. He had been passing R.J. Reynolds Tobacco Co. checks for sometime now. This was in violation of his own credo, but probably was a result of the disruption of his plans by the Newport, Rhode Island arrest. So it was that on February 16, 1951, Courtney Townsend Taylor entered a jewelry store in downtown Mobile, Alabama.

Taylor purchased a necklace at that Mobile jewelry store and it was the necklace that was to choke his freedom for many years to come. The clerk in the store remembered a local credit bulletin indicating a person was passing bogus R.J. Reynolds Tobacco Company checks. He called his store manager and the manager telephoned the Mobile field office of the FBI. The FBI responded immediately and sent agents into the downtown Mobile streets in search of Taylor. Meanwhile, Taylor had passed a second check at another jewelry store. For some reason, the credit manager at this jewelry store also was suspicious and followed Taylor into the street. He attracted the attention of a Mobile police officer who was directing traffic and the patrolman stopped Taylor. As the patrolman asked for Taylor's identification two Mobile FBI agents had spotted Taylor and he was taken into custody by the agents and Mobile police. During his arrest he continued to deny his identity and of course produced false identity credentials. However, after he had been fingerprinted he did admit to being Courtney Townsend Taylor. As they searched Taylor they found checks and identity credentials issued reportedly by the Pennsylvania Department of Revenue, the Pennsylvania Motor Vehicle Registration Department, the Pittsburgh Bank Note Company, the Postal Life Insurance Company, and others.

During the course of Taylor's arraignment, he was interviewed by FBI agents and again revealed some of the personality characteristics and mental capacity that marked him as a unique individual amongst 20th century forgers. Taylor was a bonafide speed reader. He could race through a typical novel in a little less than two hours time. He could also read longhand notes upside down and as a result could completely read the transcript of an interview before the arresting officer had even completed his interrogation. Taylor showed no particular remorse during his arrest and rationalized his activities by noting that he only defrauded those merchants of capable of withstanding a loss. In a Robin Hood-like gesture, he noted that he never defrauded stores where he knew the clerk might be personally accountable for accepting a bad check. Neither did he at this time indicate that if he was later released he would do anything other than he had been doing for the last 25 years, namely papering the American scene with a new set of bogus checks.

Taylor was returned to Providence, Rhode Island to face prosecution with the accomplices arrested at Newport. He was sentenced in Providence and then returned to the Southern District of New York, New York City. The indictment there was one of the most massive Federal indictments ever returned against an individual. He pleaded guilty to 225 separate counts of Federal violations within the Southern District of New York alone. By this time U.S. attorneys throughout the United States were lining up to take their turns against Taylor. He was sentenced on June 22, 1955 to 15 years in prison but seven State jurisdictions had already placed detainers against Taylor pending the completion of his 15 year term. From the period April 14, 1950 when Taylor was released from Onondaga County Penitentiary to February 16, 1951 it is reported that he passed at least 734 fraudulent checks. There is little doubt that he probably passed more checks than this, but that some merchants didn't report the loss. Taylor's last sentence was executed April 22, 1964 and involved eight years for the transportation of forged securities in Interstate Commerce.

The case of Courtney Townsend Taylor is significant in many respects. Taylor was able to first obtain, through the voucher route, practically any corporate check in the United States. Secondly, he was able to successfully counterfeit and forge those very identity credentials that the business community holds so dearly. Third, he passed an inordinate number of checks when one considers the alert notices that the FBI and other agencies had provided against his method of operation. In fact, Taylor had many near misses where the hand of lady luck might have been

held away had the merchant exercised reasonable business pro-
dence. In a Des Moines, Iowa hardware store Taylor presented a
set of identification cards while cashing a check. Carelessly he had
inserted three or four identical checks within the identification
card set. As the clerk glanced through the identity cards he
spotted the duplicate checks and refused to cash Taylor's check.
However, apparently sufficient notice was not provided to local
authorities or to the FBI to produce an arrest while Taylor was in
Des Moines.

At another time, Taylor, while using the alias Rodney S.
Hickson, inadvertently signed his name Hickman. A store manager discovered the error but merely corrected Taylor rather than
reporting the incident. In 1950, Taylor visited a St. Paul shop
where he had previously passed a check in 1943. Both checks were
on the Alka-Seltzer Company. The store manager had retained
the old check and showed it to Taylor by way of curiosity. He
didn't even realize that he was getting stuck a second time. As
mentioned previously, Taylor at one point was handling checks
reportedly drawn on the Louisville and Nashville Railroad. He
passed five of these which were incorrectly dated January, 1950,
during January, 1951 before anyone called it to his attention. On
one of Taylor's passes through Chicago he selected a street and
cashed checks in every other store along Michigan Blvd. On his
next trip through Chicago he filled in the gap by hitting every
alternate store within the same section. It was a deliberate risk,
one that was unnecessary, but one which provided an insight into
the character of Courtney Townsend Taylor.

In Albany, New York, during one of his check passing forays,
Taylor became frightened by the action of the store manager and
must have left without cashing an unendorsed check. Someone in
the store took the check, endorsed it with the alias that Taylor
was using at the time and deposited it for collection. Whoever did
this had to forge Taylor's alias in order to collect on the check.
Taylor might well have commented "these days you just can't
trust anybody".

Frederick Douglas George

On one wall in the Documents Section of the FBI Laboratory
in Washington, there is an unusual map of the United States. This

map seems to be completely criss-crossed with lines and small numerals. The map is a route map for Frederick Douglas George, check forger and traveller extraordinary. For a period of 26 months, from December 6, 1951 to January 28, 1954, Frederick Douglas George visited practically every major city in the United States. Behind him he left a trail of confused and angered bank tellers.

George apparently began his criminal career in the Louisville, Kentucky area and had once used the alias of Harold S. Gibson. This particular alias was adopted by FBI agents and was to be used in referring to the case as the investigation proceeded. The "Gibson" case, began slowly on a raw December day at Albuquerque, New Mexico in 1951. A man, using the alias Robert Thomas, had stopped in two Albuquerque banks and presented a number of checks for deposit to his account. Following these deposits he had drawn a check for cash, in the amount of $50.00 each time, and had departed. This was the beginning of an operation which would grow in intensity and scope for 26 months. During his career, George would utilize more than 1800 separate aliases. He would attempt to disguise his handwriting and it was only through the most painstaking examination by FBI handwriting experts that the checks were finally traced to one source.

In the history of forgery, the case of Frederick Douglas George has some recurring similarities but also some distressing variations. With regard to similarities, it should be noted that George used the same MO in nearly all of his check cashing operations. George would appear at a downtown bank and go directly to a teller's window. He would have a deposit slip in duplicate plus from two to seven checks for deposit to his "account". The account would, of course, be fictitious. George never attempted to open up an account at any bank. However, the 1800 aliases that he utilized were so plausible sounding that a bank teller, who cannot possibly remember the names of all the depositors, would assume that George had an account and was depositing these checks to that account. George never attempted to cash the fraudulent checks but rather deposited them to an account. The checks were nearly always drawn on out-of-state banks and appeared to be payments to a professional man by various organizations and individuals from out of state. The deposit slip and its duplicate had been previously picked up and prepared. The total amount of the deposit varied from a low of $400.00 to a high of $2,000.00. George also utilized the time period to his advantage. He would appear at a lunch hour or near closing time when the volume of bank traffic is high.

After he had presented the bogus checks for deposit and had received his stamped duplicate deposit slip, George would then present a counter-check drawn on the victim bank. These checks were usually for small amounts. In many cases, they represented less than 10% of what he was "depositing". As George began his career in Albuquerque, the checks were for $50.00 but gradually, as his confidence soared, he increased the amount to $150.00.

George would select downtown banks or banks that were within a short distance of each other. By careful planning, he could hit three or four banks within a period of fifteen minutes and then be on his way out of town. Utilizing this technique, he could often net up to $500.00 per day. In some cases, the tellers became suspicious of the account name and decided to check. As they turned or left to check their files, George simply walked out of the bank.

George's operation as a forger bears significant similarities in that he conforms to the recidivist pattern and repeats his MO with little variation. However, he does make some significant departures in that he selected banks as his prime target. Most forgers are well aware that banks are the most difficult place to pass a forged check. And the statistics for check forgery bear out this fact. But George concentrated solely on banks. Another point of significance is George's use of aliases. There are very few cases in which one individual used as many aliases. This factor is significant because, as law enforcement and banking officials recognize, the use of aliases often provides an identifying link to a particular criminal.

In addition, George also deliberately attempted to disguise his handwriting. Handwriting experts are aware that handwriting can be disguised to such an extent that even an expert will be unable to positively testify that such a person wrote a specific check. George may have been aware of this and attempted to take advantage of it. But, while this factor may be true for a selected signature, it begins to weaken as the forger produces more and more samples of his "disguised" hand. Now we must consider elements such as his printing on the deposit slips, and the spacing and form that he used in filling out the checks. A repeat pattern soon appeared and a basis for identification became evident.

During the first month George was active, he moved from Albuquerque to Chicago, to Glendale, Arizona, Palo Alto, California and then to San Francisco. Most of his travel was by air and here again we find one of the difficulties encountered by modern day forgery detection and prosecution. The wide availability of airline flights made it possible for George to be in several parts of the country within a single day. His MO allowed him to hit two or three banks within a quarter of an hour and be on his way back to an airport for a trip to another city. His pattern of airline flights, as shown by the FBI map, does not seem to follow any logical or repeat sequence. He would frequently backtrack on himself before jumping to a completely separate area of the country.

As George moved about the country more and more data began to accumulate in his file. There was little in his prior arrest records to tie him to this operation. In addition, at this point in his career law enforcement agents had not been able to produce a photograph of George. He remained something of a mystery, but his fame was spreading.

On January 28, 1954 George arrived in Galveston, Texas. He hit several of the Galveston banks within a one hour period and left town. It so happened that the FBI Resident Agent in Galveston was at the Galveston Police Department when the information on the victimized banks reached the department. The Resident Agent recognized the MO of Frederick Douglas George and an intensive local search was begun. The Galveston Police Department determined that the suspect had taken a taxi from Galveston to Houston on the afternoon of January 28th. He had departed the taxi near a hotel in downtown Houston. Houston FBI agents checked and determined that a person using the name D.T. Martin had been at the hotel and had then made a reservation on a Braniff flight from Houston to San Antonio, Texas. The flight had already departed and was scheduled to touch down at San Antonio at 4:29 P.M. The San Antonio FBI was alerted by phone and through cooperation with the local police, Frederick Douglas George was arrested as he stepped from the plane at the San Antonio airport. Under intensive interrogation, George finally admitted to a long list of federal counts and was returned to Louisville, Kentucky to face trial on an indictment handed down by a Federal Grand Jury. On April 9, 1954, in Federal Court, Louisville, Kentucky, Frederick Douglas George pleaded guilty to six counts of check forgery and received sentences totaling 12 years.

George Lester Belew

The FBI Document Examiner sat looking at the check on the desk in front of him. The check was forged but it contained a thumb-print. The thumb-print itself was unusual enough, but in addition there was something wrong with the print. The document examiner had previously worked in the FBI Identification Division and he knew that this thumb-print was somehow incorrect. The man who had produced that print was George Lester Belew, one of the more violent check forgers of the past two decades.

Many times check forgers are referred to as "non-violent" criminals. Courtney Townsend Taylor was known to have bragged that "the pen was the only weapon he needed". However, the case of George Lester Belew reveals that not all check forgers are non-violent criminals.

George Lester Belew was born on a small family farm on October 31, 1913 at Mt. View, Missouri. His education was limited to a grammar school program but he subsequently successfully worked as a male nurse, clerk, artist, mechanic, etc. In addition, he was able to successfully impersonate a war correspondent, a writer, and a medical doctor.

Belew's first brush with the law took place at the age of 17 when he earned 10 years for forgery and was sentenced to the Iowa State Reformatory. From the very beginning Belew revealed a confidence talent which would mark the rest of his criminal career. Belew went before the Iowa Parole Board and was out of Amamosa within four years after his sentencing. Within two months of his release on parole he had taken off to Miami, forged a series of checks, and had been arrested. He was returned to Iowa to be sentenced to 15 years for check forgery. Again, with typical false repentance, Belew managed to be released in five years.

Seven months later he popped up in Manitoba, was apprehended on a fraudulent check charge by the Royal Canadian Mounted Police, and sentenced to a term at Stoney Mountain Penitentiary in Manitoba.

For the next several years, Belew was in and out of various jails, including the U.S. Penitentiary at Atlanta and at McNeil Island, Washington. During this period, Belew became an accomplished breakout artist. Sentenced to jail in Phoenix in March, 1944, he pretended illness and was transferred to the hospital. He quickly sawed off the leg irons and escaped. Quickly recaptured in Cleveland, Ohio, four months later, he attempted a repeat performance by eating soap and biting his tongue to expectorate blood. This time it did not work. He was returned from Cleveland Cheyenne jail did not hold him for long when, with the aid of an accomplice, he escaped at gun point. By the end of 1952 Belew was accomplice he escaped at gun point. By the end of 1952 Belew was back at the U.S. Penitentiary in McNeil Island, Washington. He was scheduled to serve the remainder of an eight year term but was released on January 31, 1953. Following his release, he began one of the longest and most successful portions of his check passing career.

Belew, like Frederick Douglas George, now began an erratic route pattern which would take him through 45 states and result in the passing of hundreds of fraudulent checks. Beginning in February, 1953 Belew posed as a truck driver, writer, war correspondent, doctor, military officer, etc. and worked his way through the United States passing fraudulent checks in bars, restaurants, etc. By September, 1953, a federal grand jury at Fargo, North Dakota, had returned an indictment against him and the FBI had issued an Identification Order.

During this period, a strange quirk of forgery detection took place. A fraudulent check was received at the FBI Laboratory in Washington and was positively identified as having been written and endorsed by Belew. In looking into the history of the check, authorities were dismayed to find that an entirely different person had been arrested and sentenced to a ten year penitentiary term for having passed the Belew check. During the latter person's trial he had been positively identified as the individual who had endorsed the check in the presence of a witness. As a result of the FBI Laboratory examination, the wrongly convicted individual was set free. This is one of the few instances in which George Lester Belew did anyone a favor. Had he not become so notorious, and his handwriting identifiable by the FBI Laboratory, the other individual might have had to sit out a ten year sentence for a check he had never passed.

Eighteen months after Belew's release from McNeil Island, he was in Hays, Kansas, attempting to pass a fraudulent check at a drugstore. The druggist accepted the check but then notified the Ellis County Sheriff's Office. Before Belew could leave town he was arrested and brought to the Ellis County jail. Within five days, Belew had managed to escape by throwing a pail of hot soapy water into the face of a sheriff who entered his cell. With an accomplice, Belew beat the sheriff about the head and then escaped in the sheriff's car. An area-wide manhunt ensued involving road-blocks, air-ground searches, etc. But Belew managed to escape. His accomplice was not quite so fortunate and was apprehended at Jefferson City, Missouri, within five days. This particular escapade by Belew had gained him a spot on the FBI's ten most wanted fugitives. Six months went by and Belew continued to forge and pass his checks. Now nearly all of the checks contained inked prints which appeared to be thumb-prints. The catch was that these thumb-prints did not match the FBI Identification Files for Belew's prints.

By January of 1955 Belew had worked his way to Savoy, Illinois and had registered at a local motel. The motel owner had been circularized by the FBI and recognized Belew's photo. He notified local police and the FBI and Belew was again taken into custody. In Belew's room, police officers found another box complete with check forging materials and which included fraudulent identification cards bearing Belew's photograph and the mysterious thumb-print. By this time, FBI Document experts had a good hunch as to Belew's thumb-print. They requested that the arresting officers take toe print impressions from Belew's feet. An examination of these impressions revealed that the "thumb-print" had actually been made by the right big toe of George Lester Belew. Belew was subsequently sentenced to the U.S. Penitentiary at Leavenworth, Kansas, but contracted infectious tuberculosis and was transferred to the U.S. Federal Hospital at Springfield, Missouri. Upon recovering Belew was sentenced to a nine year term at Duluth, Minnesota beginning on March 16, 1955. During his incarceration at Duluth, he composed a poem "Repenting For His Life of Lawlessness" and dedicated to "All The Youth of America Whoever Think Crime Will Pay". The poem received national publicity, but at the point of this writing we are not certain whether the poem was in earnest or another in the long line of Belew's con efforts designed to free him for further forgery forays.

Thomas E. Brown

The name Thomas E. Brown is fictitious. The true identity of this forger has been withheld because he has been kind enough to provide us with the exact details of a check forging operation which he operated. Thomas E. Brown is a former convicted forger who has cooperated with the American Banking Association in providing information on forgery activities. Mr. Brown's case is important because it provides the exact modus operandi of the forger as described in his own words.

Thomas E. Brown, like Frederick Douglas George, worked the downtown banks and his modus operandi had some similarities with George's. However, Brown cashed actual "personal" checks rather than the deposit-counter check routine used by George. In the case of Brown the forger would check in at a large, well known downtown city hotel, and then proceed directly to the financial district of that city. He would carefully scout the financial district, noting the geographic location of the largest banks in the district. Following this, he would stop in at the special service counter of each of these banks. Pretending to be a newly opened account, he would ask for some checks until "the ones I ordered arrived". The service clerk would give him a half a dozen or so with no account number encoded. I might note at this point that this procedure has since been altered in·many banks. Brown would then stop in at the office of the bank itself and obtain a list of the directors of the bank, perhaps through an annual report. The list of directors was particularly important because these were the gentlemen who were reportedly going to be "writing" the checks that would be fraudulently cashed. Once the forger had obtained the list of the various bank directors, he would note their companies affiliations and if the companies were local, as was often the case, he would stop by at the various companies to pick up an annual report. In some cities the annual reports were available in stock brokerage firms and in libraries.

The next day would find Brown at a local public library with a copy of the city directory. By this time he had selected the names of the payers of the various checks. It was now important to make a list of payees. From the city directory, he would obtain legitimate names, addresses, number of children, etc. for the persons on the payee list. Following this, he would telephone the bookkeeping department at each of the target banks and verify the account of the person to whom he would be drawing the check. Thus, he would establish that certain parties did, in fact, have legitimate accounts at these banks. I might point out that this procedure while applicable in medium size cities became much more difficult in large cities such as New York, Chicago, etc. It is assumed that in these cases a verification check was not possible. The customary approach that Brown would use in this telephone contact was to ask whether a check for $600.00 was good for the account of Mr. John Doe, a name of one of the directors. Occasionally, the banks would refuse to answer such a question unless he could provide some more particular information on the bank branch, etc. Generally, however, Brown was able to obtain the information through the Accounting Department.

By this time, the forger was armed with the three vital factors for a successful operation. He had the right name of the payer, verification of the bank balance, the right documents, and signatures, which although they may not be perfect, were good enough. The signatures had been copied from the annual reports in which the prominent director, signed his name in the course of the company's report presentation. In copying the directors' signatures, Brown would use the signature simulation technique. From a collection of pen points he would select one that corresponded with the model signature on the director's annual report. After 15 or 20 trials, he was ready to fill out a check. The basic principle in copying that Brown employed was not so much the configuration of the individual letters as the character of the letter. Brown defines character as the appearance of the letter indicating whether the man writes rapidly, slowly, painstakingly, shakily, etc. It was also important to obtain the correct slant and general proportion of letters throughout the signature. Following this signature simulation, the forger would place each of these checks in a distinctly marked envelope and prepare himself for the final stage in his operation.

Selecting a taxi, he would provide the taxi driver with a list of addresses and identify himself as a bank messenger. The taxi

would take him on a route through the financial district, stopping
and waiting as Brown darted in and out of the individual banks.
He usually took no more than five minutes inside of each bank. On
one typical day, Brown managed to hit as many as thirty different
locations in a central city area. Brown would concentrate on
branch banks. Each check was supposedly from the bank's headquarters office, but by presenting it at a branch office it remained
within the branch bank system. This avoided the three day
clearing house delay that the forger might have experienced in
passing his checks. Brown utilized the George system in that he
would fill out deposit slips in duplicate and deposit the smaller
part of the amount and obtain the larger amount cash. He would
also utilize the human factor and attempt to pick a young man or
woman teller who was plainly new to the operation. With typical
confidence man poise, the forger would present the check and
deposit slip and ask for a major portion of the check in large bills.

FORGERY AND ORGANIZED CRIME

"La Cosa Nostra is the largest organization of the criminal underworld in this country, very closely organized and strictly disciplined. They have committed almost every crime under the sun..." - *J. Edgar Hoover* -

Inevitably, when one discusses organized crime and its possible relationship to forgery operations, one quickly uncovers a familiar group of doves and hawks. The doves belittle any attempt to link organized crime, and in particular the La Cosa Nostra, to large scale organized forgery operations. The hawks, on the other side of the debate, wish to attribute a very large portion of all forgery operations to organized crime-connected influences. In reality, the truth lies somewhere between these two positions. In the course of preparing this study, I have had some well intentioned and serious law enforcement people, who certainly should know better, comment that they did not observe organized crime operating in the field of forgery. One wonders about their powers of observation.

To build the case for direct links between organized crime and major forgery operations we must not simply consider the plain fact that acknowledged La Cosa Nostra members have been apprehended and convicted for forgery operations. Rather, we might better look beyond this truism to compare the characteristics of the organized crime operation and its striking resemblance to the needs of the professional forger.

To begin with, organized crime is located in all of the major urban areas. The crime of forgery is primarily committed in large urban centers. Here the anonymity and centralized financial resources of the city make a most tempting target for the professional forger. And the cities are where the La Cosa Nostra is. The President's Commission on Law Enforcement and the Administration of Justice conducted a survey of 71 U. S. cities. The police departments in these cities were questioned regarding the existence of organized crime within their cities. In 80% of the cities over one million residents, organized crime was active, in 20% of the cities with populations between 500,000 and one million, and in 20% of the cities with populations between 250,000 and 500,000 organized crime was also present. In over 50% of the cities between 100,000 and 250,000 police indicated that organized crime existed in their cities. Therefore, organized. crime is obviously well entrenched in the same hunting grounds that the professional forger utilizes. (Task Force Report; Organized Crime-1967).

Next, we know that the professional forger must have detailed technical knowledge of how legitimate business operates. He is familiar with banking operations, channels of commerce, etc. The ordinary burglar or holdup artist does not have this kind of knowledge. Organized crime also has a good working knowledge of both banking and legitimate business operations. The reader will remember when, in 1957, 75 of the nation's leading organized crime figures were apprehended at a meeting in Apalachin, N.Y. Quite naturally, all of these gentlemen were in illicit businesses. But in addition, at least nine of them were in the coin machine vending business, sixteen were in garmet manufacturing business-es, ten owned retail grocery stores, seventeen owned bars or restaurants, eleven were in the olive oil and cheese importing business and nine were in the construction business. The remainder were involved in such diverse industries as automobile agencies, coal companies, entertainments, funeral homes, race tracks, laundry services, trucking, waterfront activities and bakeries. (Select Committee On Improper Activities in the Labor or Management Field, *Final Report* - U. S. Senate Report no 1139, 86th Congress, 1960, Page 487-488). Therefore it is obvious that organized crime is well entrenched in legitimate businesses and has a good working knowledge of the technical aspects required for forgery schemes.

But of even greater significance is the fact that organized crime has the two "C"'s. These are *contacts* and *cash*. Both are essential to large scale forgery operations. Such operations frequently require the setting up of fronts, the purchase of printing equipment, the corruption of banking and financial firm employees, etc. And as far as cash is concerned organized crime certainly has its share.

It is estimated that illegal gambling, the mainstay revenue source of organized crime, provides an annual intake of at least

$20 billion each year. The profit to organized crime on this gross intake is somewhere between $6 and $7 billion each year. In the words of the Kefauver Commission Report "These profits provide the financial resources whereby ordinary criminals are converted into big-time racketeers, political bosses, pseudo-businessmen and alleged philanthropists." The author might append that it also provides the revenue to finance the most intricate of forgery schemes. Narcotics is the other principal source of organized crime revenue and it produces, on the heroin trade operation, approximately $350 million annually of which $21 million are probable profits to the LCN Group. (McClellan Committee Narcotics Report S. Report #72, 89th Congress, First Session 120 (1965)).

The other half of this equation is the "contacts" side. Here organized crime, by its very nature, has what large scale forgers desperately need. Once credit cards, traveler's checks, corporation checks, etc. are forged, time becomes of critical importance. The credit card company, bank, enforcement agency, etc. will race against time to alert all possible acceptors of the forged instrument to the possibility of its misuse. In this case it becomes a race between the two groups. Unfortunately, organized crime often wins this race. They are not hindered by bureaucratic red tape and in some cases may have more pressing motivations to quickly move the illicit merchandise. To understand how the contact side of this equation works, we might digress into some basics about the organized crime organization.

At the present time there are between 2 and 4,000 hard core "family" members of La Cosa Nostra operating in 24 separate "families". These families are located in the major cities of the United States. Most cities have at least one organized crime family, although New York is known to have at least five. Each of these families has authority to engage in a full range of organized crime activity. Like its legitimate counterpart, organized crime has well defined staff and functional positions. At the top of each family is a "Boss" or "Don". Immediately beneath him is an "Underboss" or "Sottocapo". Next in line, and of special interest to the student of forgery is a staff vice president or counselor, designated the "Consiglieri". Further down the line we have lieutenants or "Caporegima" and then the "Soldati" or "Button" men.

In some of the cases cited later in this volume, it will be shown that organized crime families in one city, for example New York, have been able to move a large quantity of forged instruments within literally hours to other parts of the country and to obtain distribution before banks, hotels, or enforcement officials could be notified of the original theft.

One of the most valuable functions that credit card forgery provides to organized crime is the so-called "funding operation". By this, we mean that various operatives of organized crime families can utilize stolen, forged or fraudulent credit cards to pay for their everyday travel and living expenses as they travel throughout the world on "business" trips. For example, a courier smuggling in heroin from Turkey might utilize the credit card to pay for his air line ticket, hotel expenses, meals, car rental, etc. Since the card is stolen, or fraudulent, it will be difficult to trace the movement of the individual during the trip. The card in effect provides not only the means of financing the trip, but also a false identity which masks the operative's movements.

It is well known in Federal law enforcement circles that most of the persons in the upper echelons of organized crime, and this includes the first three or four levels of the organization chart, are under close surveillance by U.S. agents The latter group is most interested in determining the expenditures of these various mobsters in order that they may confront them with a discrepancy between their reported income and actual living expenses.

A few years ago, in an attempt to complicate the life of the IRS surveillance teams, the mob switched over to an extensive use of cash. However, IRS agents were still able to trace many of the travel and entertainment expenses regardless of the fact that they were paid for in cash. Now, the mob has switched to the use of credit cards (stolen). The fraudulent credit cards allow them to live high without any direct record of their expense. The expense appears in the name of a third party who later renounces the charges when he discovers that his card has been fraudulently used. This scheme has been used extensively during 1965, 1966 and 1967. However, recently, the New York organized card group ran into one small problem.

Federal agents discovered that a Long Island and Brooklyn, New York, group was stealing late model Cadillacs and ferrying them to Atlanta, Georgia. In Atlanta, they were transferred to a local madam for resale and distribution in the South. The couriers who drove the cars from New York to Atlanta utilized stolen or fraudulent credit cards. One of these couriers was recently arrested in Atlanta on a charge involving $200-$300 worth of fraudulent credit card charges. He pleaded guilty and to his surprise was given a 5 year sentence. Within a few days, a private jet arrived in Atlanta and produced $25,000 bail for this individual while his case is before the Appeals Court. This is just typical of the operations of organized crime utilizing these cards.

IRS agents have been so successful in their approach to organized crime that over 60% of all criminal convictions of organized crime figures, between the years 1961 and 1965, resulted directly from tax investigations conducted by the Internal Revenue Service. Contrast this record with a typical enforcement record gained on gambling arrests and convictions. Cook County, Illinois provides a graphic example of the latter problem. Between 1963 and 1966, gambling arrests in Cook County outside of the Chicago area, produced 11,158 arrests. Of these arrests 76.2% were dismissed and only 16.3% resulted in any conviction at all. Only 17 jail terms were imposed and only 4 of those were in excess of 30 days. (Blakey-Unpublished Report on Local Law Enforcement Response to Organized Crime-January, 1967 - Task Force Report; Organized Crime 1967).

Although the author does not have statistical validation of this point, my impression after interviewing many police officers, federal agents, prosecutors, etc. is that the record for forgery conviction of organized crime figures, is not much better than the gambling arrests and prosecution record. The number of convictions may be higher but the length of the jail sentences is in no way commensurate with the value of money obtained or with the fact that it is part of the pattern of organized crime.

In the past organized crime has been concerned with "traditional" crime sources of revenue and these sources have proved lucrative as previously noted. However, one must not delude oneself into believing that because lucrative areas already exist, such as gambling and narcotics, that organized crime will not be interested in similarly lucrative areas such as forgery and counterfeiting. This is certainly not the case and recent arrests and convictions confirm this point.

One argument made by the "doves" on this subject is that the lower scale "Soldati" or "Button" men have made their own personal decision to get into large scale forgery operations and that the people at the top of the family have been unaware or disinterested in this type of crime. Nothing could be further from the truth. To begin with the organization of the La Cosa Nostra does not allow for this type of free enterprise. Cressey, in one of the best studies in this area, points out that "because of the illegal character of organized crime, a leader's fame and fortune can be seriously damaged if improper decisions are made at a lower level. Decision-making is therefore concentrated at the top of the hierarchy" (the Functions and Structures of Criminal Syndicates - Donald R. Cressey - Task Force Report; Organized Crime - 1967). These "Button" men had to have the approval of their superiors in order to engage in and execute some of the forgery operations for which they have been apprehended and convicted. Indeed, lately the Federal Bureau of Investigation has even been successful in apprehending some of the higher echelon in connection with forgery cases and has brought conspiracy statutes to bear in these cases.

Organized crime, like most present day social organizations, is undergoing steady change. As with business organizations, technical competence will become the yardstick of rank in the near future. Organizational positions will not automatically go to those who have spent an apprenticeship in slum condition petty thefts. Highly technical skills and familiarity with complex business operations will be an absolute necessity. In fact, this phase of the change has already occurred. The family members of organized crime are most cognizant of this need and they are busily training their blood relatives to prosper in the new technical economy. The sons and daughters of crime family members are increasingly college educated. Even here, the clanishness of the Cosa Nostra shows a particular organization quirk. It is known, for example, that one particular U. S. college has in its enrollment a very large representation of the sons or close relatives of La Cosa Nostra family members (Task Force Report; Organized Crime - Page 56 - 1967). These young men are being trained in the latest business administration, accounting and legal techniques. When these "students" are returned to the La Cosa Nostra we can expect an even greater emphasis on crimes of fraud, such as forgery and counterfeiting. Forgery is a "cleaner" crime than many others.

And these second generation family members have been educated to a "cleaner" environment, be it on a social basis or on a crime preference basis.

In the following chapters, you will have an opportunity to observe some incidents involving organized crime and forgery. Through many of these cases run a common thread of modus operandi. The thread begins with a "money mover" who recognizes the potential for illicit gain through large scale fraud involving forgery. The money mover apparently calls such an opportunity to the attention of the family "counselor". Operational groups then prepare for the actual execution of the plan. In many cases, it follows a recognizable pattern. The seed of the pattern is the corruption of one or two key individuals. These individuals may range from lowly route postman to a financial vice president or a water commissioner. Regardless of their position, they have key access to financial documents which can be forged, misrepresented and then redeemed for cash.

The organized crime group is not niggardly in spending. They will setup extensive fronts to complete a forgery operation. Nor are they adverse to becoming partners with skilled professional forgers. While La Cosa Nostra is strictly an Italian or Sicilian organization, they do not discriminate against business connections with entrepreneur forgers of other nationalities. In many cases they provide the distribution mechanism for the illicit fruits of a particular forger or counterfeiter's labor.

Consider some of the interesting "coincidences" that link organized crime to some of the major forgery operations that have occurred during the past few years. The $407,000 theft of American Express Traveler's Checks, separately reported in this volume, was accomplished by the nephew of New York Mafia Boss, Joseph Colombo. This nephew, Maurice Savino, was joined by one Vincent Potenza, listed by the Federal Bureau of Investigation as a member of the Carmine Tramunti "family", successor to the late Thomas Luchese. In the course of the investigation of this case, one prospective government witness, John Anthony Panarello, was wiped out by the mob before he could testify in the conspiracy. His car was burned and Panarello was found shot twice in the head in a Catskill Mountain roadside ditch.

In another case, still under investigation at the time of this writing, three suspects, all with organized crime links, have been indicted in an American Express Card counterfeiting operation. One of these defendants is the relative of a Revere, Massachusetts, member of the organized crime syndicate.

The Brooklyn, New York District Attorneys Office strongly suspects that in the J. W. Mays case financing for the operation came from Buffalo, New York. In fact, one of the convicted members of the conspiracy was an alleged courier for the Buffalo, New York "family".

In Chicago, the local organized crime branch had a specific "financial department". This department dealt in crimes such as forgery, fraud, and embezzlement. The head of this department was arrested on federal charges and is now serving a federal sentence. In the Chicago credit card fiasco, reported separately in this volume, Postal Inspectors had ample evidence that lower echelon organized crime members were involved in "scam" or "bust-out" operations in collusion with local merchants.

Another example of the direct link between organized crime and major check forgery operations occurred late in August of 1968. The U.S. Secret Service and the Federal Bureau of Investigation working together, uncovered a scheme which allegedly could have produced a million dollar pay-off. In this particular scheme, it is alleged that organized crime figures, specifically the "banker" of the Brooklyn Mafia, arranged to set up a checking account using the name of a Wall Street brokerage house. The scheme involved the theft of incoming checks from the brokerage house and their subsequent deposit in the fraudulent account opened in the name of the broker. The checks deposited to this fraudulent account were then subsequently drawn out of the account. It relied on the cooperation of an employee at the legitimate stock broker's office who apparently would steal random checks as they arrived at the brokerage.

In this particular case, the conspirators are charged with a conspiracy to transport and actually transporting a stolen $17,000 check from New Jersey to New York. The defendants were arrested in the case and they are known to have direct link with organized crime in the Brooklyn area. This particular case is interesting because it highlights the fact that organized crime does have "banking or financial specialists". These are individuals who operate specifically in areas such as embezzlement, fraud, forgery, and counterfeiting.

Elsewhere in this report, as the reader observes how airline tickets stolen on one coast soon appear on the opposite coast, how stolen trading stamps all seem to come to rest in one city, how airline tickets stolen in three separate sections of the country come to be on the person of a single individual and this individual in turn connected with organized crime, one can hardly escape the conclusions previously noted. It might then seem a simplification to say that organized crime is responsible for professional forgery and that the destruction of organized crime would remove most professional forgers from the scene. However, this would be a delusion because, considered against the mass of forgery, organized crime can contribute only a small portion. While this portion is an important portion, it is far from a majority. It has been estimated that 55 to 60% of all forgeries are committed by "amateurs", the remaining 40% involve some small gangs, entrepreneurs, lone wolf operators and finally organized crime. It is difficult to put a figure on what portion organized crime contributes to the total dollar volume of forgery losses. However, an educated guess would probably put this figure around 10% of the total forgery loss in the United States.

However, even in the world of crime things are seldom static. With the advent of a checkless society and the proliferation of credit cards, we can expect to see organized crime play a much larger roll in forgery type fraud. There are several reasons for this anticipated increase in activity. First, forgery is a non-violent crime which is likely to produce relatively small sentences and not arouse too much public outcry. It is also the conspiracy type of crime which is ideally suited to organized crime operations. In addition, it is the type of crime where much of the arrest risk can be delegated to pushers and lower echelon members of the syndicate.

One of the most important tools for the prevention of this type of criminal expansion lies within the provisions of the new "Omnibus Crime Bill". This bill, with its major emphases on the prosecution of organized crime on a local or statewide level, will provide a major impetus toward the detection and prosecution of the "financial" end of the organized crime syndicate.

Another promising sign in recent days has been the appearance of select federal "Task Forces" specifically designed to combat organized crime. One of the first locations established for these forces was Brooklyn, N.Y. in the heart of Mafialand. This task force has been particularly effective and was in fact cited for its excellent work by the Republican Party task force on crime, in the preparation of its report for President Nixon. At the time of this writing there are five task forces in full operation with new groups coming on stream each month.

Basically, the task force consists of a special group of Justice Department lawyers aided by supervising agents from many federal agencies whose jurisdiction involves Mafia-type crimes. There are agents from Internal Revenue, Narcotics, Immigration, etc.

The Task Force moves into a specific geographic area. The area usually coincides with the boundaries of a Federal Judicial District. An intelligence estimate is prepared on all organized crime activities within that area. From this report certain key activities, or more properly individuals, are selected. By coordinating the interests and jurisdictional capacities of the many federal agencies it is often possible to find a specific area where a local crime figure has inadvertently stepped across the line into public illegality. When this step is discovered the Task Force pounces and another member of the "family" disappears from circulation.

At the present time the Task Forces, because of limited manpower, are concentrating their up-tight surveillance on the first two or three levels of the organizational structure. As Congress appropriates more funds (the department has asked for 100 additional Assistant U. S. Attornies) the Task Force will turn their attention to ever lower levels of the structure. When this happens, then maybe, the promise of the doves that organized crime has little connection to forgery will be realized.

Bibliography

Barzini, Luigi, **THE ITALIAN** (New York; Atheneum, 1964)

Blau, Peter M., **THE DYNAMICS OF BUREAUCRACY** (Chicago; University of Chicago Press 1955)

Crawford, Frances Marion, **SOUTHERN ITALY AND SICILY AND THE RULERS OF THE SOUTH** (London; Macmillan, 1900)

Cressey, Donald R., **THE PRISON; STUDIES IN INSTITUTIONAL ORGANIZATION AND CHANGE** (New York, Holt, Rinehart & Winston, 1961)

Feder, Sidney and Turkus, Burton B., **MURDER, INC.**, (New York; Perma Books, 1952)

Johnson, "Organized Crime; Challenge To The American Legal System, 53 Journal of Criminal Law, Criminology and Police Science 399, 402-404 (1962)

Klein, Malcolm, Editor **JUVENILE GANGS IN CONTACTS** (Englewood Cliffs; Prentice Hall 1967)

Lewis, Norman, **THE HONEST SOCIETY** (New York; G. T. Putman Son, 1964)

Martin, Raymond V., **REVOLT IN THE MAFIA** (New York; Duell, Sloan & Pearce, 1963)

Mori, Cesare, **THE LAST STRUGGLE WITH THE MAFIA** (London; Putman, 1933)

Moynihan, Daniel T., "The Private Government of Crime" **REPORTER** July 6, 1961 Pages 14-20

Reid, Edward, **MAFIA** (New York; New American Library 1964)

Reiss, Albert J., Black, Donald, **STUDIES OF CRIME AND LAW ENFORCEMENT IN MAJOR METROPOLITAN AREAS, VOLUME I and II** (Washington; Government Printing Office

Sondern, Frederick, Jr., **BROTHERHOOD OF EVIL; THE MAFIA** (New York; Farrar, Straus & Cudahy, 1959)

Tyler, Gus, **ORGANIZED CRIME IN AMERICA** (Ann Arbor; University of Michigan Press, 1962)

Volitho, William, "The Natural History of Graft" **THE SURVEY**, 63; 130-140, April, 1931

Wilson, James Q. Editor, **CITY POLITICS AND PUBLIC POLICY** (New York; John Wiley & Sons, Inc., 1968)

Woetzel, "An Overview of Organized Crime; Mores vs Morality", Annals, May, 1963

Task Force Report; Organized Crime - Task Force on Organized Crime, Presidential Commission on Law Enforcement and Administration of Justice; (Washington; Government Printing Office)

"Organized Crime and Illicit Traffic in Narcotics, Part I, 1953" - Permanent Sub-Committee on Investigation on the Committee on Government Operations (McClellan Committee)

Proceedings - First National Conference on Crime Control, March 28-29, 1967 (Washington; Government Printing Office)

MISCELLANEOUS FORGERIES

Miscellaneous Forgeries is probably an inadequate title for this section, but I must confess that this part of the book is a potpourri of forgeries that doesn't lend itself to simple classification. It does illustrate the range of forgery in the world about us. There is literally nothing that our fellow man won't forge or counterfeit. For example, recently the FBI reported on a midwestern college student who had developed an interesting sideline. He had obtained some 1,243 cancelled round trip railroad tickets. Now you might think that there is nothing as worthless as a railroad ticket that has been punched and thus cancelled. That is why you are not a forger. This student grasped the latent value of these tickets.

The student simply obtained a 3/16 metal punch and positioned it over the conductor's punch-out. He cut a new smooth round hole, taking the conductor's irregular punch hole cleanly out of the ticket. Next he placed some scrap ticket stock on his work bench and proceeded to cut a series of 3/16 inch disks. He then inserted these disks in the holes cut from the "cancelled" tickets and sold the tickets for new. The disks were held in place by transparent tape. Small potatoes you say? Not necessarily; this student sold more than $5,000 worth of tickets before apprehended. But the railroad ticket really is small potatoes when compared to some other miscellaneous forgeries.

Collateral Stock Frauds

Most thieves, and certainly nearly all forgers, are reticent to walk into a stock brokers office and try to palm off either a counterfeit or stolen and forged stock certificate. For one thing, they wouldn't be paid for a week or so. They would also be putting the suspect certificate before the eyes of many people with daily

experience in handling stock certificates. Although some forgers
do occasionally try this (and most often get caught), the majority
take the route of the collateral security method.

This method involves the forger first setting up a front as a
legitimate businessman and then applying for a loan. He explains
to the banker that, since his business is just getting started, he is
willing to leave some stock he has as security or collateral for the
loan he is making. If the stock is a well known issue the banker is
usually more than happy to make the loan. When the stocks are
handed in, at the time of granting the loan, the banker may only
give them a perfunctory check since he is usually primarily
interested in seeing that the correct number of shares are being
handed in.

A few years ago in Texas it was discovered that three separate
banks had loaned money on the same stock certificates. The
certificates were allegedly counterfeit. This type of counterfeiting
is fortunately rare. Among the more recent cases was the discovery
by New York banks that Shell Union Oil Co. stocks were being
counterfeited in 1960. In 1962 an 8,000 share counterfeit certificate for the Kayser-Roth Corp. appeared as collateral for a large
bank loan in Florida. The latter certificate didn't even look like
the genuine certificate. It was a complete fabrication.

Up until the early 1960's the counterfeiting and forgery of stock
certificates was a relatively rare occasion. This is no longer the
case. As the author has pointed out before, the forger thrives
amidst activity. The current bull market in stocks is made to order
for the counterfeiter and forger. Stock brokerages are quite literally swamped with paperwork. The Securities and Exchange
Commission has shut down the market on Wednesdays in an
attempt to allow the brokerages to catch up, but even this
mechanism hasn't answered the need. The brokerages are desperately short of people. In many cases they are taking anyone that
can move. Such a situation does not promote security.

Recent news stories have linked organized crime groups here
with British gangs interested in the collateral security potential of
stolen and forged American stock certificates. New Scotland Yard
recently arrested a 39-year-old New Yorker and accused him of
conspiracy in the alleged resale of stolen American stock certificates in England.

Meanwhile back on the home front our own thieves and forgers
have been equally busy. A thief lifted 28 bonds from the offices of

Fig. 4   Hand engraving of a stock certificate for intaglio steel plate printing. Four separate engravers will work on this plate *(Courtesy of American Bank Note Co.)*

Dewey, Ballentine, Bushby, Palmer & Wood and then allegedly
used 8 of these bonds in collateral security frauds at banks in
Englewood and Fort Lee, New Jersey.

Counterfeit securities are even more promising to the forger as
a collateral security dodge. The counterfeit securities are completely bogus. They are "cold". They haven't been obtained
through the commission of a robbery and hence are not "hot
listed." Morton Kirmayer, 42 years old of Woodmere, New York is
alleged to have taken advantage of this fact. Kirmayer has been
arrested and charged with passing $374,000 worth of counterfeit
Standard Oil Co. of California and International Telephone ar.d
Telegraph certificates at the Franklin National Bank of Long
Island. The stock certificates were to be collateral "security"
against a quarter of a million dollar loan.

Another financial whiz tried to pass $404,000 dollars worth of
counterfeit Indiana toll road bonds. New Jersey F.B.I. agents
picked up this man and charged him with the interstate transportation of stolen property.

I am afraid that these cases are only the top of the iceberg.
There is little doubt that both organized crime groups and
entrepreneur forgers are cashing in handsomely on the bull
market in stocks and bonds. With the rash of security trading that
has taken place in the past few years, this problem has exploded in
scope and intensity. Security and police officials are naturally
reluctant to discuss the situation at the present time. It is
noteworthy, however, that the New York Police have set up a
special squad to handle this type of investigation. The squad is
located in the First Precinct adjacent to the Wall Street district.

Trading Stamp Forgeries — *90 Million Green Stamps*

Not even the small innocuous trading stamp has escaped the
attention of the country's forgers and counterfeiters. Although the
counterfeiting of trading stamps has not been a major problem,
threatening the financial stability of any of the trading stamp
companies, it nonetheless has been irksome to three or four of the
major trading stamp suppliers.

In the marketing of the trading stamps, the trading stamp
company usually sells the trading stamps in 50,000 stamp lots.

These are worth about $150.00. They are sold to service stations, stores, etc.

The counterfeiter of trading stamps is likely to produce the stamps and to then take them around to various service stations, stores, etc. He will advise the establishment that he was formerly in business and that in going out of business he had a great deal of these stamps left over. He is willing to sell them at a "discount". Thus, the stolen or counterfeit stamps are "discounted" to the retail merchant. It is hard to believe that the merchant accepts this story on face value, since he should be aware that anyone left with a batch of trading stamps, upon the dissolution of his business, could redeem them with the stamp company for their exact cash value. More likely, the merchant purchasing these stamps sees this as a good opportunity to "save" on his stamp purchase cost.

Perhaps the theft and subsequent resale of the stamps is an even greater problem than the forging of the stamps. In 1966 Sperry & Hutchinson experienced a major burglary from one of their warehouses in the Chicago area. The burglars, who have never been apprehended, took some 90 million S & H Green Stamps. In redeemed value they were worth quarter of a million dollars. The break in this case occurred when a ghetto resident in Los Angeles appeared willing to sell millions of stamps to a co-operative merchant in the L.A. area. The merchant advised the stamp company and a trap was set for the seller of the stamps. The "buy" was set up for Pittsburgh, Pennsylvania. FBI agents and security personnel from the company picked up the stamps and their passers in Pittsburgh when they attempted to complete the rendezvous. The stamps had been stolen in Chicago, trans-shipped to Newark, N.J., and then returned to Pittsburgh for the rendezvous.

There have been recent attempts at the counterfeiting of trading stamps, notably in the Chicago and Cleveland area. During the 1958-1959 period a local counterfeiter in Chicago attempted to produce Top Value and S & H Stamps. He made a photo offset plate but apparently was unsatisfied with its "muddy" appearance and took it to a local photoengraver for touch-up work. The photoengraver notified police and the forger was apprehended.

From news clippings it would appear that Top Value has had other problems with counterfeiting. The Kostura Brothers were reportedly active in the Cleveland, Ohio area, and particularly in Parma, Ohio in the counterfeiting of Top Value Stamps.

Other companies are alleged to have had difficulty with counterfeits such as Blue Chip on the West Coast and "Merchants Green Stamps" in the New York-New Jersey area. In the latter case, a Bronx printer was manufacturing the Merchants Green Stamps along with Con Edison Corporation checks. Con Edison security personnel broke the case and discovered plates for the Merchants Green Stamps in searching the print shop in the Bronx, N. Y.

There are a variety of safety measures built into the trading stamp design. For security reasons these are not discussed in this report. It suffices to say that the stamp company personnel are capable of detecting the run of the mill counterfeit. Apparently, the more sophisticated counterfeiters, who would be capable of severely complicating the life of the stamp company, are more interested in more profitable lines such as U.S. currency.

There is one interesting sidelight to the trading stamp forgery and theft operations. This centers about the relationship of Chicago to this type of activity. For some reason, the problem seems to be accentuated in the Chicago area. Stamps stolen or counterfeited in Chicago pop up in other places in the United States. Conversely, when a Clovis, New Mexico S & H store was burglarized, the stolen stamps in turn soon appeared in the Chicago area. On the surface, there would appear to be a good working liaison for the sale of these stolen stamps, and the focal point for such liaison appears to be in the Chicago area.

In addition to the forgeries of trading stamps, the stamps themselves also provide the basis for a variety of confidence schemes. One of these is a variation of the classical scam or bust-out operation. In this scheme the con man sets up a "local" stamp company. He prints a great deal of stamps, usually utilizing the name and similar imprint of a stamp company from another part of the country, and contacts any of the local merchants who may have a legitimate stamp such as S & H. He talks them into using his stamp and "takes back" the legitimate S & H stamps. He quickly redeems the S & H stamps for cash and then, before any substantial expense can be involved in redeeming his own stamps, he departs.

Another scheme involves the confidence man who trades on his victim's ignorance of international monetary affairs. He convinces his victim that he is a traveling businessman who regularly visits England. In England S & H utilizes "Pink Stamps." These stamps, if obtained in England and returned to the United States, may be redeemed in cash here. Of course, they are worth exactly the same dollar amount in each country.

The con man tells his victim that he can purchase $100 worth of "Pink Stamps" in England and cash them in at S & H company offices in the United States for $200.00. He explains this situation as being due to the "variance in national currency." He will usually take a couple of hundred dollars of the victim's money and supposedly purchase the stamps. He will show the purchased stamps, which are real enough, to the victim and announce that he is going to trade them in for $300-$400. He will then pretend to trade them in, obtain the funds, and return the doubled money to the victim. This portion of the campaign is a teaser. The victim now believes that this is a legitimate business operation and will proceed to invest several thousand dollars in the belief that such a practice actually works. Once the con man has the larger sum of money he will depart the scene.

Coin Forgeries — *The Mis-Struck Penny*

As pointed out previously, the forgery of or counterfeiting of coins, is relatively rare in the United States. Counterfeiters these days don't spend much time on making counterfeit coins, particularly in view of inflationary pressures and the cost of materials that go into the coins. However, there is one exception to this; that is, in the area of rare coins. In this category, there is sufficient profit motive to counterfeit a coin because its value is often several thousand times more than the face value of the coin itself. There have been several interesting cases in the last several years involving either the counterfeiting of a coin or the forging of a coin by the addition of a fraudulent mark which is reported to be an imperfection that the mint failed to observe.

There are mint coins with imperfections or with accidental special markings. And there may be even an attempt to counterfeit this unique coin. In other cases a "mis-struck" coin is "created." One of the most interesting recent cases involved the U.S. Postal Inspection Service in the breaking of a penny counterfeiting operation.

Coin collecting is one of the nation's fastest growing hobbies and much of its exchange occurs in the New York metropolitan area. Early in 1964 advertisements began to appear in nuismatic journals advertising a mis-struck 1964 P penny. It was reported that this penny, produced at the Philadelphia Mint, had a multiple image of Lincoln and that the word "Liberty" appeared in double and triple images. The journal notices advertised the penny at a price of $75 a piece. Several governmental agencies showed an immediate interest in the coins and, because most of the purchasers utilized the mails, U.S. Postal Inspectors were called into the case.

Postal Inspectors report that in April 1965, Victor Piacentile, also known as Victor Pease or Peace, began the marketing of these "mis-struck" coins. Shortly following his sale efforts, he allegedly joined forces with William Sheiner, a New York coin dealer operating under the title of Bronx Coins. Sensing that there would be some skepticism about these coins, Sheiner staged a public unveiling at a New York hotel. At this publicity event, Sheiner opened a "sealed" Federal Reserve Pouch which contained rolls of pennies. As might be expected, the bag contained an assortment of "mis-struck" pennies. It was stated that these pennies, received in a pouch with the Federal Reserve Seal on it, conclusively proved that the coins had been obtained through legal channels and had not been altered prior to their distribution by monetary authorities.

Meanwhile, Postal Inspectors were working with Mint authorities in Philadelphia to determine whether or not such an error could occur. After extensive examination, the U.S. Mint found that while the pennies were genuine, the errors could not have been introduced at the Mint and must have been produced after distribution. The forgers were indicted for mail fraud, fraud by wire and conspiracy.

In the trial that followed, U.S. Postal Inspectors demonstrated how the Mint had found it impossible to duplicate the errors. They produced extensive motion picture studies of Mint procedures and measurements which proved that it would have been impossible to strike the coins at the Philadelphia Mint. They also supplied evidence that the constant mixing of coins at the Mint during their processing made it nearly a statistical impossibility for the number of "mis-struck" coins produced by the defendants to be present in any single Federal Reserve pouch. In fact, the Philadelphia Mint tried to reproduce the marks on the 1964 P penny and were unable to. The defendants had alleged that the pennies had been produced in the Philadelphia Mint due to a "rotating die". However, engineering and physical testimony revealed that such a die manipulation would not have produced the impressions.

The final conclusive proof came when the Postal Inspectors demonstrated the fraud involved in connection with the Federal Reserve pouch itself. One of the Inspectors inserted a note in the pouch and sealed it; and later, in full view of the court, succeeded in extracting that note. The extraction was performed by manipulating one fold of the cloth of the pouch through the seal. This fold could gradually be pulled through the seal until a large enough opening existed so that the note, or pennies, as the case may be, could be inserted or extracted from the pouch.

Piacentile and Sheiner were convicted and the judge noted "it is clear that the Government had sustained its burden of proof on the issues of knowledge and intent on each count of the indictment. The coins in question were altered after leaving the mint".

During the course of the investigation, more than 4500 altered pennies were found in possession of the defendants. If they had been marketed at their advertised price of $75.00 a piece, their total value would have been approximately $335,000.00. As it was, it is estimated that the defendants did manage to sell approximately $30,000.00 worth of the fraudulently marked pennies.

Art Forgery — *The Dutch Masters*

The field of art forgery is a subject unto itself and a number of fine books have been written in this field. Other excellent volumes, such as Alexander Klein's *Grand Deception*, also cover this subject. The author has chosen one particular case in this field. This case best illustrates the skill of the art forger as well as revealing some interesting facets of the forger personality.

In the present era of inflation, many peoples, particularly the Europeans, have become interested in art purchases as a hedge against inflation. Thus, the market for art products has broadened considerably. With this exposure there is perhaps more demand for the "masters" than there is supply. Under such a situation, a tempting opportunity for profits arises from the forgery of master artwork. The evaluation of whether or not a piece of art has been done by a particular artist is, in the final analysis, a very subjective evaluation. It is true that aided by infra-red photography, x-ray analysis, spectrographic analysis, etc. the art expert can provide more reliable indices as to the authenticity of the work of art. The following case illustrates how even these methods can be foiled by the master art forger.

Hans van Meegeren was an obscure industrial artist who in 1945 rocked the art world with his announcement that he had successfully forged Vermeer's and other Dutch Masters. The case begins in pre-war Amsterdam. In 1937 an Amsterdam lawyer, during a routine purchase, uncovered an unusual painting. The painting depicted a Biblical scene. The lawyer sought to have it further evaluated by art experts. The experts closely examined the painting and excitingly proclaimed it "a new Vermeer". One of the experts, in his evaluation excitingly described it as "every inch a Vermeer". Collectors and curators from around the world bid for the new discovery and a museum in Rotterdam was successful in purchasing it. The new painting, designated "Emmausgangers" was purchased for the sum of $270,000.00. It was put on show at a large exhibition in 1938, accompanied by Rembrandts', etc. and was proclaimed the hit of the show.

Months passed and then another painting, "The Last Supper", was also discovered as a Vermeer work and was sold for $800,000 to a private collector. Still another painting, "Christ and the Adultress," also sold for over $800,000. The latter two paintings did not produce the publicity that the first painting did, but nevertheless they were also certified as "absolutely genuine."

Late in 1945 the Dutch Government, in the course of an investigation concerning the sale of historical works of art to one of the top Nazis, ran across the name Hans van Meegeren. From the initial results of the investigation, it appears that van Meegeren did have some connection with the sale of the paintings. The artist was imprisoned on these charges and during his brief confinement he became ill and despondent. Near collapse, he broke down and revealed the forgeries he produced prior to World War II.

Art critics, familiar with his regular works, immediately scoffed at the possibility that such an artist could produce anything similar to Vermeer's artistry. However, to prove his case, van Meegeren was released from jail and under supervised conditions produced a new "Vermeer" to prove his point. The interesting point here is that van Meegeren did not copy Vermeer's actual subjects. Rather he copied the master's style.

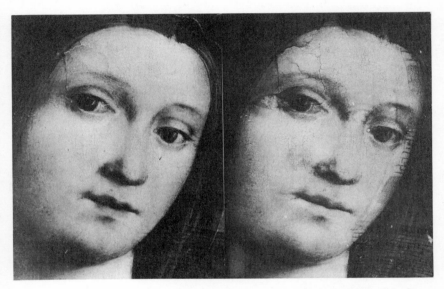

Fig. 5 The use of infra-red photography to detect alterations in art work. The photo on the left is the painting as it appeared to the naked eye. The photo on the left has been taken with Kodak Infra-Red film and a Wratten No. 87 filter. *(Courtesy of Eastman Kodak Company, Rochester, N.Y.)*

As we look into van Meegeren's psychological profile, we find an artist frustrated and rejected by the critics of his own day. In order to support himself, he prostituted his art in producing paintings of nobility, families and commercial subjects that would sell to the public. He did produce his own original abstracted form of art which was ignored by the critics. His forgery became not only a method for illicit monetary gains, but perhaps even more significantly, a form of revenge against the critics who had ignored him. Hans van Meegeren was imprisoned in 1947 and shortly after his imprisonment for a one year term, he died.

An investigation into his methods revealed that van Meegeren made a patient study of the materials and methods of the 17th century artist he had chosen to impersonate. He scoured the countryside for materials which would match the actual materials used by Vermeer. He obtained antiques that would provide suitable background materials for his subjects. In one case, he is even alleged to have paid $2,000 for a single tube of paint — Lavis Lazuli, necessary in the faithful reproduction of Vermeer's work. Van Meegeren also developed baking techniques which would artificially age and oxidize the paint surface in order to complete the simulation. Ironically, in death his own works, because of his success as a master forger, became much more valuable than they had ever been during his life.

Stamp Forgeries

Postage stamps, the rare and valuable variety, are a natural for forgery. In researching this aspect of forgery, the author was particularly impressed by the skill of two stamp forgers who stand head and shoulders above all the rest of their colleagues.

Jean de Sperati — Aix-Les-Bains, France

One of the true old masters of stamp forgery resided in the small French town of Aix-les-Bains. Much about his methods of operation is still unknown. de Sperati was so adept that in 1954 the British Philatic Association decided that they no longer could fight de Sperati and had best join him. Thus, they bought him out—paper, inks, dyes, etc. It was only after their purchase that they came to fully realize the extent of de Sperati's effort. During his career he turned out over 500 varieties of stamps which were worth more than $5 million if completely circulated and accepted. His expertise was so complete that he fooled nearly all stamp experts and was in fact called to testify in court trials attesting to the fact that his materials were in fact forgeries and not legitimate. There is little doubt that a high percentage of his material (forged stamps) still rests in some of the finest collections throughout the world.

Raul Ch. de Thuin — Merida, Mexico

The town of Merida sits basking warmly on Mexico's Yucatan peninsula. It is a quiet, dusty Mexican city of sunlit streets and simple Mexican townsfolk. On one of the streets in the old section of Merida, toward the edge of town, is a decaying mansion. A rusted iron grillework protects the house from the street. The grounds are overgrown with vegetation but the remnants of what once was a garden can still be distinguished. On the front of the house there is a sign — *Se Vende Esta Casa* (this house for sale). Inside, the house is cluttered with boxes, fish tanks, broken chairs, etc. In the midst of all of this lives a small, intent man, looking much younger than his 76 years of age, and his name is Raul Ch. de Thuin. Here in this sleepy Mexican city resides one of the world's foremost forgers and counterfeiters.

I have never met de Thuin. And yet, during the course of investigating this case through the American Philatelic Society, I feel I know him well. He is a most unusual counterfeiter. de Thuin is an artist... an artist from another age.

The name of de Thuin is unknown to most of the public, but to many stamp collectors he is a living legend. He has been described by the American Philatelic Society as operating "the most gigantic counterfeit operation ever to flourish in the Western Hemisphere." He operated it all by himself. Raul de Thuin is a lone wolf.

The success of a forger can best be measured by how long he stays in business and by how well his product is accepted. How good was de Thuin? It is hard to provide an exact answer but consider some of the facts. de Thuin operated for more than 30 years producing literally thousands of faked and counterfeit stamps. Many of his products were accepted, advertised and sold by some of the world's leading stamp firms. Some of his products were received, inspected, and certified as "genuine" by the world's foremost stamp accrediting body. As late as December 13, 1966, Harmer Rooke & Company, an extremely reputable New York City stamp auctioneer, was offering a block of six of Canal Zone #15 as Lot #189 in their catalog. This "rare item" was listed with a catalog value of $1900.00. The block was a de Thuin counterfeit. In May of 1962 a London firm, H. R. Harmer Ltd. offered at auction a "Mexican collection" with a catalog value of $80,000.00.

They advanced the Mexican seller $8,000.00 on this valuable collection. The collection was soon discovered to contain a large percentage of de Thuin counterfeits. The auction was then cancelled.

In order to grasp some of the significance of de Thuin's work we must first appreciate some basic facts about stamp collecting and stamp values. Stamps are often the signature of a country. But countries, or more particularly political regimes, are far from stable. In the course of the many revolutions that have occurred, particularly in South America, there have been alterations in stamps. These alterations, often took the form of *overprints* or *surcharges*. The term *(overprint)* is used to indicate the imprinting of additional words, or letters on a basic postage stamp of a country. This is sometimes done to convert an ordinary stamp into an air mail stamp or to commemorate a special event of national significance, or in some cases to temporarily obliterate the face of the former dictator until a new batch of stamps can be ordered.

A *surcharge* is a device where the country changes the face value of the stamp by overprinting a new denomination. For example, a 2c stamp might be changed to a 4c stamp through such an imprinting. This practice was caused by shortages in particular denominations and, as with the overprint technique, was a temporary or provisional step until new stamps would be obtained from a printer with the correct markings or denominations. As we might expect, there were a limited number of these stamps with overprints, surcharges, or other special markings. In stamp collecting scarcity is the name of the game. The scarcer the item, the greater its value. These stamps, because of the fact that they were temporary or provisional, and naturally produced in short runs, were quite valuable; and where there is value, we will quite naturally find the forger.

Raul Ch. de Thuin was never a man to let value or opportunity elude him. Over the past thirty or forty years de Thuin has allegedly been involved in many different types of illegal activities. de Thuin reportedly had the "privilege" of visiting some of the better prisons throughout the world during his years of active participation in the fraternity of counterfeiters. Mexican news media reports that he has been arrested, tried and convicted on more than one count of forgery in Belgium, France, Honduras and

Mexico. de Thuin has been reportedly expelled from some of these countries but subsequently settled in Mexico. He entered Mexico in 1931 as a Belgium citizen. It may well have been that he deliberately picked the sleepy little town of Merida as an ideal base for a world-wide counterfeiting operation. He lived here in seclusion and was generally unnoticed by his neighbors. It is

Fig. 6   The low power binocular microscope provides the document examiner with an invaluable comparison tool. *(Courtesy of U.S. Postal Laboratories, Washington, D.C.)*

reported that when he first came to Mexico he operated a house of prostitution. Apparently, there were cries of unfair competition from the local trade and he was shut down. However, he quickly worked himself into what was to be a much more profitable type of operation. No one is exactly sure where de Thuin received his training in counterfeiting and forgery. There is strong evidence to indicate that he may have been trained in Honduras by a known master counterfeiter in that region. de Thuin does have a good education and a background as an artist. He has reportedly studied at the Sorbonne in Paris and the villa in Merida has its walls lined with original paintings by de Thuin.

de Thuin made a specialty of counterfeiting overprints and surcharges of Latin American stamps. He operated for many years and might, despite his advanced age, still be operating except for one disastrous mistake that he made. de Thuin, as many other stamp experts, recognized the value of Canal Zone stamps. He began counterfeiting Canal Zone overprints and in 1950 offered a selection of these forged stamps to an American collector by the name of James T. DeVoss. This proved to be a fatal error. DeVoss was an officer in the United States Army, assigned as an Intelligence Officer on the staff of General Dwight D. Eisenhower. Col. DeVoss was also an expert in Canal Zone stamps. DeVoss quickly discovered the counterfeits and began a 16 year effort which would eventually close down de Thuin's operation, but not before additional millions of dollars of counterfeit stamps had been produced. In the U.S. alone, over a million dollars worth of counterfeit stamps, of de Thuin's production, would be circulated.

Col. James T. DeVoss is a tall, friendly and persistent investigator. In 1952 Col. DeVoss wrote an article exposing de Thuin's operation. There had been rumblings about de Thuin's operation prior to that and a fraud order had been issued by the U.S. Postal Department in 1947. But de Thuin had been able to evade the fraud order by changing the name and location of his company in Mexico. This was a device that was to enable him to continue in business for nearly 21 years after the original fraud order was signed. For years Col. DeVoss dogged de Thuin's footsteps. Stamp officials managed to have him expelled, or more correctly, his wife expelled, from the American Philatelic Society. This action cut off one source of de Thuin's "sucker" list. However, for some unknown reason, the other philatelic organizations did not reciprocate and de Thuin's wife continued to maintain membership in these societies.

The years dragged on and de Thuin continued to operate. Additional experts became aware of de Thuin's activities but he was still successful in fooling many expert committees and it was clearly apparent that the ordinary, run-of-the-mill stamp collector was a sitting duck for de Thuin. Col. DeVoss attempted to obtain cooperation from the Mexican Government in stopping de Thuin's operation. He contacted an associate at the Mexican Embassy in Washington and attempts were made to gain Mexican Government cooperation. All of these attempts failed. At this point it should be recognized that there is a single peculiarity of law which protects many stamp counterfeiters. The counterfeiting of stamps, which are no longer used for postage purposes, is a criminal offense in only four countries in the entire world. Two of these countries, the United States and Greece, make a vigorous effort against stamp counterfeiters. However, in all of the other countries, the counterfeiter of old stamps can operate with relative immunity. There was apparently no Mexican law to fit de Thuin's crime. de Thuin had good legal counsel and he was aware of his legal position.

As de Thuin passed his 75th birthday, he began to recognize the physical limitations of his age. His hand was no longer steady and perhaps his eyesight had begun to fade a bit. But even more important, Col. DeVoss and the American Philatelic Society had succeeded in getting an additional fraud order against de Thuin in August of 1965. This last fraud order updated the original orders and listed the many other firms which de Thuin was operating. Now, when American collectors sought to place orders with one of de Thuin's "fronts", the envelopes were stamped *Fraudulent* and returned to the sender. The principal source of de Thuin's revenue was being cut off and he was getting ready to negotiate.

Sometime in 1965, in contacts that he had with the APS, he intimated that he might be open for a "business proposition". In April of 1966, at a general APS meeting, in Portland, Oregon, it was decided to appoint a committee to open direct negotiations with de Thuin. A five man committee was named and the project began.

One of the first barriers concerned the American government itself. It is illegal to possess the plates or the product of a counterfeiting operation. Special approval had to be obtained through the U.S. Secret Service and the Treasury Department, for the possible acquisition of de Thuin's plates and production. Contact was made with American authorities and on December 6, 1966, the Assistant Secretary of the U.S. Treasury Department wrote to the APS stating that:

"the Treasury Department has no objections to your importation of plates used for printing false overprints and cancellations on genuine foreign stamps, as well as the stock of stamps with such overprints and cancellations in the possession of the present owner of these plates, for the purposes you have described and subject to their surrender to the United States Secret Service when they have served the purposes setforth."

The way was clear now with the U.S. government and contact was made with the Mexican government regarding the APS project. Finally, on December 11, 1966, Col. DeVoss and James H. Beal, a specialist in Mexican stamps, of Warren, Ohio, flew to Merida, Mexico. In Merida they were joined by a fellow philatel-ist, Emilio Obregon of Mexico City. Jim Beal was affluent in Spanish but Sr. Obregon was to provide the expert local dialect during the interrogation portion of the negotiation.

The APS negotiating team had no idea of what it would find when they met the master counterfeiter face-to-face. What they found was a small, 5'6"-5'7", stocky man with sandy hair, glasses, and a slight cast in one eye. They also met what must be one of the most unusual counterfeiters of this century. To begin with, de Thuin had no complicated production equipment. In fact, he did not even have a printing press. de Thuin operated with the most rudimentary equipment, improvising presses from small blocks of wood, and operating principally with small metal photoengrav-ings that had been prepared by a local, unsuspecting photoengrav-ing house. Although not a stamp collector, de Thuin was certainly in many respects a stamp expert. He recognized which stamp varieties most readily lent themselves to his peculiar brand of counterfeiting. Recognizing this, he began a systematic search operation that would provide the necessary counterfeit materials.

Later, it was revealed that de Thuin was on the mailing list of many stamp auction houses throughout the world. There was a good reason for this. de Thuin would purchase old lots of letters from various liquidated estates. He was particularly interested in estates which might have letters and envelopes for "covers" from South America. He would purchase whole lots of these letters and they provided the "raw material" for many of his counterfeiting operations. de Thuin would, for example, obtain a genuine old envelope, at a cost of practically nothing, affix a genuine stamp of the period to the envelope and then cancel it with a marking which would greatly increase the value of the stamp. It is important to recognize here that the envelope and the stamp were genuine. They would pass any test of age or evaluation. What was counterfeit was the cancellation.

In order to perfect the overprints or surcharges, many of which were produced by letterpress imprint, de Thuin would obtain a legitimate overprinted stamp on an approval basis from a stamp brokerage house. He would meticulously copy the overprint on to a plain paper surface. He would in fact fill this sheet with many other overprints and rule a border around the overprints so that they appeared to be a specimen page of illustrations in a book. Then, contacting a local photoengraver, he would ask him to make a plate for his "book" and the photoengraver would produce a complete plate. Upon receiving the completed plate, de Thuin would proceed to cut the plate apart so that he had the individual overprint or surcharge impression that he wished. He would then attach this plate to a small block of wood, carefully ink the surface by hand, and impress this overprint on the "ordinary" postal stamp thus greatly increasing its value.

But de Thuin did not only produce overprints and surcharges, he also counterfeited complete stamps. His method was somewhat similar in that he would obtain a legitimate rare stamp from an unsuspecting dealer on an approval basis. The stamp would later be returned, but in the interim, de Thuin would have made a painstaking hand reproduction of the stamp. This reproduction would again be made into a metal plate by the unwitting local photoengraver. de Thuin was astute enough to recognize the limitations of photoengraving in connection with its ability to match a genuine intaglio engraving. Therefore, he only counterfeited stamps which did not use fine line engraving. Many of the oldest and most primitive stamps, and most valuable, used single line, simple line designs. These were easily counterfeited by de Thuin. In fact, they have been counterfeited by a number of other parties but never with de Thuin's accuracy. He also had access to paper of the same age as the original stamps. In addition, through research he had been able to obtain the formula for old inks. Some of the formulas he utilized were over 100 years old. In addition to reproducing surcharges, overprints and complete stamps, de Thuin had one other ace up his sleeve. On the backs of many valuable stamps is a small imprint designating the name of the dealer who had handled the stamp. Sometimes this is a single word, a set of initials, etc. This imprint signifies to the buyer that this particular dealer has handled the stamp and has found it "genuine". To provide a further link in the wall of legitimacy that de Thuin was building, he successfully counterfeited these dealers' marks and in fact his collection contains the dealers' marks for some of the largest and most reputable stamp auction houses in the world.

There is little doubt that de Thuin, when it came to penmanship, was a genuine artist. Col. DeVoss relates one case where de Thuin counterfeited an overprint stamp worth $150.00 using nothing but a pen and ink. In other words, he drew the overprint completely free hand. The stamp was passed as genuine. In the previous chapter dealing with fraudulent check operations, we referred to the process of "raising." In a real sense this is the primary basis for de Thuin's operation. While many of his raising operations, through the use of surcharges and overprints, involved no more than a few hundred dollars, there is one instance in which he raised a Honduras stamp (Honduras No. 178) cataloged at 20c, to a rare Honduras air mail which is cataloged $30,000.00. This must certainly go down as one of the most dramatic raising operations in the history of forgery.

Besides de Thuin's unusual equipment, the APS negotiating team found an unusual man. de Thuin, despite the fact that he has remained quiet and aloof to his neighbors, was not above bragging about his counterfeiting operations and even his sexual exploits. For example, he once recounted that he had 400 mistresses and 250 illegitimate children. We do know that he has been married three times while in Mexico and that he probably was married a number of times prior to his entrance in 1931. While the world's primary reference to de Thuin is in the field of stamp counterfeiting, there is reason to believe that he was engaged in other illegal activities. In fact, in 1966 when arrested by the Mexican government for alleged exporting Mexican artifacts to a New Orleans dealer, he successfully proved that the "artifacts" were actually counterfeit reproductions he had made himself.

After four days of difficult negotiations, Col. DeVoss and James Beal, with the assistance of a Merida attorney, were able to conclude a contract with Raul de Thuin which hopefully put the old counterfeiter permanently out of business. The American Philatelic Society purchased 1636 separate cliches (plates) used to counterfeit stamps, overprints, and surcharges. They also purchased all his original drawings, his files, correspondence, and a complete record of his sales and accounts. The latter accounts were to provide some interesting information. It became evident that de Thuin had acted in concert with some American stamp dealers. These dealers would have de Thuin custom-counterfeit a particular rare issue and split the proceeds on a 50/50 basis. As a result of the account records, one of the country's leading stamp dealers, located on the West Coast, was expelled from the American Philatelic Society. An examination by Col. DeVoss and James Beal, of the plates provided through the transaction, revealed that over 50% of the counterfeits were stamps and cancellations of Mexico. de Thuin did not forget the rest of the stamp world and apparently produced fraudulent issues on 42 separate countries.

The contract negotiated between de Thuin and the American Philatelic Society provided for three principal points. First, it provided that the APS would obtain full publication rights for de Thuin's stamps and for a complete history of his philatelic activities. Secondly, he agreed to cease and desist from the production or sale of philatelic properties. Third, he agreed to subject himself to the tribunal of his own country or any country selected by the APS, in the event that he violated the previous point. In addition, he signed a notarized confession, confessing to being a counterfeiter. Thus ended, we hope, the career of one of the world's most unusual forgers.

PERSONALITY PROFILE

In reviewing the many forgery case histories, and in the course of observing forgers and interviewing the arresting officers, it occurred to the author that there might well be some basic personality profiles common to the forger. It was thought that perhaps a composite of characteristics might be valuable to law enforcement agents in sifting possible forgery suspects, and also in generally providing a closer look at the psychology behind forgery.

In order to construct this profile a survey technique was employed. A compendium of over 1000 prisons or correctional institutions was gathered and from this list 114 major penitentiaries were selected. The staff psychologists at each of these penitentiaries were requested to contribute their own observations on forgers they had interviewed and tested.

As might be expected, the results of this type of survey are both encouraging from the standpoint of the volume of data provided, but also discouraging because of the lack of consensus on many points. Nonetheless, much of the data accumulated has a validity and significance that requires publication in a report of this type.

The reports from some penal institutions were much more complete than from others. In some cases, the institution did not have a staff psychologist or the psychologist they had was unable to provide any data. In other cases, the psychologist had generalized feelings about convicted forgers but had not done any real study of these convicts. Several institutions had done specific research in this area and the writer is particularly indebted to Maurice J. Keyser of Southern Michigan State Prison, Kenneth P. Harty of New York's Sing-Sing Prison, George Levy of Colorado State Penitentiary, William C. King of the U.S. Bureau of Prisons, Lawrence B. Eskin of the New York City Correctional

Institution, Jack Plummer of Oklahoma State Reformatory and
Olov G. Gardebring of North Dakota State Penitentiary.

Listed below are some of the principal characteristics that go
into building a personality profile. There are no absolutes here.
And indeed there is very substantial deviation from any norms
that we might draw from the complete tabulation of these characteristics. Nevertheless, woven within these characteristics are
some of the principal personality elements of the major class of
forgers as they now exist in the U. S. A.

1. SEX

The sex of the vast majority of forgers is overwhelmingly male.
The ratio of male to female forgers varies from 4-1 to 10-1. On a
national basis, it probably more closely approximates the 10-1
ratio. The female forgers encountered in this study usually were
working as members of a forgery ring or were working with their
husbands or companions in a husband-wife team type of operation. Professional forgers were almost exclusively male. The
author ran into one case of a forgery ring in Chicago which was
completely female and involved more than a dozen suspects, but
this is the exception rather than the rule.

However, we may expect to see more female forgers in the near
future. Professional forgers, operating in ring organizations, have
been quick to recognize the camouflage possibilities of using
attractive female "pushers." In one recent case in New England,
the mastermind of the forgery ring was allegedly recruiting coeds
from as far south as Alabama to utilize them in check pushing
operations.

2. AGE LEVEL

Most observers report the typical level for male forgery suspects
as in the early thirties. This is the age level where the first
conviction is most likely to occur and it would appear that many
forgery careers begin in the late twenties or early thirties. The
Michigan State study reveals an age level range between 27 and
47. This study also revealed a lower age group with a median age of
23 but this age group is not completely typical of the experiences as
reported by other penal institutions. At Sing Sing Prison and
other New York institutions, the median age level is 30 to 35.

One important fact to remember in age level statistic reporting is that we are reporting age levels of the average convicted forger. This is not necessarily the median age level of forgers in general. Indeed, because of the strong recidivism shown by forgery suspects, we might well expect the national median age level to more closely approximate the adult median.

The range of age levels for forgery suspects nearly matches that for all humanity. The author has encountered, through the courtesy of Postal Inspectors, forgery suspects ranging from a low of 7 years of age for a postal money order forger to a high of 80 plus years for a lifetime forger now incarcerated in a Texas penitentiary.

3. INTELLIGENCE

It is a valid generalization to report that the intelligence level of forgery suspects nearly always exceeds that of the mean intelligence level of the criminal population. Most forgers score in the High Average to Bright Normal range. The Michigan State study reported an average intelligence rating of between 114 and 117. Of course there are exceptions to this generalization and these exceptions normally occur in connection with more routine, petty forgery operations such as the theft and forgery of welfare checks as encountered in urban areas. There will also be cases where an individual is convicted of the crime of forgery, without actually having been a "complete" forger. This occurs in cases where a forgery ring has individuals who are assigned to the theft of checks as part of the general forgery operation. When apprehended such individuals, who usually have IQ levels below 100, are also charged with forgery as well as mail theft, etc. They are not, however, forgers in the true sense of the word.

Even lacking the statistical data provided by penitentiary studies, one might well surmise that the intelligence level of many forgers is well above the intelligence level of the general criminal population. Forgers approach the personality profiles of confidence men, and the latter have been shown to have above average intelligence levels. In addition, even the most cursory inspection of some of the forgery schemes, as outlined previously, would reveal an above average intelligence level and a good capacity for organization and detail. The reader must take care not to equate intelligence, an innate characteristic, with "sense". If the forger had any sense he would be in a legitimate occupation rather than squandering his intelligence and life in forgery.

4. SOCIAL SKILL

The great majority of forgers reveal a distinct extrovert personality. They are highly verbal and often seem to possess an intuitive judgment in their social contacts. Harty reports that the forger has "the ability to manipulate most social situations in his favor".

Nearly every psychologist and law enforcement agent interviewed reported that forgers were "good talkers". They possess the ability to talk themselves out of situations and this, of course, complicates the enforcement problem. It also provides a clue to the general non-violent character of the forger. In a majority of cases they do not need to be armed because they possess the social skill to talk themselves out of most impending arrest situations.

Many forgers are reported to be friendly or likable and some of their "straight" social contacts were genuinely shocked to discover that the individual in question was a professional forger. Indeed, in retrospect, social skill is one of the most important tools of the forger. Without it his life expectancy as a forger is extremely limited.

5. RACE

Forgery suspects are primarily white male adults. There are some Negroes in forgery operations, but they are in a distinct minority when compared to the total criminal forgery population. Negro forgers primarily operate in and around the ghetto and pass welfare checks, social security checks, etc. in bars, food chains, etc. Only rarely do you find the Negro forgery suspect operating in banks, hotels, airlines, etc. The reader will remember that the physical appearance of the forger is often an important factor in the successful completion of the crime of forgery. In general, the bank teller, store clerk, etc. finds it easier to believe that a white man is a prosperous, solid citizen than he does a black man. In a curious way, the crime of forgery mirrors the innate social prejudices of the nation.

As far as counterfeiting and forgery go, there are nearly no Negro operatives. In this study, the author ran into only two cases where a Negro was both counterfeiting checks and forging them. One of these cases involved a small print shop in the Bronx, New York, counterfeiting trading stamps and utility company checks. The second case involved a forger-counterfeiter in Cleveland, Ohio who was producing a small quantity of postal money orders.

From a long range standpoint, this "inequity" between Negro and Caucasian forgers is almost certain to be erased. Many Negroes are now obtaining the graphic arts skills basic to counterfeiting and forgery operations, and others, through their exposure to the prison population are becoming apprised of successful forgery modus operandi.

6. MOTIVATION AND PROBLEM SOLVING

It is an obvious truism to relate that the motivation for forgery is economic. Obviously the forger forges because he wants or needs money. However, more to the point, we might consider why he chose this particular route to wealth. In this consideration we will of necessity examine his approach to problem solving. Harty reports that his observations reveal that the forger's approach to problem solving is directly related to his inflated self image. He solves his problems not so much on the basis of what the immediate facts and solutions are, but rather on the basis of preserving his image. Keyser reports that the forgers he has studied have come up with problem solutions that are either evasive or impulsive.

From the author's own analysis of convicted forgers, it often appears that the crime of forgery followed previously unsuccessful adventures in other forms of criminal activity, i.e. burglaries, robberies, etc. Very few professional forgers started their criminal career initially in the field of forgery. Many of them had juvenile arrest records for a variety of crimes. Apparently, at some stage their innate personality pattern coincided with the criminal personality requirements for the crime of forgery and they began their career. Once started, and successful in forgery, their problem solving dilemma was over. Forgery for some of them became so easy, that there was no other criminal recourse.

Other studies, in federal penitentiaries, revealed that forgery convicts often have relatively low frustration tolerances. Some are prone to gambling and utilize the crime of forgery to cover for immediately incurred gambling losses. Some forgers are also alcoholics and at the U. S. Penitentiary in Leavenworth it was noted that many of these types of criminals committed forgery while under the influence of alcohol. However, this observation is not to imply that the general forgery criminal population is alcohol addicted. The author does not believe this to be the case at all.

7. SOCIO-ECONOMIC BACKGROUND

In contrast to the general criminal population, most forgers are reported coming from middle class homes. Often their father has been employed in some clerical or semi-skilled occupation. A number of psychologists report that the role of the mother in these middle class families was dominant in the case of forgery convicts. They also report that the mother exhibited a frustration over her husband's mediocre earning capacity and that her attitude often presented an indictment of the father's career abilities. One can only speculate what effect such an environment had on the formation of the forger's personality. Although this observation has been arrived at independently by a number of psychologists, there is not yet sufficient data to correlate this family background with any failure traits that the forger exhibited.

Besides the above noted general categories, there are some other random personality traits which appear often enough to seem significant to forger personality analysis.

For example, many of the forgers showed a decided tendency to neatness, being neat dressers and possessed of good organizational capacities. Some have been known to keep elaborate records of their forgeries. They often utilize their verbal abilities to get them going successfully in new jobs and occupations. However, they don't have staying power and often slow up and fold under relatively light pressure.

From a physical standpoint, tests on over 400 convicted forgers at Southern Michigan State Prison revealed that they had an average physical size of 5'10" at 160 pounds. They were rated physically adequate but were not predominantly athletic from a participation point of view. Their coordination was good and they possessed normal spectator interest in popular sports.

By and large forgers are non-violent. There are conspicuous exceptions to this rule, but in order to generalize we must characterize them as normally non-violent. The social skills and verbal abilities of the forger allows him to discharge his anger and frustration in more abstract fashion than the general criminal population. Characteristic of the non-violence aspect of his personality is the forger's ability to plan and prepare at great length for the commission of his crime. Eskin has noted that "the main feature of the criminal personality is the inability to delay immediate gratification for long term goals". While this is applicable to the general criminal population it is certainly not applicable, as Eskin later notes, to the forger population.

As previously noted, many forgers spring from maternally dominated families. They often reject traditional authority and this rejection is in evidence in their behavior pattern during incarceration. They rebel against all authority figures and often are cynical about general society, institutions, and mores. They reject these institutions during their ego building, of which check passing is an integral part. Interesting enough, Eskin notes that despite their rejection of authority figures, forgers show an abnormally high incidence of arrest for "impersonating an officer". Apparently, there is some conflict and contradiction in their rejection of authority and their need to emulate authority figures.

The forger's rebelliousness often produces some degree of turmoil amongst prison officials. One forger the author studied, after having been convicted in connection with a major money order forgery scheme, was held in the Federal House of Detention in New York prior to his sentencing. This forger, a slightly built man in his late twenties, set about to organizing the prisoners and arranging for a series of protests. Prison officials hurriedly transferred him to the "Tombs" of the New York Police Department to check the outbreak of rebellion.

Finally, in fairness, we should note that forgery is sometimes not in and of itself a criminal profession. Sometimes it becomes the side effect of a principal criminal occupation. For example, a burglar may in the course of his burglary obtain checks which will later be forged and negotiated. Similarly, an embezzler may forge a check to cover a temporary situation and avoid detection. These individuals are not forgers in the true sense of the word and have not been the subject of our personality profile analysis.

SCIENTIFIC DETECTION

Introduction

The study of forgery is inexorably intertwined with the methods and techniques of detection. Indeed, had our forensic laboratories not advanced to the point where they now are, forgery would be an even greater threat to the economic integrity of the nation. In this particular chapter, the reader will be introduced to some of the basic techniques utilized in forgery detection. It is not the purpose of this chapter to provide a condensation of the many excellent books and reports on this subject. Rather, it is our purpose to introduce the interested reader to some of the principal methods used by modern document examiners. We would also like to dispel some of the commonplace myths that have arisen regarding such subjects as the dating of inks, tracing of disguised handwriting, etc. It is the author's belief that the business, financial and law enforcement community should have a clear appreciation of what the document examiner can do and what he cannot do. The successful prosecution of forgery suspects often depends primarily on the evidential material available to the investigative agency. It is our hope that by reviewing this chapter, the reader will have a greater appreciation of what materials are required for successful prosecution.

Certainly the single most important factor in the apprehension and successful prosecution of modern forgers lies in the extraordinary ability of some of our modern forensic laboratories. In any forgery there are a certain number of basic inescapable clues which the forger must provide the investigator. The principal clues are:

1. The nature of the signature itself
2. The method in which the signature was produced

3. The writing instrument
4. The ink
5. The paper
6. The mechanical (typewriter, imprinting machine, check writing machines, stamps, etc.) impression.
7. Personal identifying traces (latent prints, hair, skin, etc.)

1. The Signature

The signature itself obviously reveals the single most important clue to the detection of a forgery. Before one can study forged signatures, it is first necessary to examine some of the principal properties of genuine signatures. Document examiners have long recognized that a person's signature stands quite apart from his normal writing pattern. The signature is often produced in a flourish pattern which pays little attention to precise letter formation. The letters flow in a conditioned reflex type action. The signature for the average person is written so often, particularly in a complex urban society, that it becomes an automatic mechanism and as such may well possess a degree of originality and reproducibility which might not be possible in more primitive societies where individual attention would be given to the spelling and formation of each letter.

In examining the characteristics of the genuine signature it helps to know something of the personality and background of the individual who is reported to have signed the document. Those persons who typically produce many signatures, such as businessmen, bankers, etc. will often begin their signature without hesitation and without allowing the pen to come to rest. Since nearly all of the commercial signatures which are now under examination are of ballpoint type production, it is helpful to know something about the physics of the ballpoint pen itself. The ballpoint pen, in contrast to the older "fountain" pen, transfers a relatively high viscosity ink to the paper as the ballpoint itself revolves.

In many signatures there is a tapering or diminishing in the thickness of the line at the beginning and end of the signature. The accomplished writer, conditioned to dashing off a signature, will produce this type of genuine signature. The less experienced writer may allow the ballpoint to come to a rest position at the beginning of the signature causing either an indentation or a

Fig. 7 At the heart of the scientific detection process lies the special human skills and experience of the questioned document examiner.

thickening of the line. With fountain pens this thickening of the line is even more pronounced. Continuing our investigation of the genuine signature, we will note the effect of intervals and pauses in whucyi9cahure pattern. You have probably observed signatures which are in effect a continuous line. These are created without the pen either being lifted from the surface or without a pause in the motion. This type of signature is most often found in a short name with relatively few letters or with simple letter construction.

There are, however, many signatures in which intervals and breaks occur. These intervals are not always discernible to the naked eye since the pen may be returned to the exact same position in an envolving line pattern. The usual interval break involves the initial capital letter, as contrasted with the remaining portion of the surname. Despite their invisibility to the naked eye, these intervals or pen lifts are observable under microscopic examination and through the use of specialized photographic techniques which will be discussed later.

The widespread use of ballpoint pens has proved to be a complicating factor to many document examiners. With ballpoint pens, or many pencils, it is extremely difficult to determine where an interval or pen lift may have occurred. Cheaper variety ballpoint pens create further problems in that they may "run out of ink" creating unnatural intervals which are really not a part of the pattern of the genuine signature.

Handwriting expert, Wilson R. Harrison, has shown that some writers have peculiar signature alignment characteristics which allow for identification and determination of the genuineness of signatures. For example, a group may consistently produce a signature on, below, or above the dotted line or signature position on a document. Further evidence with regard to the slope of the signature, when contrasted with the alignment of the printed matter can also establish the genuineness of a signature.

We should bear in mind that despite the well developed motor responses that produce an "automatic signature", we nonetheless never produce two signatures which are *identically* the same. This factor can often be extremely valuable in detecting traced signatures. It will also be recognized that the slant, slope, and in fact the letter design of genuine signatures does have an acceptable range of variation between standard specimens. The existence of such variation is often a valuable proof toward the genuineness rather than the disproof that we might initially regard it as.

2. Methods of Producing the Signature

The second telltale area in which the scientific detection plays an important part, involves the signature production method. There are seven principal methods for signature production, from a forgery standpoint, and each of these methods provides telltale clues which scientific detection is capable of enumerating. The signature production methods the author refers to are:

(1) Signature by simulation.
(2) Tracing.

(3) Projections.

(4) Stamping or facsimile production.

(5) Signature splits.

(6) Spurious signatures.

(7) Disguised signatures.

(1) *Signature Simulation:* - Historically, our most gifted forgers have used the simulation technique. The simulation method is a free hand reproduction of the signature. In practice the forger

Fig. 8   An FBI Laboratory technician using reagents and a binocular microscope to examine ink from a questioned document. *(Courtesy of Federal Bureau of Investigation)*

may enlarge the signature or may copy alongside the genuine signature, sometimes making 50 to 100 copies, until he has the "feel" of the signature. As he repeats the signature, he continues to inspect it and to modify his copy so that it closely conforms to the original. This method of forgery, particularly in the hands of an expert, can be devastating. Some of the countries most dangerous forgers have utilized this technique. Fortunately, from a law enforcement standpoint, the number of individuals who are capable of this type of artistry is limited.

This method of forgery is extremely difficult to detect since the simulated signature has many of the characteristics previously described as requisite to "genuine signatures". The utilization of ballpoint pens further enhances this simulation since it becomes, as noted previously, difficult to determine the interval and pause pattern of the simulated signature as compared to the original. Forgers who use this method must possess a high degree of penmanship. They frequently are imitating signatures which, because they are "automatic", lack many of the rudiments of ordinary penmanship. This haste and disarray of letter formation, typical to professional and business signatures, actually works to the forger's advantage in the simulated signature technique.

As pointed out elsewhere in this report, the forger of traveler's checks and credit cards often does not have to simulate a signature because he has access to methods which would remove the comparison signature on the credit card or traveler's check. All that is necessary is a free-flowing spurious hand.

(2) *Tracing:* - The tracing technique, as its name implies, involves producing a signature by overlaying a piece of translucent paper on the specimen signature. For example, a light box, provided with illumination and topped with frosted glass, is utilized to provide back-lighting for the signature. The genuine signature shows through many lighter weight papers and the forger proceeds to follow the general outline indicated by the original signature. This method of direct tracing is sometimes not practical with safety bank note papers and with bills of lading, etc. which contain printing on the reverse portion of the document. In such cases the forger goes to the direct impression technique. For example, he will lay the specimen genuine signature over a piece of carbon paper and the paper in turn over the document to be forged. Then, using a fine point instrument he will go over the original signature producing an impression offset on the forged document.

Later, the line will be inked in along the guide lines provided by the tracing method. The carbon paper technique invariably leaves a residue line which, even when inked over later, becomes visible under specialized color photography inspection methods. A variation of this technique involves coating the back of the genuine document with a fine film of graphite, such as from a soft drawing pencil. This method provides greater control to the forger but again produces the graphite guide line which must be eradicated.

A soft eraser is capable of removing the line, but in so doing leaves telltale paper abrasions which change the inked characteristics of the forged signature.

(3) *Projections:* - As might be obvious to the trained photo mechanical technician, there are optical systems which allow for the exact projection of a given genuine signature on to another document. These devices, which are refined in development and use, are not publicly available. They have been utilized in security agencies for the production of clandestine documents in documentation mills. For security reasons, no further discussion of this technique is practical here.

(4) *Stampings:* - Increasingly, corporate checks are not personally signed but are imprinted with a facsimile signature. In the professional forgery of major corporation checks this method of

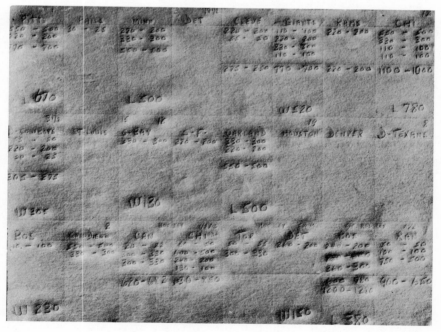

Fig. 9 An excellent example of the use of a low angle light source to reveal indented writing. *(Courtesy of Eastman Kodak Company and Captain Amedee Comete, Identification Bureau, Police Department, Montreal, Quebec, Canada)*

Example of low angle grazing light used to reveal hidden indented writing
(Courtesy of Eastman Kodak Company, Rochester, N.Y.)

signature projection is often utilized. Unfortunately, rubber stamp signatures are relatively easy to procure and to forge. Sometimes, as was the case in one recent check theft, the signature stamp or equipment used to produce the facsimile signature was stolen along with the checks. Before the checks could be recalled or payment stopped, there was wide distribution of the checks. Facsimile signatures produced with metal dies and multicolored impression ribbons are safer than rubber stamps, but are not foolproof.

(5) *Signature Split:* - Many professional forgers have come to realize that the signature materials themselves, that is, the ink or graphite impressions, are capable of being split. The technique here is to obtain a sample of the original signature, preferably while still new, and to apply a pressure sensitive facing to the signature. The facing is carefully removed, usually from a dense paper stock, and the signature is in effect "split". The signature is then transferred to a forged document where it is placed in the signature portion with the pressure sensitive sheet attached. Sometimes it is made to appear that the check has been torn at this point and that the pressure sensitive tape is merely serving as

a repair strip. These types of forgeries are quite easy to spot and are usually not used by professional forgers. This device should be recognized by the banking and business community. Any document requiring a signature, which has a torn area in or across the signature portion should be immediately suspect. Subsequent removal of this tape from the forged document might reveal that the signature is attached to the tape and not to the base paper itself. These signatures frequently are made from a pencil pick-up, and this also is a tip-off to the existence of this type of forgery. The graphite pencil outline splits more readily and with greater fidelity than the ballpoint line. The examiner is also aware of the thinness of the line before he even removes the tape. Interestingly enough some bank tellers and businessmen have been deluded into believing that the application of the tape was a security device to prevent tampering with the signature. This is one more evidence of the con man aspect of the successful forger.

(6) *Spurious Signature:* - Still another category of signature is the signature classified as spurious or bogus, that is, the signature produced by a forger, perhaps using his natural hand, and providing the name of a fictitious person. These types of forgers are particularly difficult to handle since, with the three billion inhabitants of the earth, who is to say whether a person is fictitious. In addition, many handwriting experts concede that a skilled forger can successfully disguise his hand.

There are two principal factors which act toward the detection of the spurious signature. One concerns the motor response and coordination patterns typical to an adult. These writing patterns are so firmly established that the forger, particularly if he makes a number of such signatures, may well revert to certain letter patterns which are basic to his genuine signature. In addition, his method of disguise may in turn follow a significant pattern.

(7) *Disguised Signature:* - One of the most frequent methods for the disguise of handwriting, when producing the name of a fictitious person, is to deliberately alter the slope of the signature. This simple alteration produces an entirely different visual effect. But it also creates side effects on the continuity of the signature, and alters some of the features in individual letter design. In documents which require extensive use of disguised handwriting

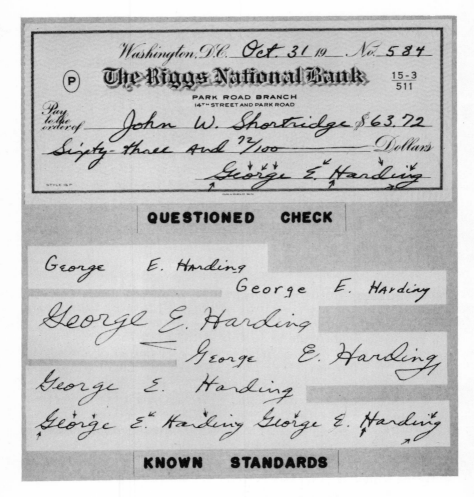

QUESTIONED CHECK

KNOWN STANDARDS

Fig. 10   *(Courtesy of Federal Bureau of Investigation)*

there is always the possibility that the forger will slip back into his normal slope angle. The difficulty with check and credit card spurious signatures is that they usually only offer two or three words of specimen to examine and compare. However, in the case of many recidivists the standards are extensive enough to prove conclusively a pattern of disguised handwriting. Harrison, in a statistical study of the variation of slope as utilized in disguised handwriting, has shown that the change from a forward to a back slope is seven times more popular than a change in the reverse method. It is quite obvious that most people write with a slight forward slope.

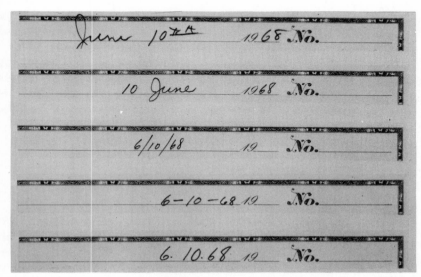

Fig. 11 An illustration of one element of the form method of document examination. The date may be written in numerous ways. Forgers tend to repeat the form although they may attempt to disguise their hands.

Another reported technique involves changing the natural letter design. For example, the forger may, in forming his capitals, go from a block to a cursive style. He may also arbitrarily insert capitals in words or artificially break vowels in an attempt to visually alter the signature appearance.

Another means of disguise involve reversion to printing, with the signature taking on the appearance of block letters sometimes joined by one or two cursive letter forms. Alteration in size is still another method. The latter method is really not effective because of the possibilities of photographic enlargement of the hand-writing. However, it sometimes causes difficulty because of the tendency of the ink, when placed in close proximity to cramped letters, to flow together and obscure the letter pattern. In the practice of large-scale forgeries, it is more likely that the forger will dash off the fictitious names with no practiced attempt at either changing the slope, the rhythm, fluidity, or character formation of the signature. These mass produced signatures will be scrawled into what is hoped to be a semi-decipherable form. In this case there are certain repeat patterns which the document examiner is aware of and which offer a good chance for detection. Many writers, for example, have a difficult time of ridding themselves of the habits of cross-over ornamentation, flourishes, etc. These idiosyncrasies tend to persist even in the disguised hand. A second, and more obvious method of detection lies in the names used by the forger during the course of his operation. There is almost an uncontrollable instinct to utilize a set group of initials. Statistical accumulations of forged signature specimens frequently provide damning evidence in this respect.

3. The Writing Instrument

The nearly complete shift in American writing habits, from conventional pens to the ballpoint pen, has produced certain difficulties with regard to scientific detection. The ballpoint pen is, quite frankly, not as good a writing instrument as the conventional fountain pen. Signatures made with a fountain pen, or even with pencil lend themselves more readily to comparison and analysis. This is not to say that ballpoint pens and the signatures they produce are not capable of analysis, because they are. Rather, it is to point out that the ballpoint pen, by the very nature of its erratic writing pattern, produces additional difficulties for the document examiner.

The writing instrument in itself, sometimes becomes an aid toward scientific detection in that it may be found on the person or property of the suspect. Test patterns performed with the suspect pen may add one more item of evidence to the detection test. Seldom, however, is the pen in and of itself sufficiently unique to provide a major point in the detection process. The pen does offer significance in that it has a specific ink cartridge and this, as we shall now see, does provide some basis for analysis and detection.

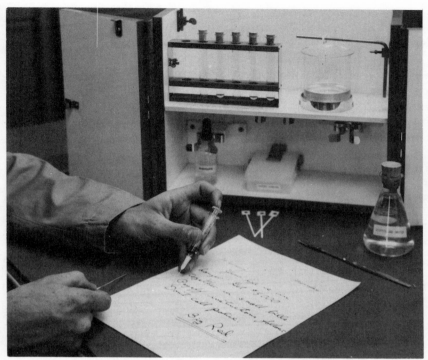

Fig. 12 A minute quantity of water is applied to a questioned ink using a hypodermic syringe. This prepares the ink for the lifting of a chromatogram. *(Courtesy of Federal Bureau of Investigation)*

4. Ink

The quick analysis of the ink used on a suspect's document would seem to be an ideal method to determine that the forger had indeed been responsible for this particular piece of work. However, the problem is much more complex than this. The single signature offered by the forger of a credit card or check does not provide but a minute amount of material which is available for analysis and comparison. Secondly, there are vast quantities of standardized pens manufactured both in the United States and in Japan which utilize strikingly similar ink formulations. Most people, including some law enforcement officers, have no conception of how little actual material is required to actually produce a signature. A single ounce of ink solids might produce five to ten miles of ink line. In a signature, measuring no more than three or four inches of ink line, there is an infinitesimal amount of material to deal with.

This attempt at analysis is further complicated by the fact that we do not wish to destroy the suspect document. Faced with these problems the document examiner relies on a number of techniques. Among these are the chromagraphic analysis of the inks, ultraviolet comparison testing, infra-red analysis, and neutron activation analysis.

Fig. 13 After the droplet of water has dissolved the ink, it is transferred to the chromotography paper by a blotting action. *(Courtesy of Federal Bureau of Investigation)*

The first step that the document examiner takes is to chemically classify the ink. The primary inks are usually organic dye based inks with further classifications of carbon based inks, iron gallotannate inks, fast set alkaline inks, etc. It can be established which chemical class of ink is involved in a particular signature. Proceeding one step further down the line, it will also be possible through spot test and through chromographic means to isolate the particular dyestuff as coloring materials for the inks. The real catch comes when a comparison is attempted between two inks from the same brand of manufacture, and it should be noted that several different ink cartridge manufacturers might conceivably use the same ink producer's material in fabricating their cartridges.

Despite all these limitations, forensic scientists have brought the analysis of minute quantities of ink, through nondestructive means, to a high degree of precision. It suffices to say here that with all of the limitations imposed by a relatively small sample, it is still possible, given the will and resources to test, to closely identify a particular ink. This, as with the other clues mentioned, provides a further link in the evidence-building chain connecting a forger to his handiwork.

5. The Paper

The use of the term paper in this instance can be partially misleading since forged signatures which occur on credit cards and on some other identity documents often do not take place on a paper surface. Nevertheless, for the purposes of general comparison paper is the basis for most forgery operations.

In some cases very little consideration has to be given to the paper because it is self-evident that the paper is genuine because of evidence indicating that a group of checks were stolen or fraudulently obtained. However, particularly in the case of facsimile checks, which the researcher is likely to encounter in the professional check forging operation, paper can be of significant value in the scientific detection process.

Some years ago safety paper was introduced for check production purposes. Initially this paper was very difficult to obtain publicly and there were limited number of check printers. The safety paper provided two safeguards in that it hindered erasures and alterations and also because of its restricted availability, made the production of counterfeit or facsimile checks much more difficult. Today the situation has changed. One of the factors producing the change has been explosion in the number of checks used in the American economy. This vast increase has created a situation where there are innumerable printers who are producing check books. In addition, the safety paper has been utilized for other non-check purposes, sales promotions, etc.

There has also been an increase in the number of firms producing this type of paper. All of the latter factors acting in concert have created a situation where safety check paper is not too difficult to obtain commercially.

In addition, there is also the possibility that the check counterfeiter or forger will overprint blank stock with a pattern which appears to be a safety pattern, but which in reality is simply a decorative pattern. The widespread change to IBM type cards for corporation checks has also complicated the picture with regard to the availability of check materials.

There still exists in the public mind, the romanticized version of the importance of a paper water mark. As it would happen, water marks have fallen into disfavor somewhat and are not nearly as widely used to identify paper as the general public would believe. For one thing, the paper manufacturers sometimes maintain a relatively sporadic record of the use of watermarks in their production. At times, a better picture can be obtained through the records maintained by "dandy roll" producers whose rolls are used to make the watermark on the paper.

The chemical analysis of paper is the subject of several separate volumes and it suffices at this point to note that very precise chemical analysis of paper is possible and that this analysis can determine whether two specimens documents are from the same batch of paper production.

Tracing paper to a particular manufacturer, and then to a particular production lot is sometimes complicated to the point of impossibility. However, from the standpoint of the study of forgery, paper characteristics themselves offer some simple parameters which are of use on nearly an immediate basis. To begin with we can consider the nature of the paper itself. Facsimile checks are seldom produced on papers which have the exact physical measurements of the original check. Paper for check manufacture is produced to precise specifications. Its thickness can be calibrated within a thousandth of an inch and it will be consistent on all of the checks from that particular manufacturer for that particular job.

Check stock is specified according to the weight of the paper and this in turn is measured in terms of dry weight per three thousand square feet of paper. Other simple physical measurements on the paper, such as exposure to ultraviolet and infrared radiation, can be particularly revealing. The type of alteration the forger is most likely to make usually involves an erasure, a tracing, or an alteration in the face amount of the check. In cases where we assume that the paper is genuine we are therefore concerned with the effect that the forger's action may have had on the surface of the paper. Nearly all papers exhibit a degree of fluorescence when exposed to ultraviolet light. The forger may have made a skillful alteration or addition, even tinting the background as required,

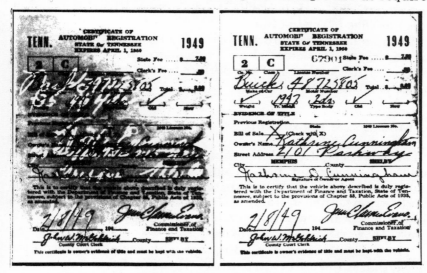

Ultraviolet photography was used to reveal alteration in this Tennessee auto registration form. The vehicle had been stolen and then sold using a fraudulent certificate of registration. *(Courtesy of Federal Bureau of Investigation)*

which escapes detection under ordinary light radiation. However, this alteration often becomes quite visible when exposed to ultraviolet radiation. In addition, the ultraviolet radiation may also reveal the original outline of the erased portion of the document. This is possible because of trace elements in the original marking instrument which, despite the best erasure attempts, may remain imbedded in the paper fibers.

lighting the check or suspect document with a powerful light source. This light source, as it penetrates the paper, may reveal alterations which would not be visibly apparent when viewed from a single light side.

Some researchers have noted that modern check papers are often sized with a coating which, as it ages, gradually loses some of its hold-out properties. Thus, in comparing the date of a particular check with a suspected forged signature, we might observe a

variance which would be due to the changing holdout characteristics of the paper sizing. If, for example, the date had been written
in earlier, the line would appear, under microscopic examination,
as a sharp straight pattern. As the paper aged, the holdout
characteristics of the sizing would deteriorate and subsequent
writings on the surface would produce more of a feathered or
irregular edge to the ink line.

In summary, paper provides a scientific clue as to the origin of
the document, its potential age, a comparison of the age of the
various writings on it, and as a surface for the collection of latent
prints as noted later.

6. Mechanical Impression

The professional check forger must often employ instruments
besides the ballpoint pen to effect his forgery. Many of the
professionals have been known to use one or more typewriters,
check writers, rubber stamps, etc. All of these instruments are
used, singly or in concert, to create a cover of legitimacy to what is
a patently worthless piece of paper.

The point to bear in mind is that with each addition to the
check, that is the use of a typewriter, check writer, stamp, etc. the
forger provides the document examiner with one more tool valuable to the detection process.

A. *Typewriter Detection:* Ironically, many forgers somehow
believe that their handwriting is much more personal and
traceable than the impression of a typewriter.

The fact is, however, that the typewriter will often be of more
value in revealing a document's origin than any other writing
instrument.

To those of us who live in the mass produced, automated
society, it is difficult to conceive that a particular machine has a
personality of its own, but this is certainly the case with typewriters and innumerable convicted felons bear eloquent testimony
to this claim. The forger, as well as the general public, is generally
oblivious to the minute differentiation that exists between typewriters. There are a host of variables which provide that each

Fig. 14 Using typewriter standards, an FBI Laboratory technician compares typewriting on a questioned document. *(Courtesy of Federal Bureau of Investigation)*

typewriter shall have its own signature. Among the more significant variables from a scientific detection standpoint are:

(1) The type script design itself.
(2) The wear characteristics of the type script.
(3) The alignment properties of the machine.
(4) The impression characteristics of the machine.
(5) The transfer properties of the ribbon and the constitution of the ribbon itself.
(6) The mode and manner in which the typewriter is operated.
(7) The care and maintenance of the machine at the time of suspect use.
(8) The handling or gripper characteristics of the machine.

(1) *Type Script Design:* The general public and the forger are aware that there are different types of type "faces". However, they are unaware of the range and extent of variations within

seemingly similar faces. The two most popular typewriter styles are the "pica" and the "elite". Type design specimens which are maintained in the National Typewriter Standards File by the Federal Bureau of Investigation, revealed that although maybe a dozen manufacturers may be utilizing a "pica" type design, there are quite distinct differences between each of these manufacturers. There may be some letters which will be closely alike, for example the letter "o", but other letters and numerals will show strikingly different design even when examined without the benefit of microscope.

It should be noted that American typewriter manufacturers produce their own type faces and thus each has a distinctive type face. In cases involving the suspect's use of foreign typewriters, the problem is further complicated. Foreign manufacturers often do not produce their own type. They buy type from various commercial sources for fabrication into their machines. However, the sample spacing of the machine, its back impressions, etc. still provide identification characteristics regardless of the difficulty encountered in type design of European machines.

Even the most professional forgers often provide an accommodating trail as they travel about the country using a single portable typewriter to provide transcript notation onto the face of the forged checks. Others, slightly more ingenious, seek to cover their trail by using rental typewriters. However, this is merely a delaying tactic. Specimens from these machines are available and law enforcement officials in an area have facilities to circularize notices to typewriter rental agencies concerning the description and M.O. suspects.

(2) *Wear Characteristics:* Having established what make and model of typewriter was utilized by the forger, we now proceed to those detection clues which will pinpoint the exact machine. One of the most valuable of these is the wear characteristics of the machine. It can be recognized that as a typewriter is used, with its constant impact of type face against paper and platen, certain wear points in the type design will appear. For example, the serifs of certain characters will become softened or worn. The entire section of a

character may miss altogether. These minute wear spots provide the typewriter with a "signature" all its own. Some enterprising forgers, who have utilized the same typewriter, recognize this basic fact and may in turn attempt to periodically alter the type face by artificial wear, such as filing or emery abrasion. However, these attempts are visually detectable to the experienced analyst and the forger lacks the intricate technical knowledge of design face wear necessary to simulate the wear that actually occurs in the type face.

(3) *Alignment Properties:* No typewriter is so precise an instrument that it does not possess certain alignments, or more correctly misalignments, which help to establish its identity. The document examiner, by placing a carefully constructed grid over the typewritten specimen, and referring to a reference standard produced from the suspect machine, is able to closely evaluate the misalignment properties of the two specimens.

The alignment feature is also valuable in forgeries involving "later additions." When a typewritten portion of the check is completed, and the check then removed from the machine, it creates a situation where subsequent additions or changes are practically impossible. It is merely impossible to return the paper to the machine in the precise alignment in which the original notation occurred. This factor is useful in discovering whether or not all of the typing on the face or back of the check occurred at the same time.

(5) *Ribbon Transfer Properties:* The typewriter ribbon itself naturally becomes an integral part of the signature of the machine. At times the ribbon will be faulty resulting in what appears to be type design defects and this in itself is a signature characteristic of the machine. As with ink, it is also possible to chemically classify and analyze the impression characteristics of the ribbon and to narrow the detection search that much further. Simple visual checks, for ribbon comparison purposes are possible with reagent solutions consisting of 5% glacial acetic acid and 95% ethyl alcohol. These agents provide a quick color comparison for the toner or dye used in the ribbon marking medium.

There are three principal types of ribbons in use today, i.e., Mylar, polyethylene, and fabric. The fabric, in turn, is divided into silk, cotton and nylon. There are about seven varieties of nylon and three each of cotton and silk. The fabric ribbon transfer provides clues in that a thread count through the offset impression is possible. There is also the distinct possibility that neutron activation analysis could pinpoint a particular roll of ribbon and link it to the suspect document.

(6) *Mode and Manner of The Operator:* One of the common fallacies, with regard to typewriter identification, concerns the amount of value that the stroke pattern of the typist lends to identification. The well trained typist produces a document which is so uniform that identification by individual typing habits is often a fruitless task. Since the touch pattern of the practiced typist is so uniform, we are much more likely to derive information on the identity of the person through a close examination of the individual's spelling, punctuation, word division, transposition of letter combinations, etc. This can best be obtained through the oral dictation of a test paragraph to the typist suspect. Typists, particularly those operating on manual machines, may produce a signature all of their own. Their manner of typing, with its consequent pauses and variations in impressions properties etc., introduces another variable which the document examiner is quick to grasp. The principal hope in the linking of a typist to a particular machine lies in the type of training which the forger might possess. If he has been trained in a standard typewriter course, then the problem may reach the point of impossibility. However, many forgers utilize hunt and peck typing techniques which are more individualistic and which provide better chances for the document examiner to trace the typist pattern to the particular machine.

(7) *Care and Maintenance of the Machine:* We frequently can learn a great deal from the amount of care and maintenance a particular machine has received. The most frequent observation concerns clogging of the design faces with ribbon particles. This clogging produces a characteristic type signature which is identifiable, particularly when multiple forged checks are involved.

The clogging of design faces is quite evident when it occurs in the extreme. However, it occurs in the extreme. However, it also occurs in smaller variations and these variations, when photographically enlarged, provide a further clue to detection.

The clogging of design faces is quite evident when it occurs in the extreme. However, it also occurs in smaller variations and these variations, when photographically enlarged, provide a further clue to detection.

(8) *Handling Properties of Machines:* The typewriter often produces additional identifying marks which are of value. For example, it may produce "carbon trees" or smudges on the back of the machine due to previous use. It may also create characteristic wrinkling of the leading edge of the check as it is inserted in the machine. The machine, due to old or loose rollers, may produce a misalignment, as mentioned previously. Guide bars or holddowns may also provide characteristic impressions or abrasions on the surface of the check which are observable under ultraviolet radiation. These marks are often reproducible when law enforcement agents obtain possession of the suspect machine.

Check Writing Machines:

Certainly one of the foremost deterrents to the "amateur" check forger is the utilization of the check writing machine by both large and small businesses. These machines, in their smallest model, can be purchased for less than $150.00 and provides a good first step towards check security. Of course, it should be pointed out that the "professional" check forger will acquire the use of one of these machines either by theft or by purchase.

As the Burroughs survey pointed out, nearly 53% of the check forgery cases involve raising the amount of the check or forging the signature portion. Since the amount being raised is often a crucial part of the forgery, check writing machines provide a deterrent to this activity. The check writing machine is a form of imprinting device which presses a ribbon or ink covered type face into the paper fibers of the check. This impression is of such strength that it actually shreds the paper fibers and produces a series of minute cuts in the paper itself. The check writer uses type face designs which make it extremely difficult to "raise" the original amount to a higher numerical figure. In addition, many models utilize multicolored ribbons. These ribbons thus produce a multicolored impression further complicating the forger's attempt at "raising". The design of the impression is such that the vulnerable ends of the amount impression are closed by the addition of the company's name and the dollar symbol at one end and the "cents" symbol at the opposite end. This prevents obvious alteration and expansion. Some machines, such as the Burroughs machine, produce a sliding prefix which prevents the insertion of numerals before the true amount.

The shredding action on the paper, as typified by the check writer operation, produces a situation where it is more difficult for the forger to apply any type of ink marking material to this area. The more absorbent cut edges of the paper will soak up, with a darker pattern, any coloring material which is applied to them. The exception to this, is if the paper surface is sized in some manner, before such a color alteration is attempted. Fortunately, the technology of such a spot sizing operation is beyond the technical capabilities of 99.5% of the forgers. The remaining small percentage of professional forgers will acquire their own machine.

This brings us to the identification of particular check writing machines. The Federal Bureau of Investigation maintains a Check Writer Standards File which includes type specimens of all of the known check writing machines. As new models are introduced, these machines are sampled, classified and identified. There are a variety of other types of machines also available, some of which are integral parts of fairly automated check processing and disbursing equipment. As mentioned previously, each of these machines has a particular signature and suspect checks can be identified as to the type of machine that was utilized, the approximate year it was produced, and given sufficient standards, even the exact machine that made the impression. From a standpoint of comparison, the check writer impressions, like their typewriter face counterparts, also show signs of wear and deterioration which allow them to be identified. However, it must be admitted that there are not quite as many points of comparison available between check writers when compared with typewriters. In addition, the alignment, etc. characteristics of the check writer machine are not as readily available for comparison. It is equally true that there are not nearly as many check writers in use and from this standpoint tracing may be more easily done than with typewriters where literally millions of machines are in use.

Since the modern check writer frequently uses a ribbon type impression, it is sometimes detectable due to the ink offset provided by the ribbon, the void characteristics of the ribbon, or,

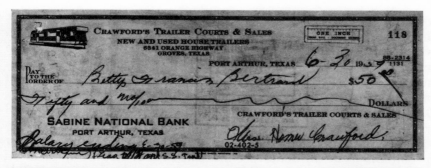

Fig. 15 Top check is as it would appear to the naked eye. The bottom check illustrates the use of ultraviolet fluorescence to reveal a raised and altered check. *(Courtesy of Eastman Kodak Company and the Texas Dept. of Public Safety, Austin, Texas)*

in the case of apprehension of the suspect and the machine, from the actual ribbon itself. The ribbons ordinarily do not have a great number of impressions developed along them and minute inspection of the ribbon might conceivably produce a corresponding set of numerals and characters which would identify the suspect and the machine.

The professional check forger is somewhat hindered by the size and weight of the check writing machines. They are not readily inserted even in their compact model into travelling cases. Unfortunately, recently an imported unit has made its appearance which can fit easily within an attache case. We can think of no other purpose for portability than to facilitate this type of operation.

The document examiner, given the various clues accorded by the imperfection of the check writer type faces, is in a good position to identify the machine. Sometimes forgers come into possession of machines through robberies involving the theft of both checks and check writing machines. At these times, they also come into the possession of signature stamps. The signature machine also produces an impression signature usually from a multi-colored ribbon, and the impression is uniform in depth and profile. It is extremely difficult to forge one of these impressions. However, it should be noted that the professional forger will manage to gain access to a counterfeit signature or will manufacture a counterfeit stamp. There are known M.O. methods for producing both the signature and the impression mechanism on the amount portion utilizing extreme compact, easily accessible equipmenh available on the general market. For the purposes of security these methods are not contained in this report.

To provide security to the check writing machines many of them are equipped with various devices to hinder or foil their theft and use. Most of them have key operated mechanisms and some in turn have alarm devices which go off when the machine is moved from its original position in an office.

The trend in signature machines is to produce a more complicated facsimile signature. In addition to the outline of the signature itself, many of the machines now introduce a seal or monogram in the signature imprint along with a series of broken dotted lines to create additional problems for facsimile counterfeiting. For the vast majority of forgeries, which involve amateur operations, these are effective counter-measures. But we should not delude ourselves into believing that they prevent the professional forger from operating, because they quite frankly do not. However, as has been pointed out numerous times before, they force he professional forger to add one more mark to the check which can aid in his eventual detection and prosecution.

Stamps and Stamping

The insistence of many banks, for the better identification of their check cashers, has led to a wider use of the "certified" check. The certified check, as most readers are aware, certifies that the issuing bank had the face amount of the check on deposit and in escrow for payment against that check. In many cases the face of the check is stamped with the words "Certified" plus a certain signature section for a bank officer. The face may be also imprinted with various devices. Some of the more enterprising forgers have recognized that the existence of such a stamp on the face of the check provides a greater legitimacy and that it lulls the receiver of the check into a false sense of security. In fact, this type of notation on the face often makes it possible for the forger to pass a higher value check.

There are many difficulties, in connection with detection, posed by the use of the stamp. To begin with, the stamp, when black ink is used, may in fact partially obliterate a portion of the writing which would be valuable for reference standard comparison. Thus, some of the identification characteristics of the written portion of the check may be destroyed. However, the stamp itself, like all other marks that the forger prints on the check, can lead to his downfall. There are a known variety of stamp pad inks and the ink itself lends itself to analysis and possible tracing to the forgery suspect. But, most significantly, the rubber stamp is usually produced in such a manner that it has microscopically discernible defects which again give it a signature all its own. It is nearly impossible to exactly counterfeit a particular rubber stamp because of the wear and other peculiarities associated with the individual stamp. The counterfeiting forger could exactly match the type face design and its proportional spacing and alignment, but he would have difficulty matching each and every line in the stamp. Indeed, the bank stamp, as it is used, probably doesn't produce two impressions that are identically the same. The latter factor sometimes complicates the presentation of the evidence. But there are enough unique identifying traits that the bank stamp can be positively identified. In addition, there is the matter of the bank officer's signature which has to be satisfactorily forged or counterfeited.

From a detection standpoint, there are available reference files, which indicate some of the type faces utilized by stamp manufacturers. In addition, detection in tracing is sometimes possible through the stamp producer himself in the event the forger utilized a professional or commercial stamp firm. Often, the stamp firm puts a sample stamp on its various bills, thus providing a permanent record of the impression, and maintains these on file for a period of years. Thus a check-back through the local rubber stamp manufacturers may reveal the existence of this particular stamp. As with everything else associated with this subject, the actual production of rubber stamps is not so complicated and so unique an operation that a professional forging ring could not, and in fact has not already, produced their own rubber stamps thus by-passing the previously mentioned means of detection.

7. PERSONAL IDENTIFYING TRACES

Quite obviously when the forger handles the check, there is a good possibility for personal contamination of the check surface. This contamination is most likely to occur through an inadvertent fingerprint of the suspect. But there are other factors, such as minute particles of hair or skin which may become part of the check. Indeed the environment of the suspect, the dust present, etc. may become a portion of the check. For most practical purposes detection by personal identifying means is limited to fingerprint examination. Although recently, with the development of neutron activation analysis, there is some movement toward more exotic types of identification and tracing.

As the suspect, or for that matter anyone else, handles the paper surface, his finger contact surfaces imprint the paper with a mixture of salt and fatty acids which leave telltale traces on the paper surface. In most cases the suspect documents arrive in a police laboratory sometime after their actual handling by the forger. Therefore, many of the dusting techniques, which are effective on non-absorbent surfaces, do not apply with check specimens. One of the most popular present methods is the use of "ninhydrin" (1, 2, 3, Indantrione Hydrate). A dilute solution of this indicator, in dimethyl ketone, can be sprayed or swabbed onto the suspect areas of the check. The outline of the fingerprint will become visible as a deep blue-red stain. This reaction occurs in the presence of heat and is a reaction between the ninhydrin and the minute quantities of fatty acid deposited on the surface of the check.

One of the occasional difficulties with the ninhydrin treatment involves the reaction of the indicator with one or more of the materials which may be used either in the finish of the paper, the sizing, the safety overprinting, etc. This may produce a staining which would make it difficult to present the suspect document in

Fig. 16 A mixture of ninhydrin and methyl ethyl ketone is sprayed onto a suspect Postal Money Order by a chemist at the U.S. Postal Laboratories in Washington. After drying the ninhydrin will reveal the presence of fingerprints. *(Courtesy of U.S. Postal Laboratories, Washington, D.C.)*

evidence. It is possible that this staining could be localized to a non-signature portion of the check and the specimen still preserved for evidential purposes.

With severely stained specimens a second reaction, involving the reaction between iodine fumes and the fingerprint impression, has also been found to be useful. The iodine fuming is an extremely sensitive reaction in that it will readily yield even light fingerprint impressions. However, the resulting impressions must be photographed quickly because of their transient nature.

Despite the effectiveness of the ninhydrin process, the law enforcement agent is often faced with the fact that only one or two prints appear on the check. Unless the other factors in the modus operandi point to a particular criminal, identification with simply one or two latent prints can become extremely difficult. For example, consider the following statistics drawn from an actual case study by The New York State Identification and Intelligence

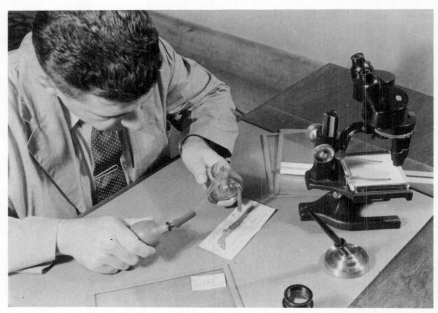

Fig. 17 An FBI Laboratory technician uses an iodine fume test to develop latent prints on a suspect document. *(Courtesy of Federal Bureau of Investigation)*

System Report. This report indicates that given two fingerprints, both on the right hand, one of which is from the index finger and is an ulnar loop with a ridge count of 9, and the other from the right middle finger with an ulnar loop and a ridge count of 12, a list of one million possible suspect cards would produce 45,000 separate candidate prints. The problem becomes even greater if only the right middle finger were obtained. In this case, 370,000 prints could be selected from a file of one million. However, many state and federal agencies have recognized this problem and have created, in addition to their general fingerprint file, a separate smaller file. These are so arranged so that it is possible to search them on a finger by finger process. These smaller files usually contain only a few thousand prints and are of primary value to specialists who are in turn looking for a specialist in a particular area of crime.

One report indicates that "latent prints are not widely used in attempting to identify criminals and are more widely used to confirm identification or to eliminate suspects". *(Task Force Report; Science and Technology, Report to the President's Commission on Law Enforcement and Administration of Justice, prepared by the Institute for Defense Analysis.)* Sometimes, the submission of prints by one law enforcement agency is of distinct value to other agencies interested in the same individual. For example in 1968, 31,404 fugitives sought by state or local law enforcement agencies were identified by fingerprints submitted to the FBI by agencies other than the agencies wanting the persons.

Photograph for Forgery Detection

The photograph, with all its modern potentials, remains one of the single most important tools available to the document examiner. Photography not only provides a valuable evidential material, but it also directly establishes the existence of forgery in many cases. Most laymen are vaguely familiar with the limitations of the human eye, in connection with their ability to see extremely small objects or objects extremely far away. However, they are generally ignorant about the limitations of the human eye to observe minute differences in color, texture, spectra absorption, etc.

The first and foremost point we should resolve is that photography, for the purposes of forgery detection and prosecution, is the province of a qualified document examiner. A commercial photographer, no matter how well intentioned or skilled, is extremely unlikely to possess the specialized knowledge required for document photography. Nothing is more disconcerting than to have a court presentation utilizing photo reproductions of a suspect document which fail to capitalize on the forensic possibilities of modern day photography. In addition, the document examiners are often called upon to examine check specimens in which the original is retained by a bank or commercial institution and a

Xerox or photostat reproduction is forwarded to the document examiner. Needless to say, this severely inhibits the photographic possibilities for detection. Wherever possible the original document should be placed in the hands of the examiner. Many of the copying processes, while suitable for commercial office routines, are completely unsuitable for documentation examination.

Types of Photo Reproduction:-For most recording and evidence purposes a two-dimensional type photo is required. The exception to this involves cases where angular photography may be suggested as a means to illustrate the impression characteristics of the forgery or the existence of tracing, etc. However, for most photos the two-dimensional photo is the type utilized. It is in this area where commercial photography often produces an unsatisfactory example because of the variances in lighting and the consequent variances in emulsion thickness in the finished negative.

One of the simplest methods of copying is referred to as *reflex* copying. In essence reflex copying involves using the original document, check, etc., as a negative and allowing a light source to pass through the suspect document and onto a slow, high contrast photo paper. Exposures of this variety naturally take some experimentation because of the differences in density of the suspect document. In general the exposure may range from 30 seconds to more than a minute.

A second type of reproduction is the *photostat*. Photostats are very often confused with photographs. In practice, the photostat is made with a special camera which produces no film negatives. The photographic paper is actually in the camera itself. The negative is a reverse of the image. This process projects the image from the suspect document into the camera and directly onto the paper. The size of the image is controlled through bellows arrangements in the equipment. This process produces a two-dimensional photo which is suitable for many primary comparison purposes, but often lacks the detail obtainable by fine grain conventional photography.

The third process, of conventional photography, is generally understood by most persons. In this process the suspect document is held in place, such as in a vacuum plate, is evenly illuminated and photographed. A regular photographic negative is produced and from this negative enlargements or reductions are possible. By varying the type of film and its grain qualities different degrees of detail are possible. Most of the photographs produced for document examination utilize conventional variations provided by filters, lighting, etc. In the majority of cases the photographer still utilizes the black and white process. There has been an increase within the past four or five years in the use of color photography. The utilization of Kodak Ektacolor print film has been valuable in establishing patterns of ballpoint pen marking, particularly when this writing is over a typewritten surface. The typewriter ribbon ink acts as an inhibitor and the ballpoint pen glides across this marking without depositing ink. The application of color photography in such cases does provide the document examiner with a good contrast photo useful for detection purposes.

Within the field of conventional photography, the document examiner utilizes such variations as color filters to balance the light and photo emulsion properties during the photo process. He

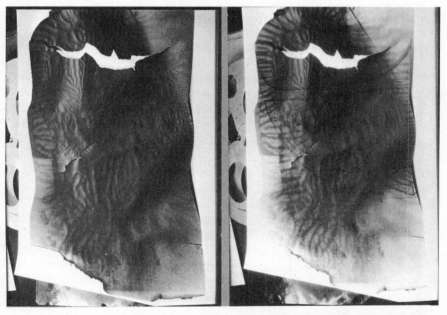

Fig. 18 Charred paper can also be restored through infra-red photo techniques. Photo on the left as it appeared to the naked eye. Photo on the right made using infra-red photography. (Courtesy Eastman Kodak Company, Rochester, N.Y.)

also makes use of ultraviolet, infra-red and fluorescent photography to illustrate properties of the suspect document which would not be visible to the naked eye. These photographs are often produced with compensating filters which provide unusually effective detection devices. For example, some forgers may deliberately sprawl their signature or endorsement over a previously printed line or signature in the hope of partially obliterating their own signature should it later be the subject of examination.

Through the use of special filters the document examiner can "drop-out" the confusing line behind the forger's signature, thus leaving only the forged line. Variations of this same technique are also valuable in determining cases where the amount of the check has been "raised". This raising process, which is described in the section on modus operandi, invariably uses a different type of ink. Since the various inks either fluoresce or absorb infrared spectra at varying rates, it is possible to obtain a special photograph which will "pop-out" the raised portion of the check. The altered line will appear in different color print thus graphically illustrating the fact that the check has been raised.

Standards or Comparison Materials

Forgery is the type of criminal offense in which we often find that there are no witnesses to the event other than the documents themselves. On the face of it, it would then appear that it is obvious we have extensive need for comparison handwriting standards. The most basic axiom that the businessman, bank officer, law enforcement officer, etc. can apply is: "We cannot obtain too many comparison materials, but we are very likely to obtain too little."

Second, and an equally important axiom, concerns the fact that we should be *comparing like materials.* In the case of a forger, where we are dealing with a check or credit card, we should be comparing signatures, dates, locations, etc. that are on checks or credit cards and not on letters, registration forms, blank pieces of paper, etc. This is not to imply that the latter materials are useless, because quite obviously they have a very valuable function in establishing the plan, letter pattern, etc. of the suspect. But it is true that persons sometimes employ different handwriting procedures on checks, particularly in the signature section, than they do in letters, delivery receipts, etc. As previously mentioned in the "form" method, there is something to be gained from noting where the suspect placed the signature, the date, the face amount of the check, etc. The proportional spacing, in relation to the lines provided, can be extremely valuable in providing a pattern of check completion.

In civil document examination the document examiner is often faced with the need to trace the evolution of a person's signature over a number of years. As we become adults our signatures standardize. They follow a slow evolutionary pattern except for abrupt changes which may be attributed to illness or old age. From a forgery detection standpoint, most crimes of forgery, and the subsequent apprehension of the suspect, hopefully occur over a relatively short period of time. Thus, we can usually expect relatively little alteration in the basic signature pattern of the person.

In many instances in which comparison material proved a weak link in the prosecution, plain negligence was involved. In some cases innocent ignorance on the part of the arresting officer may have been a factor. He may not have known what materials were needed and consequently did not obtain them. This is a matter of liaison between the documentation and forgery sections of the police forces. In smaller police departments the educational process is not as refined and the investigating officer may not have taken the trouble to obtain the standards required for later prosecution. Secondly, the arresting officer may feel that with the physical apprehension of the forger his task is complete and there is no need to obtain additional materials.

Many police departments have recognized that there is a need to obtain more extensive samples of a forger's hand. Their methods have been to develop a standardized handwriting specimen sheet on which the suspect writes out certain words, phrases, and letter groups during his arrest. These words and letter patterns are repeated a number of times and often include numerical combinations which aid in the establishment of the pattern. Also, since spelling and punctuation are an individualistic ability, the arresting officer may dictate a series of paragraphs designed to provide a clue to the spelling and punctuation peculiarities of the suspect. This type of handwriting and pen printing classification system has been codified by a number of agencies.

Director David Purtell, of the Chicago Scientific Crime Detection Laboratory, has developed a handwriting standard system which seems to work reasonably well and which takes into account the ethnic characteristics of the Chicago area. This method evolved from a 10-15 year development project. A systematic analysis was made of all of the Chicago telephone directories. The purpose of this analysis was to develop those names which were most common to the Chicago area. A statistical analysis of the most frequently occurring names provided 17 separate names which forgery suspects are asked to write. In reality these 17 separate names contain many more names hidden within their structure. In addition, some of the first names such as Thomas, Peter, Lawrence, Davis, etc. can also be family names. The reader will note the names Novak and Kowalski. These are frequently occurring names in the Chicago area which has a sizable Slavic ethnic concentration. These names also provide letter combinations which are frequently encountered within this ethnic concentration.

In addition, Purtell's form also provides an extremely well constructed hand-print standard. From a thorough analysis of their obscene, anonymous, and threatening letter file, the Chicago police constructed a note which contains, again hidden within their structure, some of the most frequently found obscene or threatening words. Any suspect can print this message without discomfort or without challenge from his attorney. Yet, the letter combinations, when skillfully broken apart, will provide many of the words found in the anonymous letter files. A sample of the handprint method is noted below:

"The money in dollars which Dick Zass received from Virginia McLong was placed in her auto without trouble. It was laying covered by a slick cape and with luck would never be found, but a pussy jumped on the seat and killed the obnoxious trick."

The Chicago form also includes spaces for the suspect to sign his name a number of times and to fill out various numerical designations as would be found on a check. This section gives the suspect an opportunity to write out amounts, provide their numerical equivalent, and to fill in a specified date. It also provides an indication of how the suspect writes a particular address and what abbreviations he characteristically uses for such things as avenues, boulevards, roads, streets, States, etc.

In addition, the Chicago police laboratory also has a series of blank checks printed and the suspect is provided with these and asked to fill one out for a specified amount and to a particular party. These checks are valuable in establishing the form pattern which we have previously noted.

There are some problems connected with the utilization of standards forms. One of them obviously concerns the admissibility of self-incriminating evidence procured during arrest. Since there is still some controversy on the notification and admissibility of such statements, we will proceed no further into that subject at this point. There also are some conflicts of opinion between document examiners as to whether or not the letter and work patterns obtained in this manner represent a completely true picture of the suspect's handwriting. The circumstances of production are artificial and many suspects will believe that they can disguise their handwriting and certainly attempt to do so on these records. Also, from a form standpoint, the records may not simulate the spacing and design characteristics of a check. That is why, as the author has noted previously, it is much more advisable to utilize like materials for comparison standard purposes. Some document examiners also question whether or not the unusual circumstances of the production of handwriting, during an arrest period, might be subject to questioning because of the emotional effects which could alter the suspect's handwriting standards.

In the case of the professional forger the situation is further complicated because he recognizes the possibilities of incrimination through filling in these forms, and he probably will stand on his constitutional rights and simply write nothing whatever once he is apprehended. Therefore, it is incumbent to obtain all of samples of his handwriting such as might be available on driver's registration, membership cards, auto registration cards, letters, receipts, etc. in addition to as many samples of his fraudulent checks as are obtainable.

One of the typical methods of providing a writing standard, in addition to those methods described by the Chicago Police Department, is the use of the so-called "London Business Letter". This letter was described by Albert S. Osborn in his excellent book "Questioned Documents". This letter has been specifically designed so as to include all of the upper and lower case alphabet characters plus the complete range of numerals and some common abbreviations. The form is provided in such a manner so that the suspect will not be completely aware that he is providing a complete record of his handwriting characteristics with regard to each and every letter in the alphabet. The letter is as follows:

"Our London business is good, but Vienna and Berlin are quiet. Mr. D. Lloyd has gone to Switzerland and I hope for good news. He will be there for a week at 1496 Zermott Street and then goes to Turin and Rome and will join Col. Parry and arrive at Athens, Greece, Nov. 27th or Dec. 2d. Letters there should be addressed; King James Blvd. 3580. We expect Chas. E. Fuller Tuesday. Dr. L. McQuaid and Robt. Unger, Esq., left on the "Y.X." EXPRESS tonight."

Both the use of the "London Business Letter" and the use of certain standard forms, as noted previously, create problems. To begin with, if the suspect is not guilty he will make no attempt to disguise his known handwriting. The guilty suspect, particularly if he is a professional, can probably be expected to consistently attempt to disguise his handwriting and it may well be that all of the "standards" uncovered during the arrest also consist of disguised handwriting. If all of the subject's disguised standards are known by the suspect to be in police possession, he might well revert to this true hand and thus confound the situation further.

In obtaining typewriter standards, it is important that we have the suspect typist both produce a test paragraph and also provide a paragraph illustrating the use of a light, medium and heavy touch. In the case of electric typewriters, this factor is of less importance since the impression is governed by the machine itself not the typist. The investigating officer might also obtain samples of the ribbon used in the typewriter. This is valuable from a standpoint of typewriter ribbon analysis as well as frth the actual pick off of words which may appear on the ribbon itself. Many of the new typewriters use "carbon" ribbon which proceeds through the typewriter in a single pass. Obtaining such a ribbon can provide us with the complete text of a document previously written on the machine. All specimens obtained should contain pertinent information on the make, model and serial number of the typewriter from which it was produced as well as the date of production and the identification of the investigating officer. As pointed out, samples of the typewriter ribbon are valuable because of the ink transposed from the ribbon becomes an integral part of the scientific detection process.

The analysis of both fluid inks and ballpoint inks, through chromatography has been well established in forensic science. This same technique, employing thin-layer chromatography may be applied to typewriter ribbon inks. The typewriter ink may be either extracted from the actual ribbon sample or may be obtained directly from the document. In some cases, the ink is lifted through the use of an extracting solvent and a sable brush directly off the typewritten specimen. In other cases, it is transferred in a letterpress blotting action using a chemically pure filter paper. The offset impression from the suspect document is contained on the contacting, solvent saturated, filter paper and is at a later point extracted from the filter paper, condensed and then analyzed through normal thin layer chromatography methods.

Establishing the Age of Forged Documents

One of the most difficult tasks for a document examiner involves the detection of a forged document's actual age. This factor could be critical in prosecutions involving counterfeit or facsimile checks. When the problem of forgery and age is thought of, most law enforcement officers relate to the measurement of ink age as the most important barometer of the forged document's age. The problem here is that at the present time nearly all Americans are using ballpoint pens. The inks in the ballpoint pens are completely organic, consisting of an organic vehicle and an organic dye. When the fountain pen type of forgery occurred, the various inks contained inorganic materials such as iron, chlorides, etc. It was possible to measure chloride migration, for example, and to determine approximately how long ago the material had been written. However, we might quote from a recent FBI report which notes that "ballpoint inks thus far have not yielded to *any* methods by means of which the age of such writing may be determined." This factor obviously inhibits the analysis of the document, from an ink factor standpoint, during age determinations.

However, there are other factors which may be used and principal among these are the watermarks or paper stock utilized in the check manufacture. Some paper manufacturers have taken to encoding, in a disguised manner, the approximate date of production of the paper by small marks or defects which occur in the dandy roll which produces the watermarks.

Unfortunately, many papers do not contain watermarks and in other cases the original document, such as a check, is such a small piece of paper as to render extensive analysis unsuitable from the standpoint of destroying vital evidence. There is no practical method to analyze paper and to determine its age. More often, the age of a paper document is determined by what is imprinted on it than by any attempt at the analysis at the paper fibers or the sizing contained on the surface of the paper.

Erasures, Alterations, Restorations

Many cases of forgery inevitably involve erasures. Erasures, or alterations which follow the erasure, are detectable through a variety of scientific aids. In some cases the forger comes into possession of a check which does not lend itself to "raising" through character manipulation. The amount or payee of the check may have to be completely erased or obliterated in order for the forger to raise the check and change the payee. In these cases, the forger resorts to a variety of erasure methods. One of the most frequently used methods involves abrading the paper surface with an India rubber eraser, sandpaper, razor blade, sharp knife, etc. Following such erasures the forger may attempt to restore the background area through cleverly tinting the paper surface to resemble the background and then placing the payee's name or raised amount in the altered area of the check.

All of these erasures produce changes in the uppermost layer of the paper. These changes, regardless of the forger's success in restoring coloration, can be detected through microscopic examination using direct, incident or back lighting. While this method will reveal that an erasure has been made it will not necessarily indicate the original amount or the payee. Sometimes so much of the paper surface has been removed that is impossible to detect the original amount. Besides microscopic examination, with varying light sources, the document examiner may also choose to dust the surface with a distinguishing carbon powder which will be entrapped by the roughened surface area of the paper and which will slide off the smooth natural finished sized area of the check.

In addition to abrading the surface, the forger may also choose to obliterate the surface with a chemical erasure. In this case strong oxidizing agents are placed in fluid form on the dyestuff of the ink. A reaction occurs between the organic dye and the oxidizing agent which produces a colorless reaction product. The document examiner has available to him examination techniques, either by ultraviolet or infra-red light, which may reveal the existence of a chemical erasure. In addition, there are a range of reagents which will reverse the oxidizing reaction and restore the color of the original organic dye.

Some of the more clever forgers have also attempted to raise checks by overprinting the affected area with what appears to be a block design on the check. For a person receiving the check, being unfamiliar with the design, this may prove to be an initially effective strategm. Through an extremely delicate process the document examiner is able to lift the overlay area. In addition, through the use of transmitted light, it can often be determined that a previous amount was printed in the suspected area. As noted before, infra-red radiation will pass through organic dye inks and be absorbed by pencil writing and some types of typewriting and printing inks containing inorganic pigments. Thus, the use of infra-red photography will often reveal an u derlyi g area that the forger has attempted to overprint with an obliterating organic pigment film.

Uniqueness of Handwriting

Document experts again and again have come into court to testify to the fact that no two signatures are exactly alike. This assertion is often challenged by defense attorneys and elaborate proofs are necessary to show a jury that signatures, like fingerprints, are unique to each and every individual. A number of studies have been conducted and the thousands of signatures compiled by organizations such as the Federal Bureau of Investigation stand as eloquent testimony to the uniqueness of an individual signature.

Perhaps, one of the most interesting experiments concerning this individuality was performed by the U.S. Postal Inspection Service. This experiment, conceived by Laboratory Director Albert B. Somerford, involved an investigation of the handwriting characteristics of identical twins. Previous work by other researchers had shown that identical twins bore so many physical, psychological and mental resemblances that there often seemed to

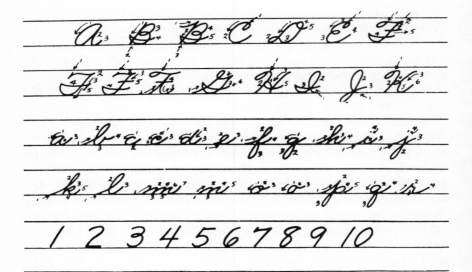

Fig. 19 An illustration of one of the several hundred different handwriting systems that have been taught in the United States. *(Courtesy of U.S. Postal Laboratories. From Colonial Writing Elements copyright by American Southern Publishing Company)*

be a unity of personality between the twins. It was reasoned that if any two individuals should have closely alike or similar handwriting then certainly twins with their very similar physical characteristics, motor response patterns, personality patterns, etc. should exhibit this similarity.

In a massive study by the Postal Laboratory, 500 separate sets of fraternal and identical twins were examined. This study required several years to complete. Six qualified document examiners, experienced and highly trained, spent weeks meticulously examining and analyzing the various handwriting specimens for these twins. It was theorized, as mentioned previously, that twins, because they were so physically and mentally alike, should show some similarity in handwriting. This similarity might provide evidence as to the possibility of identical handwriting occurring between any two individuals. A complete examination of all of these twins signatures revealed that the differences in handwriting between the 500 sets of twins were as individualistic and as unique as might be expected between any other non-related individuals in the general population.

There have been cases, some of them related in this study, where individuals have been falsely convicted of forgery only to be later exonerated on the basis of a skilled document examiner's proof that handwriting is as individualistic as fingerprints. This is not to say that there will not be marked resemblances between two individuals' handwritings. However, as with fingerprints, handwriting between two persons can never be exactly duplicated. Differences will naturally occur in the angularity, slope, speed, pressure, lateral spacing, size ratio, relative dimensions of letters, connections, pen scope, writing skill, finger dexterity, etc. In addition two persons are prevented from writing exactly the same because of their own individual mechanical, physical or mental characteristics at the moment of writing. It is extremely unlikely that two persons would possess such coordination as to perform exactly alike in connection with all of these factors. Resemblances often occur because of the penmanship training that two suspects might have received.

American handwriting instruction has become more standardized in the past decade or so. In most cases the "business hand" type of penmanship has dominated American education since 1900. The two most widely used systems are the Palmer, first introduced in 1888, and the Zaner-Bloser, introduced about 1895. To some extent both of these systems are still employed in nearly all of our 50 states. At the end of World War II the A. N. Palmer Company reported that their system was used in about 75% of the American parochial schools, but since that time there has been an alteration in that percentage because of new penmanship methods. In the same period the Zaner-Bloser Company also noted their material was being used in foreign countries such as China, Australia, Cuba, Canada, New Zealand, Mexico, Philippines, Turkey, etc.

Most forgery suspects produce clearly identifiable right hand writing patterns. Very few people are possessed with enough manual dexterity to write with either hand. Left hand writers comprise between 3 and 5% of the total population.

In connection with the individuality of a person's handwriting, it is also pertinent to note that most writers reach "graphic maturity" in their early 20s. Prior to that time the child normally passes through three different writing stages in which the nerve and motor response pattern gradually change to a more and more fixed method. Illustrated above are some of the typical hand-writing systems utilized in the United States during the past several decades. However, in addition to the many American handwriting systems, some of which are so individual as to provide a direct link to a particular suspect, we also have a problem of handwriting characteristics of immigrants and other parties taught penmanship in foreign educational systems.

In the period between 1900 and 1950 nearly 20 million immi-grants came to the United States. Most of these individuals carried with them intact the penmanship system of their native land. A basic familiarity with these systems often provides a vital clue in determining the nationality of a forger or anonymous writer who is producing a handwriting pattern not recognizable as an American hand. The Postal Laboratories have compiled a volume entitled "Foreign Systems of Handwriting." Samples from this volume, with the kind permission of the Postal In-spection Service are illustrated above. They graphically show that different nationalities do produce handwriting with peculiar indi-vidual national traits.

How these national traits can be employed in a forgery investigation are best illustrated by one incident which involved the U.S. Postal Inspectors. In this particular incident t ere were a group of 300 postal money orders stolen from a New York area post office. Sixteen of these money orders were forged and negotiated. Investigation narrowed the possibilities to that of a postal clerk, but there were innumerable postal clerks who had access to the group of money orders. Samples of the clerks' handwritings provided further narrowed the case to an individual clerk. How-ever, the clerk's handwriting appeared only on the face of the money order and this was ntt forgery per se. The endorsements were t ose of another party.

The close examination of the endorsement writing character-istics revealed that they were probably those of an individual who had learned to write in Germany. This information was passed on to the Postal Inspectors in the field and they determined that the suspect clerk was in fact having an illicit relationship with a girl of German origin. This young German female refugee was apparent-ly providing the endorsements for the checks. Quietly the postal inspectors obtained a sample of the refugee's handwriting from a series of letters that she had written to an acquaintance in

Аа Бб Вв Гг Дд Ее Ёё

Аа Бб Вв Гг Дд Ее Ёё

A B C D E F G H I J K
L M N O P Q R S T

Aa Bb Cc Dd Ee
Ff Gg Hh Ii Jj

A B C D E F G H
I J K L M N O P

Fig. 20 An illustration of the varying handwriting systems of foreign educational systems. (Extracted with permission from "Foreign Handwriting Systems" by the U.S. Postal Laboratories, Washington, D.C.)

Maryland. These handwriting samples were brought to the laboratory and positively identified as those on the endorsement. Armed with this information they confronted the suspect clerk and were able to obtain a confession and conviction.

Neutron Activation Analysis in Forgery Detection

For the past several years the U. S. Internal Revenue Service, in cooperation with the Atomic Energy Commission and with the law enforcement branches of other federal agencies, has been actively utilizing high-flux activation analysis as an important new tool in forensic science. During this period over three hundred criminal cases have received the scrutiny of the neutron activation analysis process. The Post Office Department has employed the technique for the examination of several hundred specimens from postal inspection cases, many which involve forgery and fraud.

The historical background on this test method arises out of the peculiar needs of the Internal Revenue Service to obtain minutely accurate analyses and comparisons of opiums grown in varying geographical districts. Similar needs in connection with illicit whiskey production justified the needs for this type of analytical tool.

The Internal Revenue Service first introduced physical evidence, as examined by activation analysis, in an historic federal court case, in which activation analysis accuracy was accepted by federal and state courts.

Several law enforcement agencies are now utilizing the neutron activation analysis and technique. In practice, the activation analysis process is valuable in that it is possible to analyze extremely small specimens in a non-destructive manner. The process utilizes a tank containing 60,000 gallons of heavy water and a conveying mechanism which allows about 200 samples to be treated simultaneously. A pneumatic tube propels these samples to within inches of the core of the reactor. An activation switch bombards the samples with neutrons reducing their half-lives. A multi-channel, gamma-ray analyzer then quantitatively and qualitatively determines the precise chemical composition of the physical evidence specimen. This examination technique allows the chemist to detect a large number of elements which fall into the trace category. He can detect these elements in the parts per billion range and with such precision that close matching and tracing are very feasible. In a new modification of the original system the analyzer element will punch out tapes in computer language and the computer memory banks will point out the composition from reference standards stored in its memory banks.

Fig. 21 A Postal Laboratory chemist examines a computer printout following the neutron activation analysis of suspect material. The analysis provides qualitative and quantitative values in terms of parts per billion. *(Courtesy of U.S. Postal Laboratories, Washington, D.C.)*

The results of this technique are impressive when one considers that thus far they have produced a 100% conviction ratio. This method of analysis is reputed to be one thousand times more sensitive than the most advanced spectrographic activation analysis method.

The Postal Inspection Laboratories are now involved in a neutron activation analysis project which will provide extremely precise data on various ballpoint inks. Such data would be

particularly valuable in forgery cases involving promissory note
alterations, check raisings, etc. It would also be valuable in the
precise analysis of counterfeit ink used on bogus checks and other
fiscal documents.

Besides inks, papers themselves also can be analyzed through
this new detection method. A positive conclusion as to whether
two papers were procured from the same lot could conceivably be
made through this method. However, before accepting such results, additional work will be necessary to define the extent of
variations to be found within a single block of paper.

Neutron activation could show whether two documents came
from the same lot of paper and such comparison would be valuable
in many cases of fraud and forgery. Suspected check materials
could be compared with authentic check stocks. In addition, this
analytical method could help identify burnt paper, including
checks and securities which may have been partially destroyed by
forgers in an attempt to get rid of physical evidence. Several
forgery cases have already been decided through the use of
neutron activation analysis. In one case the authenticity of a
ledger entry was questioned. The key question was whether or not
the entry had been made simultaneously with other entries or at a
point five years later as was suspected. A dilute solution of nitric
acid was used to remove the ink from bot the questioned entry and
the known entry. These were analyzed. Ink from the questioned
and known entries showed exactly the same amounts of antimony,
copper, chlorine, iridium and sodium. On this basis, it was decidee
that the questioned entry had in fact been made simultaneously
with the known entries.

In another case involving the Postal Inspectors, a stamp fraud
was uncovered when a stamp collector attempted to enhance the
value of a new commemorative stamp by meticulously bleaching
out one color of the stamp. He then claimed that the Bureau of
Printing and Engraving had "misprinted" the stamp in question.
Several of these "rare" stamps were sold to unsuspecting collectors. A fraud investigation and subsequent neutron activation
analysis showed that all of the elements of the original ink, as used
in the color for that portion of the stamp, were still present on the
paper surface although they had been changed and bleached so as
to resemble an unprinted area. On the basis of this analysis, a
fraud conviction was attained.

Fig. 22 FBI technician conducts a search through the National Fraudulent Check File. Over 100,000 check samples are contained in this file. *(Courtesy of Federal Bureau of Investigation)*

The National Fraudulent Check File

The National Fraudulent Check File was first established by the F.B.I. in 1936. It is maintained within the F.B.I. Laboratories in Washington, D.C. Contained within these files are approximately 100,000 separate check specimens. These specimens are in the form of photographs of checks and signatures as obtained through direct F.B.I. investigation and through the cooperative efforts of law enforcement agencies in the 50 States. The National Fraudulent Check File is in reality a series of files. These files act as crosschecks and as ready reference tools with which to examine various portions of the checks.

The National Fraudulent Check File is organized to contain photographs of all true names and aliases as they appear on fraudulent checks. In addition to these sub-divisions, the file is also organized to contain photographs of checks which are hand-written, handprinted, typewritten, prepared with check protectors, rubber stamps, etc.

The value of the National Fraudulent Check File lies in its unique ability to retrieve patterns of operations and characteristics of signatures, in such a manner as to positively identify the forger. Other files, such as the Typewriter Standards File, provides F.B.I. document examiners with samples of type faces, information on models and years of manufacture of both domestic and foreign typewriters. Data derived from this file, when typewriter methods are employed in preparing the fiscal document, is included in the investigative packet of a forgery suspect. In a similar manner, the checkwriter Standards File is also of value to investigative agencies. This file contains standards of the numerical type faces, i.e.; the design of the type, for all of the principal check writing machines. The Paymaster, Hedman, Todd, etc. machines are cataloged according to model, date of issuance, etc. As noted previously each check writing machine, in imprinting its numerical values, has an "identity" all of its own.

There are also sub-division files such as the National Safety Paper Standards File, etc. As noted previously, the National Fraudulent Check File contains over 100,000 photos of checks and signatures. This, however, does not necessarily indicate that there are some 50 or 100 different slots within this file system. Prolific forgers such as Courtney Townsend Taylor, etc. are well represented within the file.

One of the basic purposes of this National File is to tie-together, for the very many law enforcement agencies involved, bogus checks which are passed throughout the nation by individual check passers ranging far and wide.

Scattered throughout the country are a number of smaller index files on check forgers as maintained by urban police agencies. Some of these, such as the New York City file, actually pre-date the National Fraudulent Check File. However, many of these are indexed in manner substantially different from the National Fraudulent Check File and of course different from each other. The National File is extremely valuable in that it provides for a central repository for all types of fraudulent check cases. In addition, it also provides various law enforcement agencies with a vital cross-check on each other's indexing system. The purpose of the National Fraudulent Check File was not necessarily to eliminate local index systems as used by local law enforcement agencies. The needs and dimensions of these local index systems fit the specific requirements of local law enforcement climate and it is important that such local systems also be maintained.

F.B.I. Operation Prochek

In these days of automation it was only a matter of time before the talents of the computer were turned toward the problem of identifying forgers. The F.B.I. has initiated a system, designated "PROCHEK" which stands for "Professional Check Passers".

The F.B.I. system operates essentially as a sophisticated information retrieval mechanism. It encodes all of the known data on the suspect, and the crime. It then sorts out those previously programmed suspects whose prior history meets the details provided in the suspect case.

It has been variously estimated that there are many hundreds of hard core, top flight "professional" check forgers operating in the United States. These are the "cream of the crop" and represent a serious investigative problem for law enforcement agents throughout the United States. In many cases, these forgers have prior arrest records and so detailed data exists on the operations of these forgers. Personnel at the F.B.I. Laboratory have searched their records, contained in the National Fraudulent Check File, and created a library of data on such known individuals.

At this point it is probably too early to tell how effective PROCHEK is going to be. A great deal of data must be programmed into the library of the computer before highly sophisticated and meaningful comparisons can be made. However, this step by the Federal Bureau of Investigation is an extremely important first stage in making use of the recall capabilities of the computer.

Bibliography

Conway, James V., **EVIDENTIAL DOCUMENTS** (Springfield, Ill.; Charles C. Thomas, 1959)

Curray, A. F., **METHOD OF FORENSIC SCIENCE** (New York; Interscience Publishers, 1964)

Galland, Joseph F., **HISTORICAL AND ANALYTICAL BIBLIOGRAPHY OF THE LITERATURE OF CRYPTOLOGY** (Chicago; Northwestern University, 1945)

Harrison, Wilson R., **SUSPECT DOCUMENTS — THEIR SCIENTIFIC EXAMINATION** (Sweet & Maxwell, Ltd. London, F. A. Praeger-New York)

   FORGERY DETECTION, A PRACTICAL GUIDE (New York; Frederick A. Praeger, 1964)

Hilton, Ordway., **SCIENTIFIC EVALUATION OF QUESTIONED DOCUMENTS** (Chicago: Callahan & Co. 1956)

Karch, R. Randall., **HOW TO RECOGNIZE TYPE FACES** (Bloomington, Ill.; McKnight & McKnight Publishing Co., 1959)

LaFave, Wayne R., **"DETENTION FOR INVESTIGATION BY POLICE"**; (An analysis of current practices) (Washington University Law Quarterly 1962)

Mehta, M. A., **IDENTIFICATION OF HANDWRITING AND THE CROSS EXAMINATION OF EXPERTS** (Bombay; N. M. Tripathi, Private, Ltd., 1961-

Piven, Herman and Alcaves, Abraham., **EDUCATION AND TRAINING FOR CRIMINAL JUSTICE** (Washington; Government Printing Office)

Sutherland, Edwin H., **PRINCIPLES OF CRIMINOLOGY** (New York; J. P. Lippincott Co., 1947)

Tiffany, Lawrence P. et al., **DETECTION OF CRIME** (Boston; Little Brown 1967)

Articles

Baum, "Color Photography Used To Counterfeit Facsimiles", Banking, April, 1952, Vol. 44, Page 37

Black, David A., "Forgery Above A Genuine Signature", Journal of Criminal Law, Criminology and Police Science, Vol. 50, 1959-Page 585.

Black, David A., "Fraudulent Check Notation", Journal of Criminal Law, Criminology and Criminal Science, Vol. 54, 1963, Page 220

Black, David A., "Forged Signatures More Skillfully Written Than True Signatures", Journal of Criminal Law, Criminology and Criminal Science, Vol. 53, 1962, Page 109

Bruning, A., "A Genuine Counterfeit", International Criminal Police Review, No. 72, Nov., 1953

Conway, J. V. T., "The Identification of Hand Printing", Journal of Criminal Law-Criminology and Police Science-Volume 45.

Crown, David A. and Conway, James and Kirk, Paul L., "Differentiation of Blue Ballpoint Pen Inks", Journal of Criminal Law, Criminology and Criminal Science, Vol. 52, 1961, Page 338

Dodud, Donald, "The Cromographic Analysis of Inks", Journal of Forensic Sciences, Oct. 1958

Downey, "Disguised Handwriting", Journal of Applied Psychology, Volume 1917

Godwoon, Lindon, "The New Non-Destructive Document Testing Method", Journal of Criminal Law, Criminology and Criminal Science, 1964, No. 55, Page 280

Guven, E., "The Signature", International Criminal Police Review, Volume 53, Many, 1952

Harris, John L., "Typewriting — Original and Carbon Copies", Journal of Criminal Law, Criminology and Criminal Science, Vol. 50, 1959, Page 211.

"Disguised Handwriting", Journal of Criminal Law, Criminology and Police Science, Volume 43, No. 5, January, 1953.

Harrison, Wilson R., "The Detection of Fingerprints on Documents", International Criminal Law Review, 1958, Sept., Page 591-599.

Hilton, Ordway and Stein, E. W., "Ballpoint Pen, Use For signing Documents Considered" - American Bar Association Journal, May, 1948

"Can The Forger Be Identified From His Handwriting?" - Journal of Criminal Law, Criminology and Police Science, Volume 43, #4, December, 1952

"Problems In the Identification of Proportional Spacing Typewriting", Journal of Forensic Sciences (3) July, 1958, Page 263-287

"Proof Of An Unaltered Document", Journal of Criminal Law, Criminology and Criminal Science, Vol. 49, 1950, Page 601

"The Influence of Variation On Typewriting Identification" - Journal of Criminal Law, Criminology and Criminal Science-Vol. 50, 1959 Page 420.

"Pencil Erasures - Detection and Decipherment" - Journal of Criminal Law, Criminology and Criminal Science, Vol. 53, Page 381

"A Further Look At Writing Standards" - Journal of Criminal Law, Criminology and Criminal Science, Volume 56, No. 3, 1965

"Proper Evaluation of the Similarities in Handwriting", International Criminal Police Review, February, 1957

Naftafki, A., "Behavior Factors In Handwriting Identification" - Journal of Criminal Law, Criminology and Criminal Science, Volume 56, No. 4, 1965

Osborne, Paul A., "Discussion of The Sequence of Fluid Ink Lines and Interesting Paper Folds, Perforations, Tears and Cut Edges" - Journal of Criminal Law, Criminology and Criminal Science, No. 55, 1955, Page 412

Purtell, David J., "Handwriting Standard Forms" - Journal of Criminal Law, Criminology and Criminal Science, Vol. 54, 1963, Page 522

Smith, Stanley S., "A Method of Preparing Written Documents", International Criminal Police Review, August, 1954

Tuttle, Harris B., "Some Applications of Color Photography To Questioned Document Problems", Journal of Forensic Sciences Vol. 5, #2, Page 141

FORGERY PREVENTION

"Forgers are a plague on the whole society". - J. Edgar Hoover

As Mr. Hoover has so aptly pointed out, forgery is in fact a kind of economic disease. Like most diseases, the best hope for elimination and cure lies in the area of prevention and early detection. Forgery is unique as a criminal disorder. Unlike nearly any other common crime it is *theoretically 100% preventable.* Forgery is a crime of deception. It cannot exist in a climate where the victim refuses to be deceived. Unlike burglary, armed robbery, kidnaping, etc., forgery requires the wholehearted cooperation of the victim. The victim becomes in effect, if not in intent, the accomplice to the crime. It is for this very reason that prevention should rank first amongst the efforts of the law enforcement community against the crime of forgery.

I would seriously delude the reader if I held out the hope for the complete elimination of forgery through preventive action. No such hope exists. The more one studies this crime the more one becomes convinced that a certain percentage of forgery will always exist within our society. The move towards a "checkless" society may well reduce the overall incidence of forgery but it will certainly not eliminate it. Professional forgers, of the calibre of the men discussed in the case history section of this book, will be with us for a very long time indeed. But from a very broad viewpoint it is not this class of forgers that should be our first concern. We should be more concerned with the "garden variety" forger. This class of forger commits fully 75% of the forgeries. And this is the class of forger which effective prevention can nearly eliminate.

The writer has separated the prevention of forgery into two principal areas. The first area concerns the design, handling and issuance of the document. The second area concerns the actual use of the document. In total, there are nine separate subject areas which should be of concern to anyone seriously contemplating the reduction and prevention of forgery.

1. The design of the fiscal document

The accent these days is on modern typographical design for both banks and business corporations. Whole communities of graphic art designers have sprung up to "modernize and stream-line" company logos, letterheads, and other areas of business identity. Checks, credit cards, stock certificates, etc. have not escaped this movement. This trend toward "modern design" has been pleasing to the sales departments, stock-holders, etc. But it has been even more pleasing to the professional check, credit card or stock counterfeiter.

We must first bear in mind that 99% of all counterfeits are produced by the photolithography method. This printing method excels in simple, straight line, uncomplicated printing designs. It falters and fails badly in more complex printing designs requiring intricate borders, vignettes, etc. It is doubtful that many business firms will adopt this point, but one of the first steps toward prevention of check or credit card counterfeiting lies in the printing method itself, and the recommendation here is simple and straight forward. *For fiscal documents select intaglio steel plate engraving.*

Intaglio printing is more expensive than the offset printing. There are fewer firms able to produce this kind of work, but the firms are usually of very high caliber with good internal security arrangements. Sometimes the lessons learned on this point are painful but well remembered. A few years ago one of the country's major auto companies switched from a steel plate engraved check to a lower cost photo-offset produced check. Within months the company was hit with a series of forgeries in which a small photo offset press was used to perfectly counterfeit the company's checks. The checks were passed in small towns which had large company plants nearby. The loss must have been substantial. The company is reluctant to discuss the exact amount of loss. Within a short time after this attack on its treasury, the company returned to a steel plate engraved check process.

If for some reason, because of the small volume of documents, or other factors, you cannot use intaglio printed fiscal documents,

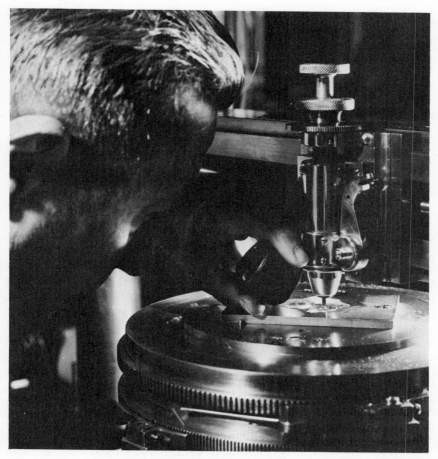

Fig. 23 An engraver using a geometric lathe to prepare a steel plate vignette for intaglio printing of a fiscal document. An engraving of this size may take up to five weeks time to complete satisfactorily. *(Courtesy of American Bank Note Company)*

you should at least use good letterpress printing techniques. Letterpress printed documents are easier to counterfeit and forge than intaglio printed documents, but they still constitute less than 2% of the forged documents. Designs, logos, etc. printed by the letterpress process still require the making of metal impression surfaces, and this single added extra step, with its resultant exposure to commerce, can provide a valuable additional obstacle against counterfeiting and forgery.

The writer has had an opportunity to examine firsthand the counterfeit checks produced in several major check forgery operations. I have examined counterfeit checks drawn on the State and City of New York, the J. W. Mays, Inc. Department Store, U. S. Treasury, U. S. Post Office Department, etc. From a graphic arts standpoint, many of these checks were very poor imitations. For example, the New York City checks were out of register. The J. W. Mays, Inc. checks used a printed signature, etc. Nonetheless, these checks were accepted by knowledgeable banks and business concerns. Even the misspelling of checks has not prevented their acceptance. Recently, in the New York City area, a series of counterfeit Macy's checks were successfully passed with the spelling "Macey's". Washington, D.C. banks were defrauded of $250,000 by a South American check forgery ring before the fraud was discovered through the misspelling of the word *"segurity"*. The point is that check counterfeiters and forgers go where the duplication is easiest. They instinctively shy away from those checks which are intricate and require more expensive and refined printing techniques. The problem is somewhat akin to keeping flies out of one's home. If you provide a screen door with a number of holes, the flies will get through without any difficulty. The object is to reduce the number of holes available so that the flies have to come through a single hole, and then you watch and prepare that hole accordingly.

The second factor in fiscal document design is *Color*. The writer is appalled at the number of checks which are printed in a single color. Likewise, some of our major credit cards are printed in one color with shade variations obtained through the use of screens or tones. This arrangement is an open invitation to the counterfeiter. Any fiscal document should be printed in more than one color. The colors should overlap at several points. This does not prevent the counterfeiter from operating but it makes his job that much more difficult. Precise color separations and multiple plates must be prepared. During the printing of the counterfeit document the counterfeiter has the problem of color registration. There is also the matter of the color itself. When you select a color use a "non-pure" color — a blend. Don't stick with a standard primary color which is easily obtained and easily matched by the counterfeiter.

Many persons may feel that they have a check with a two-color printing job. What they may actually have is a single color, usually black, printed on top of a colored "safety" paper. Safety paper these days is anything but safe. It is quite readily accessible to the skilled counterfeiter and he has any number of strategems available to obtain the more difficult paper stock. In the J. W. Mays case we saw how exact matches for the company's paper stock were obtained through subterfuge. Courtney Townsend Taylor and other master forgers had similar routes to obtain legitimate paper stock. In addition to the use of safety paper,

Fig. 24 Fiscal documents being printed by special high pressure intaglio press at American Bank Note Co. *(Courtesy of American Bank Note Co.)*

which is always required, we should also consider the printing of tones or under-tints prior to the principal printing on the document itself. Very few checks utilize this technique, except for intaglio printed designs, and we know of only one credit card which uses this technique. Here again this step does not eliminate the counterfeiter, but it is one more element in making his job more difficult and, with so many other choice targets to choose from, he is likely to pass up your fiscal document in favor of an easier prize.

Don't feel any safer because you use magnetic inks on your checks. Magnetic inks can be easily home made and in fact are readily obtained from any number of legitimate ink producers. The J. W. Mays case checks were completely printed with magnetic ink.

In the section on credit cards, the writer described the various methods of manufacture and the relative ease with which credit cards could be counterfeited. This is true for even the best of the present day credit card design. The American Express Card design, which utilizes a vignette, a simple engraved border and a background tint plate, has also been the subject of a recent counterfeiting attempt and this case is now before the courts in the Southern District of N. Y. At the time of this writing one of the defendants named in the indictment is a fugitive and the writer cannot disclose further details on this counterfeiting attempt. Nonetheless, it is sufficient to say that the cards produced were, in the opinion of one of the prosecution attorneys, "very good matches" for the American Express Card.

It is obvious that some real steps have to be taken in this area of fiscal document design. The credit card is a form of "instant credit" and further safeguards have to be built into it. There have been a number of recent technical advances including the use of encoded names or numerals on the credit cards, photos, etc. as described previously. The card companies continue to be reticent about employing these features either on the basis of alleged customer reluctance or on the basis of additional cost to the credit card company.

It is reported that some credit card companies also use what is known as a "check digit". This digit is intended to aid security personnel in quickly determining whether a number is legitimate, or whether it has been invented by a counterfeiter or forger. There are any number of ways that such a "check digit" system can work. For example, consider the number 044-910-80. In this number the seventh digit, the digit 8, is the check number. This digit must always equal the sum of the second and third digits. If the sum is ten then the check digit is zero. If the sum exceeds ten then the check digit automatically becomes the second number in the sum. Within this same number you can also see that the check digit might be coded so that it is the difference between the fourth and fifth digit. There are literally thousands of routine mathematical manipulations that can be arranged so as to provide a check digit. One problem with check digits is that if the counterfeiter gets hold of enough legitimate credit card numbers, he can apply some basic cryptography and break the code.

The case for revised fiscal document design is a very strong one. Each week brings repeated evidence that forgers and counterfeiters are selective in choosing the document they wish to counterfeit. Economy of style and printing method only facilitates the already easy life of the professional forger.

2. Internal security handling of the fiscal document

The local printer, who meticulously prepares your letterheads, may be a good friend and reliable vendor, but he is not necessarily the best source for fiscal documents. With the proliferation of checking accounts many firms utilize their regular printing sources to produce company checks. The checks end up being printed in a plant that has no more security precautions than a menu printing plant. The employees and management, while well intentioned, take a nonchalant attitude toward the handling of checks and similar fiscal documents. There may be cases of overage or printing errors in which the waste is negligently discarded. These plants are prime targets for forgers. There is no need to counterfeit a fiscal document if you can steal it or obtain it in a wastepaper pile.

In picking a check printer, or a credit card manufacturer, be certain that you know exactly who you are dealing with and what safety precautions the proposed vendor has in force. Know the extent and manner to which his employees are bonded, the method of handling waste sheets, accounting for press runs, etc. One credit card company discovered to their dismay that their credit card manufacturer had produced two full extra sheets of credit cards which were then stolen and cut into usable blanks which in turn were sold for $50 to $100 in the New York area. There is no tabulation on the extent of the losses resulting from this incident.

Once production has been completed on the fiscal document, particular caution has to be exercised during its next stage of handling. In this area, we are concerned with the mode and manner in which the check or credit card is shipped, accounted for, inventoried, etc. The American Express Company Travellers Check case illustrates the damage that can occur through high-jacking or theft of large quantities of unendorsed fiscal documents. Checks and credit cards are simply another form of currency. When shipped about the country they should be shipped with the same degree of security that one exercises in shipping cash. It is rather ludicrous to utilize regular shipping lines and open warehouse terminals when specific, bonded, high security shipping arrangements are readily available.

As the fiscal document arrives in the bank corporation offices, etc. it should also be the subject of close security arrangements. In one recent case in New York a shipment of 14 cases of checks were made to a major insurance company. One case of these checks, prepared in manifold form for automatic processing, was surreptitiously removed. The thieves deliberately selected a case toward the end of the numerical sequence where it would be undiscovered for some time. A series of 200 separate "front" savings accounts were setup and the checks were being readied for passage as "claim" checks which would be deposited in these 200 accounts and then neatly withdrawn when the proper time arrived. Close inventory check on all of the cases in this shipment would have eliminated the possibility of this variety of fraud.

The checks or other fiscal documents must be shipped in cartons which are completely glue sealed, requiring destruction of the case in order to open them. Thieves are not above carefully opening a case of checks and removing a portion of the shipment and replacing it with filler material.

The writer, during the course of this study, has had ample opportunity to observe the security precautions exercised by many major corporations in connection with the internal and external handling of their checks. Quite frankly there is a single word which describes these precautions and that word is — *lousy*. In far too many cases the corporation, and this applies to both large and small organizations, treats its blank checks as so many other pieces of form paper which are to be gradually eaten up by the bureaucracy. Internal security precautions begin with the selection and supervision of the check printer, proceed through the shipment counting of checks, continue through their safeguarding at company locations, and culminate in the issuance of the check.

Spot checking many firms reveal that the companies utilize normal commercial shipping means to transport cartons of blank checks. This continues to be an open invitation to large scale counterfeiting. The daily news accounts of highjackings, freight diversions, etc. should provide ample warning as to the potential which is involved in the routine trans-shipment of checks. Many checks continue to be unnumbered on their face making close inventory control, in the case of random pilferage, a difficult task. The printers have the technical facilities and capabilities to individually imprint each check with an identifying number which can be utilized for inventory and tracing purposes. However, such procedures are admittedly more expensive and some companies would rather risk loss through forgery than bear the expense of this extra step.

As noted, the internal security precautions for a check or other fiscal document begin with the design and order placement for production. The key here is to know the people you are dealing with. It is not too much to ask that a company's purchasing representative visit the plant where checks are reproduced for his company and to go over the basic security precautions which will be exercised by this plant. Such a visit can be quite illuminating since in some cases there are practically no security precautions.

Secondly, the purchasing official should be justly concerned with a complete accounting of all press sheets utilized in the run. Any misprinted sheets, overage, etc., should be strictly accounted for and returned to the customer. Plates utilized in the printing process, particularly in those processes involving gravure or intaglio printing, should be closely controlled by either the printer or the firm itself. Evidence should be shown as to the security precautions for all artwork, plates, engravings, proofs, etc. utilized in the production of the check or fiscal document.

Next, the purchasing official should justly concern himself with the method by which these checks will be delivered. Lacking armoured truck delivery, the executive should receive assurances on the extent of the liability of the trucker in the event of theft of a portion of the document shipment.

Finally, as the check arrives in the company's offices, additional mandatory security precautions should be put in force. I have observed situations where a petty cash box is religiously placed in the company safe each night while cartons of blank checks stand naked in the corner of an accounting room or at best in a simple metal cabinet. The blank checks represent a potential fortune to a clever forger and should be protected with that possibility in mind.

In addition to checking to see that all of the numbered checks are properly in place, following an ordinary breaking and entering robbery, the business man should take a close look at those checks which are noted as "destroyed". One enterprising forger is known to have committed a breaking and entering routine. In his first visit to the victim company he gained access and took nothing but a sample of the stamp imprint utilized to impress the check stub with the word "destroyed" or "cancelled". This practice is utilized by firms when a mistake is made in filling out a check. The stub portion of the check is stamped indicating that the check has been destroyed and should not be entered in the balance of the book. This forger obtained an example of that imprint during his first visit to the firm. On his second visit to the firm he carefully removed some random checks from the existing book and stamped them "destroyed". Multiple bookkeepers had access to the book and it was quite a while before they discovered that the imprint was fraudulent and that the check had in fact been removed, forged and negotiated.

3. Issuance of the document

Most forgers know that if they can obtain legitimate access to a fiscal document they are half way home in their fraud scheme. By this I mean, that if they can legitimately obtain credit cards, bank accounts, etc. they avoid one of the major obstacles and hazards inherent to check forgery operation, i.e. the hazard of back-checking or verification which might uncover either a hot card, a counterfeit check, a closed account, etc. In the case of check forgeries, the successful opening of an account practically assures success for many check forging operations. Check forgers are not slow in learning banking procedures. They realize for example, that it is easier to open a savings account than a checking account. They also recognize that persons with depositor status have very little difficulty in opening checking accounts. Therefore, it is not unusual for a forger to first open a savings account and then, claiming depositor status, apply for a checking account.

The case files of check forgery are filled with major swindles, some involving sums up to and exceeding one million dollars, which have had as their integral element the successful opening of a checking account. As pointed out previously in the J. W. Mays case, 17 separate checking accounts for 17 "paper" companies were successfully opened. As the latter case illustrates, banks are not notoriously thorough in checking out the background of new company depositors. In the MO Section of this report there are numerous referrals to schemes which involve setting up legitimate looking accounts in order to have them as a deposit source for counterfeit or fraudulently raised checks. Many banks are satisfied with minimal quasi-legal precautions in opening new accounts. A new company might register themselves with the State, or in the larger swindles a whole corporation might be formed to create a cover of legitimacy. The fact remains that in the creation of these companies or corporations no specific moral or financial responsibility criteria are exercised. One cannot assume that

Fig. 25 Skilled engraver preparing master plate for currency production. *(Courtesy of American Bank Note Co.)*

because a corporation exists that it in fact exists for a legitimate purpose and not for an illegitimate purpose. This is a fine distinction but it is a distinction that forgers daily trade on with a great deal of success.

Forgers may also utilize the "sounds like" technique with which they open up a branch account of a company which has a familiar ring to the banker's ear. The wording may be sufficiently close so that the bank erroneously identifies it with a larger organization. There have even been cases where a branch account was opened and the forger successfully represented himself as a local branch manager for a major corporation. One would think that the branch bank would have had to have positive assurance and identity papers from the corporation headquarters prior to opening the account. However, they didn't.

Law enforcement reports for 1968 are repleat with instances where credit cards have been issued to fictitious persons, to known persons with poor or non-existent credit standing, and in a few cases even to deceased individuals. Obviously the wholesale indiscriminate mailing of credit cards indicates a type of mentality that is not likely to produce very thorough credit checks on those applications sent in by would-be card holders.

There are also cases where the card is applied for in the name of a legitimate party, with a good credit standing, and where the legitimate person's mail is thereafter monitored until the credit card appears in mails. At this point it is intercepted and fraudulently utilized. The writer recently applied for and received à major national credit card. At no point, between the submission of the application and the issuance of the credit card did the credit card company ever seek to verify, either by phone or by letter, whether or not I had in fact made such an application. True, they did check employment and credit ratings, but suppose that in fact I had not applied for that card. The card company did not have access to my handwriting standards and would be hard pressed to know whether or not I had made that application myself. The information contained on the application blank could have been obtained by a diligent researcher through independent methods. This technique has in fact been used successfully, yet it appears that the credit card companies have not yet been hit hard enough in this area to take the simple precautionary step of writing the "applicant" a letter, in an unmarked envelope, "thanking" him for his recent application. In addition to a low cost security check, the latter procedure might even be good public relation practice.

4. Maintaining security of the document

Perhaps the best way to maintain proper security for a fiscal document is to first cultivate a particular state of mind. In this state of mind you visualize checks, credit cards, and cold cash all within the same large box. These are not separate items but rather different forms of "currency". Once you convince yourself that checks and credit cards have the same liquidity as cash, you will find it much easier to maintain the security of the fiscal document. A check book or a check or a credit card is a key to your personal or corporate assets. As such, it should be guarded carefully. Repeatedly the author has researched cases where large financial loss might have been prevented had the individual or corporation treated its checks or credit cards in the same manner that it treated its cash. In our "cashless society" one is left with no other course but to treat the fiscal documents as completely and instantly negotiable materials. In the hands of a skilled forger, this is exactly what they are.

There are any number of ways in which we can maintain the security of our fiscal documents once they have been properly designed, handled and issued. To begin with, lets make sure that all old checks (cancelled), unused obsolete checks, out-of-date credit cards, etc., when no longer required for accounting purposes, are completely and absolutely destroyed. Do not rely on your garbage disposal service to take care of this task. More than one forger has lifted a complete set of fiscal document examples from the waste containers of an obliging firm or individual. Special security arrangements should involve the burning of all checks and the mutilation of plastic credit cards by cutting these cards into at least a half dozen pieces with the pieces being distributed into two different waste receptacles. Some businessmen are unaware of the value that even a cancelled check has to a professional forger. The cancelled check provides the forger with a complete "form" for producing his forged instrument. With modern printing techniques, it is not difficult for him to reproduce your check blank and, armed with copies of your signature, checkwriter type faces, etc., he is in a position to complete a masterful imitation. Sometimes these imitations are so effective that only the experts are capable of detecting the difference. Not too long ago, the Michigan Consolidated Gas Company and the Chevrolet Division of General Motors found $20,000.00 in bad checks circulated in a Detroit area during two February weekends. These checks were so good that only a defect in the magnetic ink imprint caused the checks to be kicked out by the automated magnetic check sorting operations of the Detroit banks. The checks ranged from $114.00 to $139.00 for the Chevrolet checks and all of the Michigan Consolidated checks were drawn for $139.00.

Next, be very careful to look over your check books, credit cards, etc. after any theft. Forgers have been known to stage a "petty theft" and surreptitiously remove checks from the back or middle portion of a check book. As noted previously, this requires rechecking the numeral sequence once in a while and such a recheck is particularly required after any breaking and entering or similar breach of physical security. Often, the security of your document can be threatened even if your document itself is well protected. Examples of this involve cases where firms have sold or traded in their old check writers, discarded signature stamps, etc. In some cases, the forger, knowing that a signature stamp is employed and recognized by the business associates of a firm, will commit a theft over a week-end procuring the signature stamp and a supply of valid check forms. Then, moving quickly on a Monday, he will paper the local towns with these forged instruments. Bookkeepers, accountants, etc. charged with check issuance, should make a routine Monday morning check on such accessory equipment as checkwriters, rubber stamps, etc.

Finally, the security of your document can be protected through the protection you provide your own signature. Banking and law enforcement officials repeatedly urge that you use a separate signature for your checks. This may involve writing out your complete name, using only your initials, using your first name and initials, etc. There are dozens of ways in which a signature can be made unique. This should be your "banking" signature. This form should be reserved for credit cards and checks. Skillful forgers must obtain a good example of your "banking signature". If you use a single universal signature form, they can readily obtain this from parcel receipts, hotel or motel registrations, mail return addresses, or any other of a dozen or more common places where you unknowingly but routinely affix your signature. Professional men's signatures are available from prescription blanks, wills and deeds, corporation reports, annual reports printed by companies, etc. Once provided with the signature "form" the forger will have little difficulty in duplicating your signature. In fact, as noted before, he need not duplicate it perfectly since signatures are seldom the same two times in a row. In addition to your signature, the "form" that you use in filling in the check is also an important element in maintaining the security of the document. There are three simple precautions with regard to form that can complicate the life of the forger.

1. Make certain that all blank spaces are tightly filled in with either writing or numerals or cross-lines so that no additional material may be written in.

2. Never make out a check to Cash unless you plan to cash it nearly immediately. Anyone finding such a check can use it the same as they would a $10 bill.

3. Date the check on the exact day that you write it. If this is a Sunday, holiday, etc. nonetheless date it on that day. Don't postdate a check and anticipate that it will be cashed.

5. The acceptance climate

When we talk of the acceptance climate, we are talking about the total environment in which the check or credit card comes to be accepted as a substitute for cash. There two principal elements to this environment. The first element concerns the people in the environment. These are the bank tellers, store clerks, cashiers, etc. who accept the check or credit card in lieu of cash. Secondly, the environment consists of the procedures, policies and technical devices that surround the check cashing operation. Each business has a particular acceptance climate. Certain businesses obviously have a more hospitable climate than others. Otherwise, we could not logically account for the fact that groceries, taverns, bars, liquor stores, etc. are easier victims than banks, hardware stores, etc. So there is obviously a difference in this acceptance climate. The point is to make this climate as inhospitable as possible while yet meeting the ordinary and legitimate needs of the vast majority of check and credit card users. This is a compromise and in any compromise a certain umber of forgers are going to slip through. However, the author's experience has shown that much can be done to change the climate towards one more favorable to the banking and business community. The first step in changing this climate involves the training that your personnel receive.

Recently, in an informal discussion with a forgery squad officer, he remarked to me that he has been asked to talk before numerous banking and store organizations on the depredations of forgers and safeguards against forgery. Yet, from his own experience he knows that the people he is talking to rarely go back to their own organization and implement their new found knowledge through training courses for their employees. When a check cashing seminar is held, the department store, bank, etc. is only too willing to send one of its executives for an education. However, somewhere along the line there is a breakdown following this educational experience. The clerks, cashiers, etc. don't gain the benefit of this executive's new education. The people who require training are the front line troops. These are the individuals who are faced each day with making a check acceptance decision. Of necessity, a certain amount of discretionary authority has to be provided to even the lowest of store clerks. With this authority, should go the tools for fiscal protection.

The training of personnel begins with an introduction to the complete policies and procedures of your organization with regard to check handling. This phase is followed by an introduction to some of the more prevalent forgery MO's and is reinforced with photos, drawings, etc. of fraudulent checks. There are a variety of worthwhile publications which can be utilized to train personnel. In addition, you should regard this training process as more than a one shot type operation. Training, to be successful, has to be maintained. Schedule regular meetings to discuss this particular problem. Post enforcement bulletins, warnings, etc. conspicuously in employee lounges, dressing rooms, etc. There are a variety of posters and other visual aids available for reminder and information purposes. These create the mental awareness and alertness which is an integral part of the acceptance climate.

In addition to training your personnel you should also provide them with a set of policies and procedures which work to your advantage. It is beyond the scope of this report to detail all of the check acceptance procedures which might be encountered in widely divergent business operations. There are some common threads of agreement and these concern the limits of teller or clerk acceptance, the cashing of checks for more than the value of the goods purchased, the specifying of particular types of identification, the need for a second clerk, store manager, etc. to "okay" the check etc. It suffices to say here that there should be a specific check or credit card handling procedure well fixed in the mind of the clerk, store manager, etc. In addition, there should be a further policy and procedure to be utilized in those gray areas where there is some doubt as to the authenticity of the check or credit cards being offered. An interesting aside here concerns the case of one New York store that had a set procedure it utilized for doubtful checks. When the clerk encountered such a check he would remark to the passer "please wait a second, I have to go to the back for a moment and call the check into the computer clearing point. This shouldn't take but a moment, I'll be right back". Actually, there was no such clearing point, but the forger was unaware of this and in several instances fled from the store while the clerk was completing a routine round-trip stroll to the back of the store.

Another portion of your policy concerns the actual sale of products through the use of checks and credit cards. The forger often preys on the eagerness of a merchant to make a sale. Don't be so anxious to make a sale that you are willing to give away your product and perhaps a portion of your treasury as well. The vast majority of the public, if handled courteously and sincerely, do not resent having their checks or credit cards routinely verified. They expect that you are going to ask them for some identification, and take a few moments in comparing the maker's signature against endorsement, and in generally appraising the document. Beware of those persons who are too "busy" for this simple procedure. Don't be misled by their prosperous appearance. As we shall see later, appearance is among the most important tools of the forger.

Finally, use the technical and psychological devices available to you. American industry has produced a whole range of admirable check cashing cameras which experience has definitely proven reduce the operations of a professional forger. The forger is intelligent. He knows that the check cashing photo can often prove his undoing and that it provides the single most important link in both apprehension and in alerting the business community to his existence. If you accept checks on any volume at all, you should be protected with some type of camera device. A separate portion of this chapter illustrates these devices.

But having the device itself and installing it incorrectly or not using it at all obviously defeats its purpose. The writer recently visited a number of large resort hotels to investigate their check cashing procedures. One of the largest in the country, with several lines of people checking out at their cashier's counter, had an excellent camera device. The only problem was that the unit had been inoperative for several months. However, even an inoperative camera is better than none at all.

Law enforcement forgery experts know that the professional forger frequently cases his victim. The existence of a camera automatically discourages the forger before he ever walks into your store or bank. In addition, the existence of this device should be proclaimed by a suitable warning sticker. The manufacturer of these cameras makes such stickers freely available.

And so in the acceptance climate we have the person, the policy or procedure, and the technical equipment available to protect against the forger. All of these items make up the acceptance climate. Used together, they can make this climate very cold indeed for the professional forger.

6. The document itself

State laws regulating the cashing of checks vary somewhat but generally a bank is under no legal obligation to cash a check drawn on another bank. A store or business establishment is similarly under no legal obligation to immediately accept a check as payment in lieu of cash. However, a bank is under an obligation to pay on demand a genuine check drawn on itself. But even in this case it is permitted to delay cashing for at least five reasons. These are:

1. To determine whether the signature is in fact that of the maker.

2. To ascertain whether the maker has sufficient funds in his account to cover the value of the check.

3. Be sure that payment on this particular check has not been stopped.

4. To verify the identity of the casher.

5. To verify his legal title to the instrument itself.

Many persons are under a cloud of misapprehension in connection with their legal obligations with regard to the cashing of checks. Were they not so beclouded they might take a closer look at the instrument itself and this is the next subject for study.

There are at least five different points in which the document or instrument provides its own best testimony as to its worth.

1. Misspellings are often a good tip-off as to the value of the check. Be wary of checks in which towns, companies, etc. are misspelled. Also be wary of "odd" spellings for names which you are generally familiar with. Don't look only at the spelling contained in the hand written portion of the check but also the printed portion of the check. There have been numerous cases involving misspelled checks for which the counterfeit printer haphazardly set type and produced a title such as "Macey's" or "Segurity". Unfortunately, checks involving the latter two misspellings were in fact passed. Sometimes this misspelling can prove to be a valuable clue to the national origin of the forger. The U.S. Postal Inspectors have been successful in utilizing this single clue in the apprehension of a forger whose only mistake was temporarily reverting to the spelling common to his native land. These days, nearly everyone has a checking account and admittedly there are a large number of the people in the population who have trouble with spelling. Nonetheless, the high incidence of misspelling on forged checks does make this a legitimate tip-off.

2. Unusually formed numerals are frequently a warning sign which spells "raising". Check to see whether the numerals have been formed with an easy flowing line rather than a stilted angular motion. Sometimes, quite legitimately, persons will change their minds about the intended value of a check and make a homemade correction. Don't be afraid to remark about such a correction or to call their attention to it. Such remarks coupled with the important factor of delay often can scare off the professional forger.

3. Be especially on guard against any blots, erasures, changes in ink color, penline thickness, etc. Checks are relatively inexpensive. Most people, when they make a mistake, will simply cancel and destroy the incorrect check and make out a new one.

Also be particularly on guard against checks which have been "repaired" with Scotch Tape. One of the more ingenious forgery MO's involves the splitting of a genuine signature and its subsequent transfer to a blank check through the use of such tape. The presence of the tape is accounted for by tearing the maker's signature panel just prior to application of the tape.

4. Do not accept any checks in pencil. Pencil signatures are extremely easy to split and transfer and of course pencil checks lend themselves to all types of erasures, raisings, etc.

5. Do not accept checks with rubber stamp signatures unless you personally know the payee and maker of the check. Rubber stamp signatures are easily procured by practically anyone and rubber stamp producers and distributors make little or no effort to determine whether or not the person requesting a signature stamp is in fact legitimately entitled to it.

In considering the document, we should also pay particular attention to certain classes of checks. Experience has graphically shown that forgeries are more prevalent amongst these classes of checks. Among the checks which bear a little extra scrutiny are:

1. **Third party checks.** This type of check is extremely susceptible to fraud. Third party checks occur when a check is issued by one person to a second person and then handed your store or company to be either cashed or used as payment. The difficulty with third party checks is that the original maker can stop payment, for valid reasons, and if you have accepted and hold such a check your recourse lies in the areas of restitution action, a legal process which is often costly and time consuming, as well as economically unattractive.

2. **Blank checks.** Blank check forms were formerly issued by banks or businesses and are still sold at stationery and legal supply stores. In this type of check the maker prints in, in the outlined areas, the name, address and branch designation of the bank. These are extremely dubious types of checks as most banks are quite able and willing to provide all the printed blank checks one needs.

3. **Counter Checks.** Counter checks are not negotiable and are specifically stated to be such, but nonetheless we often find retail merchants accepting these as legitimate checks. The counter

check is printed by the bank for use by its own depositors in withdrawing funds held by that bank. They are not intended to be good anywhere else.

4. Company Checks. Checks which are issued to specific commercial organizations should be deposited to their accounts, in their own banks or cashed at the maker's bank. These should not be cashed or accepted by retail merchants or by third party banks. In some cases, one company may receive a check from a second company and believing it to be of dubious value, will seek to cash it somewhere other than in their own bank.

5. Late Date Checks. A bank or retail merchant should never accept a check made out with a date later than the date on which the check is being cashed. These "post-dated checks", if they prove to be fraudulent, can create quite a prosecution problem. To prove check fraud you most often prove that the check was in fact a negotiable instrument. If you cash the check on the first of the month and the signer made it for the 5th then the check was in fact non-negotiable until the 5th of the month.

6. Checks with varying amounts. If the numerals and the written words do not coincide, you should be at least cautious of the check. If all other circumstances appear good, you may wish to cash the check, while making payment on the smaller amount on the check.

7. Identification

The subject of identification is crucial to the entire area of forgery prevention. There are several points which bear particular emphasis in the subject of identification. Beneath all of these points is the assumption that you will ask questions of the person presenting the identification. If you are unwilling to ask questions you have automatically forfeited 90% of the value of the credential. Credentials can be counterfeited, stolen, purchased from "credential pools" operated by the underworld, or obtained fraudulently. The credential itself means nothing without your ability to intelligently utilize cross-check procedures available to you. Interestingly enough, even some of the best credentials are often shunted aside in favor of more "normal" or "accepted" forms. Agents from the Federal Bureau of Investigation and the U.S. Secret Service have recalled incidents where, when asked to present identification, they presented their law enforcement credentials. The clerks frequently became distracted and asked "don't you have a driver's license".

Among the points that we wish to remember about credentials and identification are the following:

1. Is the identification consistent with the person? There have been cases where juveniles have presented credentials for elderly persons and had them accepted because the clerk failed to closely examine the age and physical description portion of the identification document. Identification documents frequently contain information on the height, hair color, eye color, age, etc. A cross check on this takes but a second and should be basic to the acceptance of identity credentials.

2. Is there more than one item of identification offered? Multiple identity credentials are always desirable. It is quite possible for a felon to steal a credit card, driver's license, etc. It is possible that he may not have obtained a secondary identifying credential. You should try to obtain at least two identity documents and both of these identity documents should contain signature samples. The signature samples can be quickly cross-checked and then further checked against the endorsement signature.

3. Does the endorsement signature check out with the handwriting on the check? The check should be endorsed in your presence and it is basic to cross check the endorsement against the maker's signature. Often this is not done. In addition to checking out the handwriting characteristics, you should also be concerned with whether or not the same name appears. Many forgers of welfare checks, U.S. Social Security checks, etc. even make the mistake of misspelling the payee's name, or missing a middle initial, etc. This is a dead giveaway to a forgery.

4. Do not be swayed in the identification process by the fact that the person presenting it may be either a depositor, charge account customer, etc. Forgers are aware that such status gives them preferential treatment and they frequently will establish accounts simply to gain the identification as a depositor or charge account customer.

5. Evaluate the type of identity document being offered. These days there are literally hundreds of various "identity documents"

which might be available. These range from social security cards, automobile owners or operators licenses, private clubs or lodge cards, labor union or fraternity cards, special company employment identification cards such as used by telephone and power companies, fishing and hunting licenses, library cards, passports, selective service or draft registration cards, military service identification cards, school and college identification cards, all types of credit cards, etc. Nearly every one of the cards previously mentioned can be readily obtained. Social security cards are worthless as far as identification is concerned. Automobile owners and operators licenses are a bit more difficult to obtain and these are the types most frequently employed for identification purposes. However, they are far from fool-proof. With respect to that particular identity credential, the clerk should take some note to see whether the validating stamp has been properly affixed and whether the license is in effect. Forgers sometimes gain access to drivers licenses when people throw away their expired licenses. There is absolutely no fool-proof identification credential and the only positive identity procedure is personal identification through previous acquaintance.

6. Cross-check the identity credentials that are presented to you. By cross-check we mean ask specific questions. Don't be afraid to ask questions as to where the party presenting the check lives, works, etc. Particularly ask questions which relate to the document being offered. For example if a service discharge is being offered as identification some reasonable and logical questions about the unit the individual served with, when he was discharged, etc. are in order. Most identity documents also contain a statement as to the person's date of birth. Specific question like "how old are you" might unnerve the holder of a false document because he may have memorized the date of birth but failed to compute forward the actual age of the person.

Many prudent merchants are also wise enough to deliberately insert a question designed to ensnare a potential forger. For example, they may reverse the numerals on his address such as stating your address is: "757 East Main Street" when the actual shown address is 775 Main Street. They may also note that you must live next door to Joe Lawler (a fictitious person) or may state "I see you work at Binks Company, you must know my uncle

Robert in the Machine Department" in an attempt to elicit a telltale response error. The master forger may be smart enough to pass such cross checks but the country is fortunately not plagued by master forgers but rather by the semi-pro forger who will be entrapped by such procedures.

One of the simplest ruses used to confound petty forgers is for the store clerk or bank teller to simply turn the check face down, and while pretending to make out a sales slip or deposit record ask the suspect to provide his name and spelling thereon. In many cases, particularly in the forgery of Social Security, Welfare, etc. checks the suspect is in fact unable to provide the exact spelling of the name as it appears on the face of the check.

8. The passer

In the final analysis, the person passing the check provides the single best clue as to the value of the check and offers the single best source for forgery prevention. However, we encounter a parodox here because the best forgers capitalize on this point and make their appearance and mannerisms work for them in committing their forgery.

Recently the National Institute of Mental Health sponsored a research project at the University of Michigan which provided some interesting insights into peoples' ability to judge a person's "honesty". In this survey, conducted amongst 200 men and women students, the respondents were asked to evaluate honesty under three separate conditions: (1) watching and hearing an interview; (2) hearing the tape recording of the interview; or (3) reading a transcript of the interview. The listeners and readers scored far higher than those who had personal contact with the interview through actually watching and listening to it. The Michigan researchers concluded "The watchers were distracted by facial expressions, gestures, etc." This is exactly the type of distraction that professional forgers rely on. Therefore, the most important point we can stress here is not to rely singularly on the appearance of the person, or his manner. In particular be aware of:

1. Glib or distracting talkers. Experienced forgers frequently attempt to dominate the conversation in order to prevent any

questions that may arise about themselves. This procedure also deliberately creates an air of self-confidence which disarms the teller or store clerk. This technique of distracting conversation is often combined, by the professional forger, with the presentation of checks during a busy period of the day. These two factors, the pressure of the business routine combined with the distracting conversation, allow many checks to slip by that might otherwise be detected.

2. Beware of "uniforms". Many forgers utilize their personal appearance to their own best advantage. We have numerous cases where the forger will procure a military officers uniform, a priest's habit, a corporate uniform such as a service station overalls with the oil company name affixed, vending machine company uniform, cleaning service uniform, etc. In all of these cases, the uniform is deliberately arranged to provide camouflage for the person. The uniform is intended as a form of identification. Some forgers, including one who recently worked in New York area even utilized doctors or nurses uniforms in the time tested technique that tellers or store clerks will be less suspicious of a professional person. The mere fact that the suspect has a uniform on should not deter one iota of precaution in handling a suspect check.

3. Juveniles are another suspect group. Most juveniles do not have legitimate access to a checking account and are bound to be a second party endorser which creates potential credibility hazards with regard to their possession and passing of a check. Their use of a credit card should be even further questioned. Despite the latter reservation, we have cases where two or more juveniles, gaining access to their parents' credit cards, have successfully traveled around the world utilizing one or more of the major national credit cards to charge air-fare, hotel bills, restaurant charges, etc.

4. Intoxicated persons are a further check hazard. One parole officer told me that a number of forgers at the U.S. Federal Penitentiary in Leavenworth had passed checks during various drunken sprees. The inhibitions preventing false signatures, etc. are apparently relaxed by alcohol.

9. Circumstances of passing

The forger recognizes particular times of day and business circumstance as being ideal for the forging and passing of checks.

The American Banking Association recommends that you do not cash pay checks or any other checks out of business or banking hours on Saturdays or holidays without complete investigation. Also beware of checks that are presented just before closing time or during rush noon hour periods. Since we also know that certain businesses are more prone to forgery attempts, these businesses, by their very existence, should also be on-guard. In those cases where a large number of payroll checks are submitted on a Friday or Saturday, we should take particular precautions during this period. Forgers will time their visit to coincide with such activity.

Forgers also take advantage of the relief schedules at certain banks or business establishments. They recognize that during the lunch hour break individuals will be pressed into temporary service as tellers or cashiers and that these persons may not be as experienced and may be more suspectible to a check forgery operation. Particular care has to be exercised and particular caution should be drilled into these type of "replacement" employees.

Safeguards — photo and electronic devices

One of the single most important deterrents, on a merchant level, has been the development of the surveillance camera. These cameras, as typified by the Regiscope unit, provide a split image photograph of both the suspect and the questioned document. In some cases this document may be other than a check. For example, it may be an invoice, bill of lading, receipt for security, etc. Therefore, the camera devices have wide application other than check cashing functions as a forgery prevention device.

In operation the counter unit camera is placed in a position where the patron can sign a check and the unit can simultaneously photograph the check, face and upper torso of the signer. In some cases the unit is stationed several feet back from the actual counter of the bank, hotel, etc. In other cases the unit has been utilized to photograph patrons at drive-in windows of banks and similar establishments. The tripping of the camera can be performed by the clerk with either a manual switch or an electronic mechanism. The Regiscope camera contains 100 feet of 16 mm film which provides 2,000 individual exposures. Each exposure contains a split image providing a good likeness of the

Fig. 26 Example of the photos produced using the Regiscope camera. *(Courtesy of Regiscope Corporation)*

individual and the suspect document. The film utilized is sufficiently fast for daylight operations. In some cases where night utilization is necessary, such as at drive-in windows at banks where check cashing is done after dusk, a 20 watt fluorescent light fixture provides the sufficient light for the photo process.

Law enforcement agents that the author has interviewed have been enthusiastic about the camera, but have expressed two principal reservations which do not reflect on the camera but rather on its utilization. They note that in some cases glare from reflecting objects or from store lighting devices can create a problem, since the glare gets into the camera lens. They have also noted, and this has been the author's own experience, that some institutions will have the camera but fail to load them or to trigger them as required.

It is also known that some forgers will attempt to partially obliterate their face, timing their movements to the shutter release. Thus they may reach up to scratch an eye-brow or perform some other seemingly casual gesture. The trigger mechanism should be unknown to the suspect and not within his timing anticipation. A study of protection photographs shows that professional forgers will frequently change their appearance substantially in order to attempt to spoil the camera image. By and large such disguise attempts are fairly transparent to the trained investigator.

Almost without exception, the installation of these camera systems has proved to be a boom in reducing forgery losses. Police officials and financial officials alike are enthusiastic over the performance of this equipment. Police Director, J. Adrien Roberts of Montreal, has described them as "one of the most important innovations of many years". Case histories of utilization of these cameras provides an interesting insight into the effect that they have on forgery and fraud losses. Lit Brothers, a large Philadelphia retailer, was losing up to $80,000 a year in fraud losses from forged documents, fraudulent refunds, etc. Nine months after installing a surveillance camera, their losses had been reduced to 23 transactions totaling only $200.92. The security director at Rigley Supermarkets, reporting in the January, 1965 edition of SECURITY WORLD, notes that "since the Regiscope went in our losses went down almost to zero — we had had a terrific problem with stolen State and Federal Government checks".

In a single year, 1963, the Regiscope cameras in one city (Chicago) enabled retailers to recover losses of about $90,000 from checks taken in burglaries and armed robberies and subsequently fraudulently passed.

When Labor Day of 1960 arrived a highly trained gang of professional forgers moved into Columbus, Ohio. They began to work the downtown stores with a devastating effect over the long weekend. Significantly, and this is a testimony to the forgers own appraisal of photo surveillance equipment, they completely avoided all stores that had surveillance cameras in operation. Some forgers are so unnerved by the surveillance cameras that they have even attempted to get back the checks they passed, once they realized that they had been photographed. A typical example of this concerns a Kansas City, Missouri forger who was apprehended in 1960 for forging American Express Money Orders and causing them to be transported in Interstate Commerce from Kansas City to New York. This forger had cashed 55 of the money orders which had been stolen in Omaha, Nebraska. An additional uncashed quantity was found at his home. The forger was arrested when he returned to a department store the day after cashing four of the stolen money orders. He returned to the store because he feared he had been photographed by a check protection camera and he wished to redeem the money orders, thus wiping out the possibility of the photograph being utilized in evidence. His return to the store resulted in his arrest.

The cases where forgers have been identified and apprehended by check surveillance cameras are too numerous to be enumerated here. It suffices to say that hundreds of forgers have been apprehended directly through the assistance provided by these cameras. In addition to the technical support provided by the camera, the willingness of the camera manufacturers to supply expert witnesses to confirm the law enforcement agent's case has been instrumental in many convictions. In some cases the camera photo provides a final proof in criminal convictions other than forgery. One tragic case in New York illustrates this point. On an early Fall morning a New York patrolman, William J. Long, 27, and father of three children, noticed a suspicious figure moving through a parking lot. Patrolman Long suspected that the man might be looting the parked cars and challenged him. Whirling suddenly, the suspect fired four times mortally wounding the patrolman. Patrolman Long staggered to a telephone and before he died provided a sketchy description of the suspect. From clues left at the scene it was established that a Virgil Richardson, an airman serving at an air base in Las Vegas, Nevada, was a prime suspect. Richardson in his haste dropped a hat which was traced to a Brooklyn haberdashery. Richardson had bought the hat using a government tax refund check. He had been photographed with a check surveillance camera. The record of this transaction provided positive identification of Richardson, and along with other linking evidence, provided the basis for his arrest, prosecution and conviction. On November 21, 1958 Virgil Richardson, age 29, died in the electric chair in New York's Sing-Sing Prison.

Bibliography

Aughey, Theodore, "Employee Training, A Review of Procedures Advocated As A Solution To The Check-Kiting Evil" - American Banker, Sept. 27, 1961

Bloom, Murray Teigh, "Season of Good-will and Bad Checks" - New York Times, Dec. 18, 1960

Cunningham, Benjamin W., "Warning Net Stop Bad Checks" - Pacific Banker & Business, Volume 63, No. 8, March, 1966

Granahan, Catherine, "Tips To Trip The Forger" - Banking, Volume 46, No. 3, Sept., 1963

Fletcher, C. H., "Six Easy Ways To Recognize A Bad Check" - The Fraud Detection and Prevention Bureau, Chicago, Illinois

Hobbs, Mrs. Eileen, "Forgery Problem" - Woman Banker, Page 4, August-September, 1950

Hoover, J. Edgar, "Check Artist - A National Menace" - Auditgram, Volume 37, No. 3, March, 1961

Kendrick, Gerald L., "How To Discourage Forgery", - Journal of Banking, Volume 58, No. 2, Page 73

Montague, Henry., "Check Fraud Artists Finding New Method" - American Banker, Nov. 4, 1965

Nolan, Joseph, "Big Business In Bad Checks" - New York Times, August 29, 1954

Sloane, Leonard, "Personal Finance; On Cashing Checks" - New York Times, January 4, 1968

Toney, Thomas, "Hot Tips On Hot Checks" - The Texas Parade, Volume 11, No. 5, Page 4

Yoder, Robert M., "You'd Never Think They Were Crooks" - Saturday Evening Post, Volume 225, No. 40, Page 70

Young, Gordon, "Check Anonymous" - Northwestern Banker, Volume 71, No. 31, February, 1965

"Bonded Defense Against The Check Forger" - The Surety Association of America - New York, N.Y.

"How Chase Manhattan Thwarts Bad Check Forgery Artists" - U.S. Investors, Volume 68, No. 49, Page 11, December 7, 1957

"How To Trap A Forger" - New York Herald Tribune, April 27, 1947

"Is This Check Forged" - Identification Bureau, Michigan State Police, East Lansing, Michigan